Morality and the N

MORALITY AND THE MEANING OF LIFE

Edited by:
Professor Albert W. Musschenga (Amsterdam)
Professor Paul J.M. van Tongeren (Nijmegen)

Advisory Board:
Professor Frans De Wachter (Louvain)
Professor Dietmar Mieth (Tübingen)
Professor Kai E. Nielsen (Calgary)
Professor Dewi Z. Phillips (Swansea)

In this series the following titles have been published:

1 MOXTER M., *Güterbegriff und Handlungstheorie. Eine Studie zur Ethik Friedrich Schleiermachers*, 1992, X-255 p., ISBN: 90-390-0042-5   30 EURO

2 MUSSCHENGA B., *Does Religion Matter Morally? A Critical Reappraisal of the Thesis of Morality's Independence from Religion*, 1995, VIII-212 p., ISBN: 90-390-0404-8   30 EURO

3 VAN HAUTE P., BIRMINGHAM P., *Dissensus Communis. Between Ethics and Politics*, 1995, 154 p., ISBN: 90-390-0403-X   33 EURO

4 ZWART H., *Ethical Consensus and the Truth of Laughter. The Structure of Moral Transformations*, 1996, 216 p., ISBN 90-390-0412-9   27 EURO

5 PRAETORIUS I., *Essays in Feminist Ethics*, 1998, 181 p., ISBN: 90-429-0590-5   27 EURO

6 MÖLLER G., *Ethics and the Life of Faith. A Christian Moral Perspective*, 1998, VI-157 p., ISBN: 90-429-0699-5   34 EURO

7 THERON S., *The End of the Law. The Good Life: a Theological View*, 1999, VIII-128 p., ISBN: 90-429-0725-8   35 EURO

8 HERMSEN J.J., Villa D., *The Judge and the Spectator. Hannah Arendt's Political Philosophy*, 1999, VI-135 p., ISBN: 90-429-0781-9   23 EURO

9 VANDEVELDE A., *Gifts and Interests*, 2000, VIII-225 p., ISBN: 90-429-0814-9   25 EURO

10 OPDEBEECK H.J., *The Foundation and Application of Moral Philosophy. Ricœur's Ethical Order*, 2000, V-84 p., ISBN: 90-429-0852-1   15 EURO

11 TUDOR S., *Compassion and Remorse. Acknowledging the Suffering Other*, 2000, VI-235 p., ISBN: 90-429-0920-X   40 EURO

12 VAN HARSKAMP A., MUSSCHENGA A.W., *The Many Faces of Individualism*, 2000, VI-282 p., ISBN: 90-429-0954-4   40 EURO

13 APEL K.-O., *The Response of Discourse Ethics*, 2001, VIII-118 p., ISBN: 90-429-0978-1   24 EURO

14 CORTINA A., *Covenant and Contract*, 2003, X-138 p., ISBN: 90-429-1340-1   35 EURO

TOWARDS A
COMPLEX PERFECTIONISM

Peter Scheers

PEETERS
LEUVEN – DUDLEY, MA
2005

Library of Congress Cataloging-in-Publication Data

Scheers, Peter.
Towards a complex perfectionism / Peter Scheers.
    p. cm. -- (Morality and the meaning of life)
  Includes bibliographical references.
  ISBN 90-429-1655-9 (alk. paper)
    1. Perfection. 2. Ethics. I. Title. II. Series.

BD233.S34 2005
128--dc22

2005047694

© 2005 — Peeters, Bondgenotenlaan 153, B-3000 Leuven, Belgium
D. 2005/0602/1
ISBN 90-429-1655-9

CONTENTS

Acknowledgements 5

Introduction 7

1. INTERPRETATION AND PERFECTION – I:
   Existential Hermeneutics 13

2. INTERPRETATION AND PERFECTION – II:
   Perfective Hermeneutics 21

3. INTERPRETATION AND PERFECTION – III:
   Evolutionary Hermeneutics 39

4. THE LANGUAGE OF PERFECTION – I:
   Perfection as Positive / as Negative 49

5. THE LANGUAGE OF PERFECTION – II:
   Perfection Today 59

6. THE LANGUAGE OF PERFECTION – III:
   Varieties of Perfective Appraisal 69

7. THE LANGUAGE OF PERFECTION – IV:
   Aretaic Perfection 91

8. HUMAN PERFECTIVE EXISTENCE – I:
   Perfective Naturalism 119

9. HUMAN PERFECTIVE EXISTENCE – II:
   Personal Perfection 135

10. HUMAN PERFECTIVE EXISTENCE – III:
    Perfection in Practice 143

11. HUMAN PERFECTIVE EXISTENCE – IV:
    Future Perfection 163

12. ENVIRONMENTAL PERFECTIONISM:
    Nature and Narrative 181

Conclusion 199

Bibliography 201

ACKNOWLEDGEMENTS

One of the first things a relevant perfectionism should realise is that the idea of radical perfective autonomy has to be abandoned. The activity of writing itself offers a good illustration. It is, as John Passmore (1970) points out, to make oneself dependent on a multitude of other human beings. In line with this, it is clear that this study could not have been undertaken without the implicit and explicit help of a list of 'contributive perfectors'. I am most indebted to prof. dr. Bert Musschenga (Free University, Amsterdam). His role has been greatly instrumental in different ways. This includes his interest and assistance in turning this study into a volume for the book series *Morality and the Meaning of Life*. My thanks are also due to prof. dr. Johan Verstraeten (University of Leuven), from whose comments I have benefited in a later stage of my research. Furthermore, it gives me great pleasure to express my gratitude to prof. dr. William Desmond (University of Leuven) and his wife, Maria Desmond, for their help and generous encouragement. This includes the structural influence of William's thought on the concrete formation of my perfective argument, as well as Maria's linguistic revision of this manuscript from the invaluable angle of an academic native speaker. I also wish to thank prof. dr. Jere Surber (Denver University) and dr. Gerlof Verwey for their friendship and support. Above all, I am profoundly indebted to my wife, Miglena Dikova. It is unlikely that this study could have been written without her presence. Finally, I wish to dedicate this book to my mother, Huguette Scheers-De Grove, and to the memory of my father, Edmond Scheers.

Peter Scheers
January 2005
Aartselaar

INTRODUCTION

This study aims to contribute to a contemporary perfectionist reading of human (and non-human) existence. I hope to make clear that perfective and semi-perfective discourse constitutes an existentially fertile language of evaluation or estimation, offering a structural interpretation of what we are and can — or perhaps should — become. The language of perfection provides us with anthropological content and axiological direction.

Perfection for contemporary selves

Currently, we do not have a firm concept of perfection, nor a coherent one. Perfection shifts and wanders. It has been made to mean numerous things. There are several negative views of it: certain political thinkers identify perfection with a dogmatic and elitist perspective; psychologists introduce us to perfection as personal pathology; biomedical ethicists warn us against the arrogance of genetic and medical perfection. Perfection in a positive sense is explored, often in bits and pieces, under a variety of names — perfectionism, perfectibilism, virtue ethics, ethics of character, aretaics, teleology, eudaimonism, and so forth. Confronted with such a plurality of perspectives it is fruitful to stand back for a while and to attempt to move in the direction of a higher degree of clarity, depth and wholeness. In this way we might succeed in discovering perfection's particular relevance to the way of being of contemporary selves. I am especially concerned with revealing the benign working of perfection in all its forms, as it is important that we learn about perfection's real possibilities. The main question of this study is then, what can be done with perfection today?

Estimation

Implicit and explicit instances of perfection have to do with our estimation of ourselves, others, aspects of being, situations, actions, states, functions, properties, events, institutions, and so on — an estimation structured in terms of better and worse. And beyond the not yet perfect lies a higher, inspirational standard. The best of its kind, beyond which there can be no further improvement, is what we should define as being perfect in a strict sense. Something that is fair, average, good or better, but not the best of its kind — hence, improvement is still possible — then possesses partial, approximate, or relative perfection, that is, perfection to a certain degree.

Perfective and semi-perfective terminology (progression, fulfilment, realisation, flourishing, etc.) is involved in the articulation of aspects and dimensions less directly, or at least less systematically, addressed in certain other languages and perspectives. On this, Donald Walhout remarks:

> We speak of being one's real self, of developing oneself, of becoming what we can become, of achieving our goals, of perfecting our abilities, of being mature human beings; and such expressions seem to be more inclusive, more revealing, more valuationally normative than the similarly prevalent speech about satisfying particular desires, promoting particular interests, and the like, and certainly more indicative than such remote talk as that about synthesizing values, balancing pleasures and pains, and the like (1978a: 224).

The current movement of positive psychology, quite straightforwardly, insists that human existential meaning cannot be adequately understood without perfective concepts such as virtue, skill, flourishing, and so on (Seligman & Csikszentmihalyi 2000). My analysis intends to concur with this insight. We need something like the language of perfection to make sense of different human fields. Perfective estimation is at work in many areas of human concern. Through our powers of discrimination we come to see degrees of perfection— scales, distances and standards — in our varied practices and enterprises (Murdoch 1971: 71). In this manner the idea of perfection functions as a basic producer of order and direction.

Beyond perfective estimation as a system of discrimination lies the idea of perfective experience as such. Each of us has personally experienced (so it is to be hoped) that it is better to actually reach and receive perfective states in ourselves and in the things around us than not to do so. No one will argue against the fact that it is better to have a good or a perfected hammer at one's disposal than to work with a flawed tool, or against the fact that it is better to play a musical instrument with perfected skill than to be hampered by weak musical technique. Perfection, therefore, is relevant as a language of estimation exactly because it appropriately tunes in with concrete human experience. Perfective language did not suddenly appear without including a consideration for the beings we indeed are. It is clear, for example, that human selves do not easily give up their particular contact with facts of perfective fulfilment, certainly not without a strong degree of frustration and disappointment. Most of us are typically interested in progression. Existential meaning is intimately connected with positive development and the presence of completion. Who, indeed, would like to throw out his or her received or acquired perfection? It simply feels good to strive for and reach a perfective state. Perfection is pleasing. There is an intrinsic connection between perfection and satisfaction.

Complexity

I am interested in a complex reading of the language of perfection. *Complexus* originally refers to the idea of an interwoven whole, and this is what we should be pursuing — an interwoven togetherness, a tissue of questions, responses, themes and concepts (Morin 1990a: 175). Complex perfectionism is driven by the conviction that something significant is to be gained in thematic interaction or combination. The introduction of different contexts in which perfection finds a place — think, for example, of interpretation, character, future possibility, nature beyond humanity, and other issues — is likely to lead to a revitalised perfectionism, with which one can indeed live in today's context. In turn, the language of perfection might contribute to a sharpened reception of particular issues at hand. Perfection then is not only something to be understood, but itself constitutes a fruitful way to understanding.

It is best to operate in a relaxed and experimental manner — let us see where we can get with the language of perfection. While defending perfection whenever appropriate, I will not insist on the claim that perfectionism alone can successfully offer an adequate approach to human (and non-human) existence. Perhaps at a later stage, beyond the confines of this study, it will be proper to offer a more intense defence of perfection as our best language of estimation. But before this might come about, it is necessary to become sufficiently acquainted with the ways of perfection. The point is to arrive at a *recognisable* language of perfection, that is, to turn perfection into something other than a vague, magical talisman. This challenge may itself require more than one attempt. Indeed, it is a serious task to which this study only manages to respond in a preliminary manner.

One point to be stressed is that a contemporary language of perfection is not meant to confirm an optimistic view of earthly existence. We live with relative states, and this means that we live with failure, degradation and imperfection too. A real perfectionism — one for concrete persons — should not turn a blind eye to the fragility, the roughness, and the risks involved in human existence. There are no guarantees of completion. Angelic perfection is not of this world. We are always on our way, and never actually reach an absolute state.

Perfectionism as philosophical anthropology

It is important to stress perfectionism's existential ambition: it functions largely as a philosophical anthropology. The following points introduce us more closely to the idea of an existential perfectionism.

First, aiming to defend a theory of perfective subjects driven by the desire to be and determined by the effort to exist, perfectionism intends to offer a distinct version of what can be called an 'earthly anthropology' (Fink 1979: 29). Perfectionism is first and foremost concerned with 'terrestrial perfectibility' (Passmore 1970: 27). Most forms of perfection are uniquely situated on our planet. Our skills, qualities, capacities and virtues function only as benign states for the particular psycho-organic beings that we are. They serve as obvious instances of earthly perfection. Our globe directly conditions the actualities and possibilities of the human state of being. Another point is that we are only specifically and inimitably at home on earth (Morin 1991b: 22). It is here that we live with rivers, trees, mountains, with the diversity of species and cultures. As human creatures there is no better place to be. A life on other planets — perhaps after we have destroyed the benign conditions on earth — will only be a feeble imitation of what we have now on this unique planet.

Second, the idea of perfection undoubtedly deserves to be applied to realities beyond the human, as will become clear in different chapters, but perfectionism as a theory of human existence unavoidably holds the first position. The language of perfection is developed by human beings and is centrally concerned with the human enterprise. A perfective reception of non-human entities — even while implying a reaching out to something that is not human — is necessarily played out in the context of a human interpretation of natural otherness. Our reception of nature, perfectively and otherwise, in this sense constitutes an issue in perfective anthropology

Third, perfectionism as anthropology extends beyond the realm of ethics (it is, of course, possible to opt for a so-called broad conception of morality or ethics, which would include self-development, creativity and intellectual accomplishment, but it seems better to differentiate terminologically between non-moral issues of self-concern and moral concern for others). Perfective anthropology reacts to something like Bill Puka's theory of moral perfectionism. He wishes not to be occupied with fostering financial geniuses and athletic stars (Puka 1990: 49). Fine, but what about fostering musical talents and other personal creativities? These things soundly belong to human accomplishment. Consequently, we should not hesitate to posit Puka's characterisation of perfectionism as 'an inspirational picture of what we can be or might try to be' (*ibid.*: 159) against his own drive toward morality. An inspirational picture needs more than morals alone. The positive acceptance of self-regarding issues beyond morality is a great strength of perfectionism (Hurka 1993: 5). It permits us to make contact with a much larger territory. We should, of course, add that perfectionism is not to be identified with radical self-realisationism (Walhout 1978a: 228). There is a strong recognition of perfection beyond morality — of ideals of personal perfection (Norton 1976) — but morality remains an unavoidable, indeed a very essential aspect of perfective human existence.

Fourth, a great number of human earthly perfections are played out in the context of practices, that is, complex projects characterised by original internal goods, a concrete history of progression, and a singular sense of accomplishment. Good human lives are deeply determined by their immersion in a world of particular practices. Perfectionism as anthropology to a very substantial degree includes the question of practice. The connection between perfection and practice is outlined in MacIntyre (1981), as well as in liberal authors like Rawls (1999) and Raz (1999). Being an existentially significant middle between the minimal level of basic action and the comprehensive level of life story (Ricoeur 1990: 181), the world of practices constitutes a most fertile realm of perfective concern. Many of our cultural achievements are products of practices. It is therefore of capital importance to defend the presence of practice in contemporary culture.

Fifth, perfectionism is connected to a positive theory of human development. It is impossible, in fact, to defend a constructive psychology of development without a sense of perfection (a sense of better and worse, connected with stages of human personal development and achievement). A perfective scheme is a fundamental value presupposition of developmental theory as such (Kaplan 1986). In turn, perfectionism leads to a sense of development (teleology). Human perfection is, in most cases, not a matter of immediate accomplishment. It takes time to develop perfection. This is an essential dimension of the organic and human way of being. We may conclude, thus, that the idea of human perfection introduces the question of development as much as the idea of human development implies the question of perfection.

Sixth, perfective anthropology brings to light a human being defined by an intrinsic desire to accomplish things and reach ends. We need the vessel of purpose. Intrinsic motivation, as discerned by White (1965) and others (Deci & Ryan 1985), is automatically connected to perfective experience, while perfectionism immediately includes a sense of intrinsic motivation. Motivation concerns the energizing and direction of behaviour. Intrinsic motivation is to be proposed as a new motivational propensity that coheres with the presence of a variety of activities (practices). It concerns the inherent satisfaction of being involved in exercising and extending one's capacities and enhancing one's mastery. Perfectionism is not exactly a theory for passive selves without much aspiration, but rather one of active achievement.

One could name other significant characteristics, but they will appear in the course of this study. For now, we have provided perfectionism with an actual face.

The plan of this study

This study is divided into the following chapters.

The first three chapters highlight the relation between interpretation and perfection. Chapter 1 develops an anthropological reading of interpretation. I will propose an existential hermeneutics that is relevant to perfectionism (perfective selves unavoidably are interpreting selves; hermeneutics, therefore, cannot but be an essential part of perfectionism as anthropology). Chapter 2 is interested in underlining the perfective aspects of interpretation. I will propose a perfective hermeneutics grounded in the point that a defence of interpretation is possible only on the basis of a perfective scheme of better and worse. Chapter 3 relates a contemporary defence of the language of perfection to the idea of an evolutionary hermeneutics. One can attempt to prolong the language of perfection through an interpretative procedure that combines a sense of continuation with one of revision.

A second set of chapters focuses on the language of perfection. Chapter 4 deals with the tension between positive and negative interpretations of perfection and offers a balanced concept of positive perfection, which can withstand current critical and negative readings. Chapter 5 introduces a contemporary form of relative perfection. I will also clarify the position of perfection in its relation to other languages of estimation. Chapter 6 proposes a basic list of perfective concepts and distinctions. It is important to construct a broad language of perfective appraisal, expressing significant varieties of perfective being and development; only then shall we manage to approach the complexity of perfection. Chapter 7 explores the language of aretaic perfection, perhaps the most popular issue in contemporary perfectionism. I will study virtues as human strengths of a special kind in the framework of an aretaic personology for fallible selves.

The next four chapters explore different segments of a theory of human perfective existence. Chapter 8 develops a perfective naturalism. A general conception of human perfective existence is to be rationally justified on the basis of a general interpretation and estimation of humans as organic beings of a certain kind. Chapter 9 clarifies the personal or individual aspects of human perfection. Chapter 10 discusses the creation of existential meaning in the context of perfective practices. Many significant experiences of perfection are played out in practices as defined in the thought of Alasdair MacIntyre. I will sketch a perfective praxiology in close dialogue with his insights. Chapter 11 articulates a perfective possibilism. Human perfective existence is strongly defined by possibility. It is important to highlight different aspects of the question of future perfection. My analysis will be concerned with the issues of ideals, hope, meliorism, and utopia.

Chapter 12, finally, introduces natural perfection. We are not the only heroes of perfective being. I will focus on the application of the perfective concept of life story to the world of plants and animals. A theory of bio-narration can contribute to a positive appreciation of nature in terms of original meaning and perfection.

This study ends with a brief conclusion.

CHAPTER ONE —
INTERPRETATION AND PERFECTION — i:
EXISTENTIAL HERMENEUTICS

*Die Auslegung ist das treibende Moment
in der Wurzel des Menschseins.*

— Karl Jaspers

One would normally expect a study on perfection to begin with perfection and not with interpretation. However, there is much to say in favour of interpretation as our first issue.

The perfective relevance of interpretation

Three points make clear why interpretation should be included, and why it is good to begin with interpretation in the first place.

While in everyday life we use perfective language regularly, there is nowadays a strong philosophical habit to suspect perfection. Bring up perfection in moral and philosophical debate and soon a choir of critics makes its appearance, insisting that perfection is dogmatic and elitist, that it is a medieval relic. The claim is made that in times of radical plurality and construction we simply cannot deliver an interpretational ground for perfection. Interpretation itself is made suspect. Liberal authors insist that only thin conclusions about human existence can be upheld rationally — the rest is for private consumption. Postmodernist authors tell us that only a play of fictional constructions is out there. Interpretation — with its more serious undertone — is taken to be a crypto-dogmatic enterprise. Since perfectionism can only deliver rational insight into perfective thickness when there is first rationality of interpretation, we need to find out whether a more positive conception of interpretation is indeed available. To defend perfection it is necessary to defend interpretation.

A second point is that there is no gap between the issues of interpretation and perfection to begin with. Interpretation is itself an intrinsically perfective undertaking. If a defence of perfection leads to interpretation, a defence of interpretation leads in turn to perfection. Between the poles of absolutism (non-interpretative truth) and relativism (construction without rational defence) interpretation constitutes a middle position, based on the possibility of estimating different interpretations according to a scheme of better and worse. And, as suggested in the introduction, estimation of this kind is perfective estimation.

Without perfective language we cannot come to an understanding of the distinct qualities of interpretation. To introduce interpretation is, unavoidably, to introduce perfection.

Finally, interpretation constitutes a fundamental existential process. We are all interpreters and our ways of interpretation deeply enter our ways of being. The interpreting self is an essential figure within philosophical anthropology. Since perfectionism is itself a form of philosophical anthropology, it is bound to encounter the problem of interpretative selfhood.

These points sufficiently introduce the perfective relevance of hermeneutics. In this chapter I will depict the general figure of the interpreting self in the context of an existential hermeneutics. Perfective aspects of interpretation and interpretative aspects of perfectionism will be introduced in the next two chapters.

Towards a generalised sense of interpretation

Interpretation is not an isolated or confined cognitive activity, but is everywhere in human existence. We live with interpretation and there is no way to opt out. To make this point evident we need to move from a confined to a generalised sense of interpretation.

Interpretation etymologically relates to 'in between' (*inter*) and 'saying' or 'showing' (*pres*, a Latin word going back to the Greek term *phrazo*, related to the English 'phrase') (Seiffert 1992: 10). In its literal sense, an interpreter is a between-speaker, someone who acts as an intermediary between an original source and a receptor (sometimes hermeneutics is linked with Hermes, the messenger-God — this, again, underlines an intermediary role). Interpretation is then considered to be an act undertaken by a third party, whether it be a translator who articulates in one language a message written in another, or an expositor who clarifies the symbolic words of a poet or a prophet (Nicholson 1984: 3).

Four traits in interpretation stand out. First, interpretation is a public act. Translation and exposition are undertaken for the sake of others. Second, interpretation is necessary exactly because there is some incomprehension — something is not understood by someone. Third, interpretation is an activity that in principle is based upon and results in the achievement of understanding. Translators and expositors are experts in understanding certain texts or certain kinds of texts. And the communication of their understanding to others is destined to be equally successful. Fourth, interpretation is a confined undertaking, not necessary in contexts of plain discourse and shared language where understanding is spontaneous. Interpretation also does not play a role in realms beyond language.

At a later stage we find this original conception of interpretation applied to the larger world of human textuality beyond translation and exposition. Think of

Schleiermacher's general text-hermeneutics. The understanding of interpretation in connection with texts today constitutes a well-established discipline. General text-hermeneutics transcends the particularities of translation and exposition. We reach a broader sense of interpretation.

There are hermeneutic rules that concern every text. A central point is that according to general text-hermeneutics the aspect of mediation does not only lie in the fact that a messenger or translator mediates between a text and a particular receptor. The act of reading *as such* is seen to imply interpretation. Like a mediator standing between text and receptor, so too, the particular workings of our cognitive, emotive, valuational, and linguistic schemes stand between the text and our understanding of this text. There is no direct grasp of the text's meaning. In reading a text — whether as translator, expositor or as individual reader — I am automatically involved in interpretative activity. Such a generalisation of the idea of interpretation clearly makes hermeneutics something more than an occasional necessity. It also turns interpretation into an interior cognitive activity, since the process of interpretation does not need an exterior third party to qualify as interpretation. A translator, or any other reader, is involved in interpretation as soon as he or she begins to appropriate a text.

Some will perhaps argue that we are only confronted with tasks of interpretation when encountering difficulties in understanding, but this point constitutes an invalid limitation of the interpretational field. The fact that a text is an extended and complex totality, in which the meanings of parts necessarily need to be interconnected through cognitive labour, automatically implies a sense of non-immediacy. Textual meaning — even if felt to be spontaneously understood — is the result of mental work in which our preconceptions have a continued voice. Reading takes time, so a sense of anticipation (which always implies a sense of preconception) is unavoidable. It is true, of course, that the act of interpretation is most evident in confrontation with difficult, symbolic, enigmatic texts, texts written in other times and cultures, or in languages other than our own. We are especially forced to undertake interpretative work when confronted with unfamiliar symbols, ambiguities of context, and historical distance. But even when our interpretative work has become more easy, it still requires effort, albeit less intensely so. So too, reading is still interpretative when we read easy texts. There is a process of interpretational habituation and confirmation. Extensive and repeated reading of a text is likely to lead to an automatism of understanding, but this does not eliminate interpretation — it only turns earlier struggle into a fluent undertaking.

A central point to remember is that one cannot escape the interpretative nature of textual reception. Even when the complexities of symbolism, historicity, context and language are limited, we would still have the essential complexities in the reader's mind — texts are encountered only through the workings of our preconceptions (a collection of personal and communal sedimentary deposits —

ideas, concepts, expectations, valuations, experiences and convictions). The issue at stake here is that these experiences and schemes are destined to colour our reception of something as something, thereby unavoidably mediating between understanding (or misunderstanding) and the message to be understood. We cannot get rid of such mediation and this in itself is not a bad thing. Without it we would simply not be able to receive at all. Preconceptions and sedimentations constitute obstacles as well as opportunities for our interpretative capability.

Each interpretation implies a productive process of interaction between prejudgements/anticipations and confirmations/revisions, between parts and wholes. This process of mutual clarification constitutes the hermeneutic circle (Bontekoe 1996). Reading is a coloured, selective and temporal activity. We read a few lines. These lines mean something to us by virtue of an already acquired stock of beliefs, concepts, anticipations, and schemes. We then develop a provisional sense of the whole, which in turn colours our interpretation of the next part, which will again influence our sense of the whole, and so on. The circular structure of reading highlights the nature of interpretation. Without such a circular process there is no interpretation.

One must underline the deeper complexity of the hermeneutic circle in the context of textual interpretation.

In taking something as something (the question of meaning) we are at the same time concerned, whether consciously or unconsciously, with what we can or cannot do with that which we receive as a certain meaning in our current existential and hermeneutic situation (the question of application). What we interpret is furthermore something that is digested through a process of axiological appreciation (the question of valuation). A reception that appraises in a negative, positive or neutral way (which is also an axiological option) is unavoidable. We receive meanings as more and less valuable. Application and valuing, too, are undertakings taking the form of a hermeneutic circle, undertakings which need to be adapted along the way. We anticipate how we should or could apply or value certain texts and meanings. These anticipations influence our subsequent moments of application and valuation and may themselves be formatted by these further moments. Furthermore, it is not the case that reception of meaning, application and valuation constitute independent processes. They necessarily interact: our applications influence our valuations and receptions, our valuations influence our applications and receptions, and our receptions influence our applications and valuations.

We would do injustice to the hermeneutic tradition if we portray it as being involved only with the interpretation of texts. Besides a concern for texts, modern and contemporary hermeneutics is also directed toward the field of existential interpretation (Dilthey, Heidegger, Gadamer, Bollnow, Ricoeur, Lenk). This constitutes an important extension of the theory of interpretation.

16

Interpretation is proposed as the fundamental human way of being. It is not just one activity among others; we simply interpret by the very energy of our being, as part of the effort to exist. We interpret not only texts, but basically everything — textless and wordless realities included. We interpret ourselves, others, actions, history, art works, dreams, houses, streets, trees, animals, and any other aspect of being. There is an inescapable *Interpretationsimprägniertheit* (Lenk 1993: 21). Existing is interpretative from beginning to end:

> From the time you wake in the morning until you sink into sleep, you are interpreting. On waking you glance at the bedside clock and interpret its meaning: you recall what day it is, and in grasping the meaning of the day you are placed in the world and your plans for the future; you rise and must interpret the words and gestures of those you meet on the daily round. Interpretation is, then, perhaps the most basic act of human thinking. Indeed existing itself may be said to be a constant process of interpretation (Palmer 1969: 9).

Existential hermeneutics, or hermeneutic anthropology, is the philosophical study of the diversity of processes of interpretation at work in human lives as such. Interpretation becomes a cognitive instrument with practical import in a much wider and deeper sense. The regional problem of literary interpretation is now to be situated within a larger hermeneutic framework. We may leave the library, so to speak, and be concerned with interpretation as the conferring of existential meaning, wherever we are and whatever we do.

Texts and beyond

Existential hermeneutics remains influenced by the basic textual definition of interpretation.

Certain human non-linguistic realities and happenings — notably (parts of) histories and life histories — may be considered as text-analogues (Ricoeur 1986a: 183-211). The interpretation of oneself, for example, always includes interpretation of a personal past. This past is a complex sequence (or rather, is interpreted as being such a sequence) of elements, notably actions, situations, experiences, events, accomplishments. Self-knowledge arises out of an interpretation of elements and of the connections between elements. This play of connection shows sufficient similarity with the interaction of parts and wholes in text-interpretation (Ricoeur 1990: 210-211).

Of course, there are several differences between the interpretation of texts and the interpretation of life histories.

First, although linguistic and textual expressions are elements with which we may have to deal in self-interpretation, many elements of our past are simply wordless (feelings, actions, objects, events). Obviously, the wordless is also humanly interpreted through the medium of language (the interpretation of the wordless is itself linguistically expressed and is in any case influenced by the many concepts and words that have infiltrated our cognitive being), but — and this is important — interpretation does not make the wordless and the non-textual as such a sequence of words, sentences and texts.

Second, words and sentences in texts are stable and clear. We may have disputes about certain meanings, but the material forms that we perceive are at least taken as reasonably defined. This is not fully the case in the interpretation of histories and life histories. We often have to decide which traces and events, experiences and expressions to include in the text of history or of our lives. Moreover, the text of our life is still going on. It is not a finished book but an open-ended process.

Third, interpretations of personal histories are bound to become a constitutive part of those histories. The histories to be interpreted are directly influenced, transformed even, by the interpretations of those histories (self-interpretation will therefore have to include interpretation of our earlier and current interpretations of ourselves). In contrast, the interpretation of texts beyond our personal reality does not constitute an internal or organic part of those texts as such. We can only receive texts through reading, but reading is not the same as rewriting or creating.

These points should teach us to be sufficiently careful in extending the model of the text to human realities beyond the literal conception of a text.

Perceptual hermeneutics

Some are perhaps inclined to limit the breadth of existential hermeneutics. To be sure, histories and life histories are complex human realities and we may consider the interpretation of these realities as a temporal, selective and coloured process — the relations between the different parts of histories and life histories in this sense somehow match the relations between words and lines in texts — but can we really claim the same thing concerning other elements to which existential hermeneutics refers, specifically the activity of seeing objects and aspects of being? Is the immediacy and spontaneity of vision, as it is experienced by each of us, not epistemologically opposed to the mediation, indirectness, and extension that characterise interpretative activity as circular movement?

The 'naive observer' is convinced that the world he or she perceives is a passive recording of reality (von Uexküll 1984: 192). However, we should not allow ourselves to be overpowered by the 'naive' immediacy of seeing. The field of perceptual hermeneutics is in fact ineradicably a part of human hermeneutics. Our perceptions and ideas do not directly reflect reality, but translate aspects of being in terms of our cognitive structures, capacities, schemes and

18

concerns (Morin 1990b: 134). To perceive an object or an aspect of being is to see it as something. Perception is reception and reception involves interpretative mediation by a receptive organism. There is no reception without mediation; hence, reception is interpretation.

Language and culture in part determine what we see. Organic and practical inclinations, too, play a cardinal role. Things that we see in the world are used and valued in certain ways. Interpretations are formatted through the interests and orientations of the interpreter; they play a role in our selection of aspects, in taking parts of reality as something:

> Our practical interests do not merely prescribe what is selected from the environment; they also play a role in pinpointing the aspects, qualities, and features we see the things as having. The actual matter of being a hat derives from the interest we have in having our heads covered and from interests associated with that (Nicholson 1984: 36).

It is for humans almost impossible not to receive a tree in certain established ways. Furthermore, it is not inadequate to sense a hermeneutic circle at work in the human perception of things (this, of course, serves as an analytic remark, since in reality we immediately 'see' an object as something). We do not *feel* that there is a mediating process. However, our interpretation of the cognitive constitution of our visual and cerebral system does support a hermeneutics of perception and a cerebral hermeneutics. Our cognitive and perceptual system works in certain ways. Visual information is received and synthesised into diverse units, distributed among cells, and finalised into a perceptual unity. Purely on a perceptual level it is clear that we do not see objects in their immediate totality, but as a complex of sides, surfaces, and so forth, which are received as a totality by way of an interpretative process — a process we do not concretely experience as process due to the fluency of our biological, cognitive, psychological, linguistic, and cultural 'habits'. When I see aspects of a house I immediately receive it as parts of an entire house — as parts of a house to begin with — by virtue of the workings of earlier visual, practical, psychological and cultural experience, earlier valuations, cognitive and organic structure, and prejudgement. After analytic reflection, however, it turns out that I see parts of a house, which, by virtue of my sense of the whole, provide me with the interpretational togetherness of a house. If a temporal process of perception is admitted to be there, then the hermeneutic circle can in principle be introduced as a description of what will not be consciously experienced as hermeneutically circular (Bontekoe 1996: 2).

Perception differs in an obvious way from the more complex interpretations of texts and personal pasts. In most cases it does not constitute an intense drama of interpretation, but rather a background process. Moreover, the interpretation of my past may suddenly change — after crisis or tragic event, I may come to

19

see a new self with a differently interpreted past — but my perceptual interpretation of parts and aspects of reality (an object, a stone, a tree, etc.) is in most cases highly stable and to large extent static. The self is able, at times, to revise self-interpretation drastically, but is quite strongly determined — simply by being a human organism — to receive reality in certain established ways. The stability and direction of perceptual interpretation are deeply connected — this we can say on the basis of our scientific and philosophical interpretations of the environment and of the relation between organism and environment — with the elements, energies, processes and systemic stabilities found in the outside world, which constitute the source material for our perceptual undertakings. The invariant elements, stabilities, and processes we pick out can be assumed to find their source in what is originally out there.

The figure of the interpreting self

We have established that the figure of the interpreting self extends beyond textual and linguistic being. Interpretation becomes a general characteristic of the human person, including perceptual existence.

A relevant perfectionism, in its ambition to function as an anthropological perspective, cannot avoid giving a basic position to existential hermeneutics and to the figure of the interpreting self.

Perfective selves are, first and foremost, interpreting selves. How many challenges of interpretation do not await each perfective person in the course of his or her life?

Furthermore, it is not only the case that interpretation is unavoidable, but also that one can only obtain valuable and concrete self-knowledge by way of interpretational detours, this is, through a reception of signs, symbols and texts (Ricoeur 1986a: 29). This constitutes an essential finding of the hermeneutic philosophy of self-knowledge, a finding that perfectionism should take over in two ways. Perfective selves ought to indulge in an interpretative quest for self-knowledge (it better to try to know, and thus develop, oneself by way of interpretative challenges and opportunities). And perfective theory must itself be prepared to recognise its own quest as a hermeneutic enterprise.

The interpretative nature of perfective selfhood and perfective theory is, of course, based on one fundamental assumption, namely that processes of interpretation can indeed lead to a functional perfective theory and to a productive perfective existence. But this implies that interpretation is itself something of a *benign* activity. This issue brings us to the perfective nature of interpretation as such. This is something we have to clarify in the next chapter.

CHAPTER TWO —
INTERPRETATION AND PERFECTION — ii:
PERFECTIVE HERMENEUTICS

> *Interpretation is not a matter of*
> *anything-goes imaginative flights into*
> *the never-never world of free-floating*
> *fancy.*

— Nicholas Rescher

We may live with interpretation all the time, but perhaps interpretation is not really something that can be appreciated as a benign and capable process, as a *good* cognitive activity. Interpretation will then resist estimation in terms of perfective value. The figure of the interpreting self subsequently loses its place within perfectionism. Or rather, it would lead us to cancel perfectionism as a valid option. Perfectionism as a philosophical perspective on human existence is in fact based on possibilities of good interpretation. A defence of the goodness of interpretation, of good interpretations and of the good interpreter holds an essential position in the development of a contemporary perfectionism. We therefore specifically need to concern ourselves with the idea of a perfective hermeneutics.

Perfective hermeneutics, focused on varieties of goodness in interpretation, wishes to offer an alternative to the relativist argument without falling into the hands of absolutism. On the one hand, interpretation is a process without definitive ending. On the other hand, certain standards and accomplishments of interpretation can be suggested. In the same way that the realisation that a perfectly aseptic environment is impossible should not lead us to conduct our surgeries in a sewer (Robert Solow, quoted in Geertz 1973: 30), so we must also seek not to throw away available rational possibilities simply because we are so disappointed about the lack of absolute knowledge. There are shades between everything and nothing.

Interpretation beyond absolutism and relativism

Absolutism claims that a true reception of reality is possible and that we can also arrive at certain and universally valid moral foundations, values and rules. It insists that we have an immediate non-interpretational entrance or that interpretational processes can after a while result in a secure truth — a truth which then loses its interpretative character. Absolutism is highly motivated to seek an escape from interpretation because it considers interpretation to be a deeply infected process. Interpretation will only lead to relativism. To give in on something will force us to give in on everything. The figure of the absolutist self is determined by a fear that may capture most of us. In the words of Mark Johnson:

> There lurks in most of us a graving fear that, should objectivism prove untenable, the floodgates holding back the raging currents of relativism would be opened forever. We would all drown in the ensuing chaotic inundation (1987: 198).

The relativist, of course, thinks otherwise. Radical constructionist relativism (as is defended, for example, in the writings of Richard Rorty, Don Cupitt, Joseph Margolis, Nelson Goodman, Kenneth Gergen, and many others) is a direct response to absolutism, which is taken to be a dangerous illusion. Absolutists are depicted as trying to sell their own interpretations as non-interpretative truths, driven perhaps by a will to power. Interpretations not officially presented as interpretations are in fact unhealthy, manipulative forms of interpretation. A healthy attitude towards interpretation consists in accepting that there is only a plurality of interpretations. The essential point is to grant each (non-absolutist) interpretation its creative place without trying to impose a confrontation with other interpretations supposed to be epistemically or morally better. Relativism proposes an exciting play of interpretation without rational control: every interpretation is as good as any other (Rescher 1997a: 198).

Although a perfective hermeneutics is likely to agree with the relativist critique of absolutism, it is subsequently pushed towards the formulation of an alternative position, leading us away from a radicalised relativism. Perfective hermeneutics does not deny plural, historical, particular, and relative aspects of the process of interpretation. However, it does arrive at another reading of what interpretation is all about.

Radical constructionist relativism sees the interpreting self as an entity enclosed in its own interpretational productions. Each interpretation is a constructionist fiction, which has nothing to do with what is out there (otherness). We ourselves fully create what is 'out there'. Hence, the idea of discovery is abandoned for a process of making. All interpretations, if somehow 'useful', are considered equally valid. Interpretations are productive tools enabling one to enjoy more pleasure and less pain. No interpretation is ever more or less in touch with reality. We are introduced to the trivialisation of interpretation.

Perfective hermeneutics wishes to underline aspects of interpretation that are ignored or underestimated in relativist discourse — aspects which, in different ways, do invite an estimation of interpretations in terms of better and worse, and which lead to a sense of interpretational openness without absolutism. Not all interpretations are benign, to be sure. We may interpret forms of otherness without care, finesse, fairness and openness. We may misinterpret ourselves.

Existing interpretations may lack sufficient quality. We can become the victims of presuppositions and unconscious frames. But this does not cancel out a more positive challenge. Heidegger (1963: 53) tells us the following about the hermeneutic circle. We should not try to avoid the circle, nor consider it as *unvermeidliche Unvolkommenheit*. We can actually never leave interpretation (there is no escape); nor should we try to escape in the first place since interpretation does embody fertile possibilities. The cardinal issue is to stay within the hermeneutic circle in a proper way, and a primordial element of proper interpretational existence is exactly to realise that one cannot escape interpretation and that interpretation may be a positive undertaking with certain possibilities.

In the following I will highlight the principal aspects of interpretative goodness that call for a scheme of better and worse. Let us begin with the biological role of interpretation.

The vital mission of interpretation

Different creatures receive aspects of being in a plurality of ways. Indeed, the idea of one world as communally experienced by a plurality of creatures turns out to be false (see von Uexküll 1980). Each species is characterised by a typical cycle of acting and perceiving. The plurality of organic beings is bound up with a plurality of interpretations. This may perhaps suggest that the trivialisation of interpretation holds true on an organic level. However, to think so is to ignore that for each species interpretation is an activity of vital importance, quite literally so. It would be unfruitful not to receive different aspects of being in a particularised way. Meaning only appears on the basis of selectivity and the world would not signify anything at all if everything were to be seen at once without discrimination and selection. To live is to choose and to particularise. There is a benign narrowness to embrace and without this one would turn into a formless state and cease to exist (Morin 1975: 250). Without a principle of interpretative selection we would float in a sea of chaos and nothingness. A perfective scheme, stressing better and worse, may therefore take interpretation as such as something that is better to have than not to have. While we cannot escape interpretative existence — a point that may suggest the negative idea of being cognitively framed by and duped into free construction — there is a deep sense of vital goodness in interpretative life. Interpretational efforts keep us alive! There is no life without interpretation, and there is no interpretation without life. We discover a cardinal link between survival and ways of interpretation, this is, between biology and hermeneutics (Kampis 1999). Interpretation, in its biological stage, as well as on other levels, is a form of what Jankélévitch (1977: 98) calls an 'organ-obstacle': that which limits and confines us (obstacle) is at the same time an essential instrument (organ) of openness (and vice versa).

In the dramatic organic context of life and death, the same principle of survival also finds application in the particular interpretative lives of the different species. To be a successful species and to be a successful member of a species means to live according to interpretations that have distinct survival value. Each organic kind specialises in interpretations that are effective. An animal specifically has to perceive the affordances of objects, places, events, and so forth, in a proper way. Affordances of things are what they furnish for good or ill to the observer (Gibson 1982). Each member has to adequately follow effective interpretations of available affordances. Besides the general insight that interpretation as such is good, we can furthermore discriminate between better and worse interpretations in terms of their contribution to the concrete survival of members of a species. It is good to interpret as such and it is better to interpret effectively (in terms of survival) than not to interpret effectively. Organisms have to make sense of aspects of being and of each other in contexts where this matters biologically. This is also for human beings the most urgent layer of interpretation, without which there would be no more elaborated and cultured forms of interpretation. Pragmatically minded relativists, so one may assume, will as such not deny the connection between interpretation and vital utility. In their writings it is, for example, suggested that we see a giraffe as a distinct object only because doing so serves a particular human activity of survival, the activity of hunting (Rorty 1999: xxvi). We may, thus, assume that relativists do accept that it is better to have than not to have interpretation (since without interpretation we would die) and that it is better to have interpretations with greater survival value. Relativism seems to confirm the goodness of interpretation on such a basic vital level. Interpretations are a means for animals to do their best in coping with the environment.

However, the point is that radical constructionist relativism all too quickly takes the connection between interpretation and survival in the direction of *complete* interpretational closure. We never meet aspects of otherness, but only our own constructions, based on our own instrumentalist concerns. Relativism furthermore extrapolates the radical vitalist and instrumentalist role of interpretation to *all* levels of human interpretation. In its urge to extrapolate, radical constructionist relativism is also inclined, so it appears, to fuse the principle of survival with a vague but all-consuming sense of aesthetico-creative gratification. The activities of interpretation, in whatever form, are to be focused on becoming 'the best habits of action for gratifying our desires' (Rorty 1999: xxiv). For the sake of psychological and vital health, so we are told, we need the intense excitement of plurality, difference, and flux. What matters is the production of diversification and novelty (Rorty 1989: 77). Interpretations and expressions ought to serve this 'artistic' sense of excitement, and in that case

24

are considered to be 'good' interpretations. One wonders, however, whether the original goodness of human interpretation is thereby not turned into a caricature.

Let us in the following respond to the relativist interpretation of interpretation.

Beyond interpretative closure

It is important to realise that the connection between interpretation and successful survival necessarily implies something beyond radical closure, and this in at least three aspects.

First, interpretation must itself have developed as an evolutionary response to varieties of otherness. Forms of otherness endanger or contribute to the life and survival of organic beings. Interpretation is a means to deal with these forms of otherness. We need interpretation exactly because there is otherness. The evolutionary role of otherness is implied in the idea of interpretation. The task of perceptual systems is to obtain useful information about the environment. Without an 'outside' this task would simply be irrelevant. This outside forces itself upon us and into us. In this sense, we are in the world as much as the world is in us (Morin 1991a: 185). What appears is therefore not only the result of our making, even if we cannot get to a non-interpretative reception of otherness.

Second, an interpretation that is effective must somehow manage to appropriately tune in, to some degree, with aspects of otherness. Each organism is an effective interpretative response to aspects of being. Whatever fire may constitute beyond the human organism, we know that prolonged contact with fire will lead to burning and even death. We can therefore interpretatively assume that certain properties of fire are such that humans and other organic beings cannot survive its workings. We never leave human interpretation, to be sure, but as part of human interpretation we arrive at the reasonable conclusion that not all interpretations of fire are equally adequate. Fire is such that it has strong effects on organic being. Hence, there is a strong role for otherness beyond radical interpretational closure. In interpretation we can do many things with and to otherness, but we cannot do everything. The world appears to be not indefinitely malleable (Johnson 1987: 207). The environment is systemically structured in ways that narrow down possibilities for our 'useful' interpretations. This confirms the applicability of a scheme of better and worse in connection with the interpretation of otherness.

Third, concerning the relativist extrapolation of survival and aesthetico-creative gratification it is also relevant to ask whether it is not possible for us to have acquired — in the course of human organic, mental and cultural history —

other interests besides survival and personal gratification. And perhaps these interests suggest further aims and possibilities of interpretation, more profound standards of better and worse. I indeed think these other aims and possibilities can be found. This will become clear in a later segment of my argument.

Basic organic relativity

Another point that radical constructionist relativism is bound to stress is that, although a sense of better and worse may somehow be appropriate in connection with interpretational processes characterising each particular organic kind, it is not appropriate to set up an estimative scheme in terms of better and worse in comparing different species or members of different species. Good interpretations of bats cannot be said to be better or worse than good interpretations of wolves or humans. A dog receives a certain something as a thing to lie under, while we see it as a table. Each organic kind has its own original way of being and interpretation. Moreover, one may safely assume that each organic kind 'likes' its life of interpretation and would not wish to turn, even if it could, into something else. Bats do not wish to become humans, humans are not (commonly) inclined to try to become bats. Hence, the plurality of interpretational projects implies a firm plurality of valuational stances. And this clearly brings a relativist stance into view as our most relevant option.

Perfective hermeneutics does not resist interpretational and valuational relativity with respect to the different species. In fact, it gladly shares the idea of each organic kind possessing its own original (perfective) way of being and interpretation beyond a comparative estimation of species in terms of better and worse. As humans we are likely to insist that it is better to be able to undertake scientific research than not to be able, but this is not an evaluation that can matter to other animal species. A bat wishing to undertake scientific research would not be speaking anymore from a bat's position: it would not be a bat. For a bat itself, in its original way of being, it is not better to be able to do science. This is simply not a question that arises for bats. Science appeals only to human beings and makes sense only in the context of being human.

But an admission of basic organic relativity does not automatically influence the course of perfective hermeneutics in the direction of a full relativism. First of all, because humans can conclude that it is questionable to judge comparatively the values of one species over against another means that we somehow can recognise the qualitative otherness of species beyond our own. Otherness is recognised in *its being other*. This recognition constitutes a small but significant step. Relativism is in fact obliged to accept a minimal sense of human openness, since its message is directly based on the recognition of a plurality of interpretational lives. Second, to leave others to be with their original differences,

26

without imposing one's own way of being, is a moral undertaking. Perfective hermeneutics insists that it is morally better to respect than not to respect otherness. Such a non-relativist respect is in fact also suggested in relativism. Rorty, too, speaks about a moral struggle focused on devising ways of diminishing the suffering of others (1999: xxix). Third, the acceptance of organic specificity, which is confirmed in relativism, may come to play a non-relativist role in confrontation with a cultural relativism (see next point).

Human cultures

There are numerous cultures, each implying (in part) distinct languages, and a distinct interpretation of world, society and existence. In this respect it may again become difficult to keep out a radical relativist sense of plurality. Cultural relativism is perhaps the most influential form of relativism. Perfective hermeneutics, however, manages to offer a more differentiated response.

First, since as a species we share organic properties, it is possible to moderate cultural relativism. Our hands, legs, ears and eyes bring about movement, action and interpretation in a species-specific way. Our brain is constituted according to a definite structure resulting in a set of basic experiences, which we may assume to be fairly the same in every culture (Johnson 1993: 11). Experiences of pain and pleasure, of movement and effort, of harm and well-being, define the contours of our reception of the world. There are recurring structures of embodied understanding (Johnson 1987: 196). Relativism in its cultural (and linguistic) version, so we may insist, is to be qualified by the principle of shared organic being (a principle accepted by relativism in its biological version). Humans — being embedded in distinct cultures and languages — share basic organic interpretations and capacities of existence. The possibility of interpretatively discerning a shared, organically constituted set of properties inhibits the celebration of radical plurality and thereby enlarges the field of agreement concerning the human way of being.

Second, besides organic being, there are other things and aspects we share in terms of cultural accomplishment and practice. There are different sources for this. Shared organic being itself is one source. Another is the fact that cultures essentially include interaction. Cultures are not clear-cut givens, involved as they are in a process of mutual moulding or mutuality (Iser 1996: 301). This turns a concrete culture into something other than an autonomous, closed entity:

> A fully individuable culture is at best a rare thing. Cultures, subcultures, fragments of cultures, constantly meet one another and exchange and modify practices and attitudes. Social practices could never come forward with a certificate saying that they belonged to a genuinely different culture (Williams 1993: 158).

Shared cultural and practical being again qualifies the relativist focus on radical plurality. One should never exaggerate the conceptual insularity of cultures (Raz 1999: 158).

Third, it is the case that cultures often share things by way of difference. For example, cultures share linguistic competence, but this competence is actualised in different directions — think of English and Chinese. Consider also the many forms of musical being. The production of difference as such is one of the things shared between cultures and there is something deeply universal in the capacity to be different. Deviation, innovation, and particularisation find their source in the *shared* complexity of the human brain (Morin 1986: 233).

Fourth, difference beyond what we share is also to be honoured in its own terms. There are numerous things and experiences that are not culturally and linguistically shared, or only shared in part or by only a few cultures. Radical constructionist relativism is not alone in appreciating the plurality of interpretations and cultures. A hermeneutically organised theory of perfective existence will be concerned with cultural otherness in a negative sense (think of cultures neglecting basic human rights, imperialistic cultures), but the other essential part of hermeneutic reception will be in line with what has been said about respect for animal otherness. A good interpreting self will respect aspects of original cultural otherness. We can go a step further even: perfective hermeneutics is also interested in creativities and opportunities arising out of the actual experience of plurality. There is a cognitive and existential goodness in difference. Being the creatures that we are, we need the play of plurality and difference. We know quite well that we are involved in interpretation and existence in a certain way, and that in many aspects other interpretations and ways of being are possible. This is likely to lead to a productive awareness that others may in their interpretations and ways of being have something to offer. Cultural anthropology produces knowledge of other cultural, existential, and moral possibilities and actualities. To recognise plurality is, in fact, its most essential vocation (Geertz 1973: 30). Plurality is a cognitive blessing. Experience with a plurality of interpretations may lead to a process of dialogical learning and knowledge formation. To be sure, evaluative and thematic confrontation and dialogue will at times leave us in a state of perplexity, but it is, all in all, 'more comprehensive and more humanising to embrace the plurality of cultures than to be imprisoned in our own' (Hirsch 1976: 78). It is better to accept the productive risk of pluralist interaction than to be captured by interpretational monotony and existential closure. Cultural and linguistic complexity sustains our epistemological and existential complexity, creating a turbulent zone that breaks through a rigid and closed cultural determinism (Morin 1991a: 30). Someone living with only one system of interpretation will in fact never realise the interpretational nature of his or her interpretation — interpretation would not be seen as interpretation. Interpretation implies the presence of other interpretations.

Without such an interpretative awareness we shall come to lose the organised possibility of cognitive progression.

Fifth, the radical constructionist relativist may be inclined to play out the cards of incomprehension, untranslatability and incommensurability. These cards are supposed to make thematic and evaluative understanding impossible, since we would be unable to reach and compare the specific content of other interpretations, languages and cultures. Perfective hermeneutics does not deny the fact that different languages and cultures can in part be incomprehensible, untranslatable and incommensurable. But the cardinal point is not to turn particular instances of incomprehension, untranslatability, and incommensurability into an automatic and universal negative theory. There are differences and problems, to be sure, but the possibility of mediation and mutual understanding is never fully closed (Desmond 1995a: 129). A hermeneutic theory of intercultural dialogue is inclined to stress the following points:

A — As already noted, the content of a culture is itself significantly an inter-culturally established content. Together with factors of shared organic experience this offers a first robust argument in favour of the possibility of understanding, comparison, and translation.

B — Many translations and comparative dialogues do seem to work. Inter-cultural dialogue — notably when carried out by someone who is a plain speaker of the two languages being compared, or who has direct experience within the two cultures being compared — may result in the establishment of certain connections between and translation of meanings, words, practices, customs, capacities, interpretations, and so forth.

C — Words available in one culture, although without (strict) equivalent in another culture, may often be situated in broader existential, functional and societal totalities. Comparing different terminologies is not only a matter of playing out one individual word against another, but also a matter of embedding words in larger histories and contexts. In these broader settings we may come to see that a certain word or concept comes close to words and concepts in our own language, while not being exactly the same.

D — By way of linguistic creativity it may be possible to develop an approximating terminology for non-equivalent terms available in other languages. Sometimes we will use several words or sentences to express a foreign word or concept.

E — It is not because we receive a form of cultural otherness completely different from our own culture, without equivalence, that we cannot somehow understand its point and purpose, and how it has come to be. Furthermore, it is not because one does not agree with something in another culture that one cannot comprehend or translate.

F — It will often be the case that we come to understand something only to some extent. Without full understanding, we are not in a situation of complete non-understanding.

G — It is good to be aware that we will also encounter terms, actions, and interpretations that we cannot place or define in some way. In that case we honestly have to accept the limits of our capacity to understand. Hermeneutics is certainly not based on the idea that we shall come to comprehend the whole world.

H — There is, in fact, nothing wrong with an admission of non-understanding. Rather, concrete awareness about what one does not understand is likely to contribute to proper understanding in other ways. An awareness of the limits of our understanding at least will help us to prevent an unconscious misunderstanding (believing that we have understood everything when this is not the case).

On the basis of the points mentioned we can say that the incommensurabilities and untranslatabilities discovered in the practice of understanding cultural and linguistic otherness never completely control that practice. There is a substantial and evolving degree of connection, comprehension and translation — a degree sufficient to go on with efforts to understand, to compare, and to translate.

We may conclude the hermeneutic response to cultural relativism as follows. Relativism, in its official stance at least, seems to know only one response to the experience of human cultural pluralism — we should let be all interpretations and differences as they are without trying to apply schemes of estimation (minus, of course, estimation in terms of survival and excitement). Perfective hermeneutics proposes more options for responding to cultural being: to appropriately honour differences, to learn from them, to find or to confirm underlying and obvious similarities and identities whenever relevant, to install a comparative scheme of better and worse between different interpretations, practices, views, and terminologies whenever this is possible, relevant, preferable, or unavoidable.

The play of similarity and resistance

In my earlier points I have underlined certain cracks in the relativist and constructionist narrative about interpretational closure. It is now time to enlarge and multiply these cracks, notably by stressing the combined productive role of the hermeneutic principles of similarity and resistance.

The radical constructionist relativist argues that the fact that we approach otherness by way of our preconceptions must automatically lead to a complete distortion and annihilation of otherness — we only meet our own constructions.

Interpretation as such is infected by presuppositions and this makes it sure that no otherness will be received. Interpretation is then considered a kind of dense fog through which we can reach nothing, through which nothing can reach us. And the interpretative fog is produced by our stubborn and often unconscious schemes. In interpretation we do not touch otherness: we simply encounter our own productions.

Perfective hermeneutics, however, brings into play the principle of similarity. Behind the principle of similarity immediately stands another fundamental principle, namely the principle of earthliness. Most of our interpretations are focused on forms of otherness that came to be in the context of earthly being. In many instances we see similarities between one's self and others (other humans, other organisms, other aspects of being). How to explain these similarities? Should we automatically assume that such similarities are constructionist figments of our mind? In some cases this is undeniably so — think of naive anthropomorphic interpretations of animal being. In other cases, however, this is less likely. Animals move and so do we. They eat and so do we. We share certain organic capabilities and needs with other organisms and it is rather foolish to deny the rationality of these interpretationally constituted observations of similarity. For all we know, each kind of organism has been specifically developed on our planet. It is therefore quite reasonable to expect that we share certain capacities and certain responses to aspects of earthly being. This is also the case, even more so, for different human beings and human cultures.

Contrary to the principle of similarity, radical constructionist relativism is eager to stress the gap between oneself and others: others are not like us, and we do not know what they are on their own terms since we cannot reach otherness. However, constructionist authors seem to have no difficulty in characterising others as leading another kind of interpretational life. Hence, there is at least one similarity that has to be admitted under the rule of constructionist relativism: We interpret and other organic kinds interpret. But if we can observe one segment of similarity, why not other segments of similarity too?

The principle of similarity sheds new light on the interpretational role of presuppositions and expectations. Certain expectations, presuppositions and interpretational schemes, which are established on the basis of our earthly way of being, are likely to help us to understand what happens in other earthly creatures. How else could we manage to understand and recognise something as movement in other animals if we had never moved ourselves. Hence, our sense of movement constitutes a fertile presupposition or expectation by which to interpret other organisms. We can conclude that presuppositions are not automatically negative — such a negative view typically is an 'Enlightenment attitude' (Gadamer 1986). We must of course be prepared to revise schemes of expectation and presupposition, which we in an earlier phase thought to be appropriate. The internal mobility of the hermeneutic process permits a sifting out of better and worse presuppositions and expectations. Expectations can be adapted and transformed. The principle of similarity plays a productive role in this.

There is also the principle of resistance. Our preconceptions and interpretations in fact find themselves confronted with resistances beyond our personal control. Realities beyond our interpretations are out there: 'If there is something to be interpreted, the interpretation must speak of something which must be found somewhere, and in some ways respected' (Eco 1992: 43) A text, for example, is not a picnic where the author brings the words and readers the sense. Some interpretations tend after a while to fall into contradiction and irrelevance. We realise that something is wrong and subsequently proceed in a different direction. Resistances implied in the way of being of an animal, for example, quickly tell us that certain interpretations of animal being are likely to be invalid. And animals will die or get sick or suffer if we treat them according to wrong interpretation. Texts similarly have their way of resisting inadequate readings:

> [I]f jack the Ripper told us that he did what he did on the grounds of his interpretation of the Gospel according to Saint Luke, I suspect that many reader critics would be inclined to think that he read Saint Luke in a pretty preposterous way (*ibid.*: 24).

A text needs to be checked out as a whole. Interpretations may fail to address all the parts in a coherent way. We never receive finalised truth, to be sure, but we may become aware — specifically through regular confrontation with resistances — that we are on a wrong path. Precisely through their stubborn presence, resistances teach us a benign lesson. Resistance causes interpretation — textual as well as perceptual interpretation — to be under constraint. It is not a free play. Each negative experience of resistance narrows and thereby controls the positive direction that can be taken.

Radical constructionist relativism, however, will insist that resistances are themselves interpretative constructions only. We pick out whatever we want and we invent signs of direction and resistance along the way. The interpreting self is pictured as being unable to learn from its interpretational confrontations. It is unable to learn because otherness is portrayed as a silent victim that will never scream out against wrong interpretation.

In my view concrete practices of interpretation show that resistances do manage to break through our scenarios and somehow do come to direct our interpretations in a positive manner. As Mark Johnson notes: 'Things outside us talk back to us, and proclaim their presence, with a very loud voice most of the time' (1987: 204). This already surfaces on the level of basic interpretation in the biological context. An animal may interpret something as a prey, but may find out later that the object captured does not act or taste as 'something to be eaten'. There is resistance against this interpretation, coming from the object in question. It is therefore not possible to claim that all is simply a matter of radical interpretative invention. An object can only afford to an animal what it does because it is what it is. The power of being is not exhausted by our constructs. Affordances cannot be radically invented. This simply doesn't work. The otherness of resistance is to be recognised as a cardinal dimension. Wayne Booth (1988) offers a refined, metaphorical view on the varied play of resistance, which deserves mentioning. Stones, for example, are in some sense 'actors'. They actively influence the plausibility of certain interpretations in terms of invitation, toleration, and violation:

> A stone *asks*, as it were, to be considered as a mass, a weight, a solidity; it certainly *tolerates* being placed according to its origins in geological time, or even being broken down into its chemical elements or into quarks and leptons, though it might be said to express considerable surprise at the breakdown. But it will be positively *violated* by questions about its stanzaic form or its point of view as a narrative (*ibid.*: 91).

The interplay of the principles of similarity and resistance shows that human interpretation is more than a matter of closure and constructionist fiction without a sense of otherness. This surplus beyond closure makes it valid to assume there are more and less healthy ways of functioning within the hermeneutical circle. We are not fully locked up in interpretational schemes. There is movement and evolution in interpretation. Estimation in terms of better and worse can be applied to interpretations and to interpretative movements more and less appropriately dealing with similarity and resistance, notably with complex combinations of similarity and resistance. We clearly transcend a 'merit-annihilating indifferentism' (Rescher 1997a: 199). For example, experiences of resistance and similarity are important in the human understanding of animal being. A dog does not respond to aspects of being in a human way. A human interpretation that assumes dogs look at the world like we do is bound to encounter certain resistances. These resistances will guide us in the direction of a revised interpretation of the dog's different way of interpreting the world. The principle of similarity, on the other hand, is important in establishing the insight that human and canine receptions of being both constitute varieties of interpretation.

The ends of interpretation

The complexity of the hermeneutic circle in the human context gives rise to ends, interests and capacities beyond interpretational closure and beyond interpretation defined only in terms of survival and aesthetico-creative gratification. To be sure, we shall never eradicate the organic urge to survive. Also gratification will continue to play a role. These aims and needs simply continue to be. But this doesn't mean that there is no combination possible with other ends and needs. Relativism, as a theory of suspicion, is inclined to reduce those other ends and needs to cryptic expressions of the will to survive, will to power, and hedonic gratification. Perfective hermeneutics, on the other hand, strongly appreciates these new ends. They are seen to have an original presence. It is especially important to underline cognitive and moral ends and capacities.

Our ability to compare interpretations (and to compare comparisons of interpretation), combined with the interplay between similarity and resistance, suggests certain opportunities for a practice focused on interpretations attempting to reach out, as much as possible, to properties belonging to forms of otherness. This is a fresh cognitive possibility focused on arriving at understandings which are better, not so much because they only give us more pleasure or have a cardinal role in our effort to survive, but also because they allow us to make more sense of original aspects of otherness.

Though never able to fully leave our own organic perspective — human eyes will always remain human eyes — we do appear to have the power to receive otherness from different interpretative angles. This is also part of being human. For example, we can interpret animals, not only as instances of nutritional material, but also as original projects characterised by a distinct way of being and interpretation. An animal is not only something we can eat. We may not be able to reach the full content of animal otherness, but our awareness that there is otherness beyond our interpretation may nonetheless motivate us to revise existing interpretations of animal being, confronted as we are with productive resistances and with other interpretations of animal otherness, which, possibly, have it in them to unlock complementary and alternative aspects ignored in our own personal interpretative effort

One can say that, within human interpretation, the moments of application and valuation do not fully overflow or dismantle the cognitive possibility of receiving original meaning. Otherness may be interpretatively received, at least in part, through the benign workings of similarity and resistance.

Besides a larger cognitive goal — a goal which radical constructionist relativism will of course try to reduce to the need to survive and to gratify oneself or to the cryptic and unhealthy workings of a will to power — it is relevant to underline the presence of moral interest and orientation. If otherness somehow can be interpretatively received in better and worse ways, beyond a strictly instrumental interpretation aimed at survival and gratification, then we reach a ground in which to build moral concern in terms of respect, care, generosity, and fairness. We can in fact only develop moral concern for otherness if aspects of otherness are interpretatively recognised beyond the confines of instrumentalist and closed construction. In turn, moral concern may come to constitute a structural factor in the production of better interpretations of otherness.

To be good to others means to try to understand them well. A hermeneutically schooled consciousness attempts to be receptive to otherness (Gadamer 1986: 273). The moral quality of human interpretation holds an important position within hermeneutic theory. With an interpretation of otherness we automatically enter the moral question of respecting original meaning (Hirsch 1976: 85).

The morality of interpretation finds an interesting confirmation in the figure of the benevolent interpreter. One discovers the presence of this figure in several hermeneutically minded authors.

In the eighteenth century hermeneutics of Meier (1996: 17) one hears about the interpretational virtue of *hermeneutische Billigkeit* or *aequitas hermeneutica*. This virtue refers to the disposition in an interpreter to initially receive, and to try to continue to receive, signs beyond oneself as true, coherent and meaningful in line with the perfective qualities of the producer of those signs. A similar principle is sketched in Gadamer. He refers to a *Vorgriff der Vollkommenheit* (1986: 299), which states that the interpretation of texts must be based on a preliminary anticipation of the meaning, coherence and truth of the text's message. Popper (1974b: 225) speaks in the same spirit. We must recognise others as potential sources of reasonable information. In Steiner we find the hermeneutic motion initiated by an act of trust: 'We grant *ab initio* that there is something there to be understood, that the transfer will not be void' (1975: 297). MacIntyre states that any worthwhile interpretation will be governed by a principle of charity requiring us to read a text, as far as possible, so as to impute significance rather than lack of meaning, plausibility rather than implausibility, truth rather than falsity' (2002: 164). Desmond refers to an agapeic hermeneutics — agapeic interpretational generosity is to be played out according to the following rule: 'Seek the strength in the other, the point of ripeness, or if not that, seek the promise of ripeness in the other' (1995b: 125). Finally, in the context of an ethic of care, it is specified that the 'one-caring' is destined to interpret the words and acts of the 'cared-for' in the best possible light (Noddings 1984).

Benevolent interpretation implies different tasks. Not only should we initially expect to find perfection in otherness, we may also involve ourselves in constructively improving or upgrading the quality of otherness, in line with what we conceive to be its original meaning (Thom 2001). This is a form of restorative interpretation. Audiences, for example, may reinterpret certain wrong notes and other little imperfections while listening to a very fine musical performer, enabling them to hear through available minor imperfections a more idealised perfective performance. Messages and performances with a certain perfective quality invite these benign interpretative processes of sympathetic idealising. Cognitive and moral ends and capacities give rise, especially in their complex interaction, to a distinct life of interpretation resisting summary in terms of the ends of survival and gratification.

Beyond interpretative imperfectionism

Radical constructionist relativism does its best to deny moral motivation. It is determined by strong resistance to anything suggesting a rational morality. Theories of moral and aretaic being are considered to be instances of absolutism. Hence, behind ethics and aretaics stands a manipulative will to power. But one notes a particular circularity. The downfall of rational and good interpretation results in the downfall of moral and aretaic being. And the downfall of moral and aretaic being contributes to the further impossibility of good interpretation, since interpreters will lack the guidance by virtues and moral demands. The idea of the good and virtuous interpreter is, according to relativism, a fiction.

One finds here a disposition opposite to hermeneutical equity or charity, namely the disposition to suspect others, to expect only processes of manipulation in forms of otherness. The result is an aggressive reading based upon a theory of imperfection (Greisch 1977: 207-208). Texts are radically distrusted and reduced to projects of dissimulation: we should anticipate imperfection, not perfection.

However, radical constructionist relativism has the tendency to contradict itself, or at least to be ambiguous in its relation to moral being. While refusing moral being in one way it suggests its own sense of moral being. Its minimal moral demand is to let other interpretations be as they are. More often than not this sense of moral being is left unexplained in any systematic sense (systematisation itself is considered a cognitive vice). Nonetheless, such an implicitly available principle of tolerance unavoidably carries us beyond moral relativism (Williams 1993: 159). It already expresses a universal moral good (Harré & Krausz 1996: 158). Furthermore, theories of radical suspicion are never fully consequent in their own constructionist suspicion. They get involved in a 'vicious skepticism' (Keith & Cherwitz 1989). For example, they cast doubt on the possibility of interpreting written language, but do so in written form. MacIntyre points out that the genealogical project of Nietzsche and Foucault implies something other than genealogy:

> For in making his or her sequence of strategies of masking and unmasking intelligible to him or herself the genealogist has to ascribe to the genealogical self a continuity of deliberate purpose and a commitment to the purpose which can only be ascribed to a self not to be dissolved into masks and moments, a self which cannot but be conceived as more and other than its disguises and concealments and negotiations, a self which just insofar as it can adopt alternative perspectives is itself not perspectival, but persistent and substantial. Make of the genealogist's self nothing but what genealogy makes of it, and the self is dissolved to the point at which there is no longer a continuous genealogical project (1990: 54).

Grammatologists and genealogists, so it turns out, cannot coherently sustain a life of interpretational imperfection and distrust. They demand that we read their works accurately and do not want us to misunderstand their theories of misunderstanding. And they are convinced of the proper quality of what they have to say, expecting from us an appreciation and anticipation of those qualities. It is not unfair to point out that in their actual demands relativist authors bring us beyond interpretative imperfectionism.

Hermeneutic modesty

We are offered an alternative to the relativist interpretation of interpretation. We can conclude that the conflict between perfective hermeneutics and radical constructionist relativism displays itself in different ways. In each step we have confirmed the relevance of estimation in terms of better and worse. We have ended with the introduction of a sense of moral being that is destined to guide the efforts of a good interpreter. A perfective reading of interpretation harbours differentiated judgement about bad, average, fair and better interpretations. In the actual practice of interpretation one cannot get rid of those perfective qualities and demands. This is the message of perfective hermeneutics.

A perfective appreciation of the complexity and mobility of human interpretation permits us to admit that our knowledge is indeed an all too human affair without at the same time implying that all is really a matter of individual whim only The self-correcting procedures of interpretation give the opportunity to distinguish between that which is worthy of belief and that which is not (Harré & Krausz 1996: 223). It should be noted that we are, all in all, well equipped to deal with the provisional and the uncertain and are quite capable of thinking within these dramatic circumstances (Morin 1990a: 93).

The perfective interpreter will combine the psychology of assurance with the preparedness to walk in the direction of revised interpretation. This combination is essential, as otherwise we run the risk of becoming hysterical fanatics who try to convince themselves of a certainty that they unconsciously know is not available (Popper 1990: 33). We make many errors, the biggest of which is exactly to deny this and to set up a 'monopoly of truth' (Morin 1990b: 134). The establishment of a *balanced* interpretational temperament is what is at stake. A balanced interpretational temperament will never forget that one must choose between hermeneutics and absolute knowledge. There is no ultimate interpretational completion, even if at times we are entitled to treat certain interpretations as rationally appropriate (until we, again, find reason to think otherwise). Interpretative mediation always carries the risk of error. The limiting conditions on hermeneutic totality cannot be transcended: there are no absolute perfections and final stabilities of understanding (Steiner 1975: 407).

Hence, finding appropriate interpretations will never be the same as claiming that one has somehow reached a state of cognitive transparency. In the light of this we must qualify the following statement:

> Interpretation is the very process that makes the world cognitively accessible and, when successful, renders the world cognitively transparent — not in the sense that it affords direct, unmediated access to it, but in the sense that, as soon as the interpretation works, and for as long as it continues to work, there is no good reason to doubt, and considerable reason to maintain, that one does have cognitive access to those aspects of the world that it purports to reveal. *As we know the world, so it is* (italics mine) (Novitz 2001: 11).

We can certainly agree with different sides of this quotation, but the terminological jump to 'as we know the world, so it is' should be cancelled. Not having current doubts about a certain interpretation — something which we psychologically need, as otherwise life becomes a neurotic and impossible enterprise — the real hermeneuticist will, perhaps silently in the back of his mind, keep the option of revision open (Bontekoe 1996: 239). He or she will understand that it is certainly not good to be always right, since that would only constitute a sign of one's absolutist attitude (Feibleman 1952: 307). He or she will also understand that the right to feel sure does not give us the right to close our minds to the possibility that we might be wrong (Chisholm 1977: 118). Successful interpretation is not finalised truth, never to be doubted or qualified again. To speak in terms of the definitive, even if only cryptically, is to abandon hermeneutic consciousness.

Perfective hermeneutics is itself only an interpretation of interpretation, which may be challenged by other interpretations of interpretation. However, I think it is not unfair to suggest that possible revisions are likely to lead to an adapted version of perfective hermeneutics, and not to a version of radical constructionist relativism or to a version of absolutism.

Perfectionism as interpretative enterprise

The ubiquity and goodness of interpretation logically confronts us with the positive challenge of developing perfectionism as an interpretative quest. If all our receptions of aspects of being are interpretational, and if we are indeed involved in a play of better and worse interpretations, then perfectio-existential interpretation seems a highly relevant challenge. Interpretation is part of the content of perfectionism but also constitutes the cognitive means by which to build perfectionism as a philosophical project. The theory of interpretation is perfective and the theory of perfection is interpretative.

CHAPTER THREE —
INTERPRETATION AND PERFECTION — iii:
EVOLUTIONARY HERMENEUTICS

> *We inhabit an interpreted world in which*
> *reinterpretation is the most fundamental*
> *form of change.*

— Alasdair MacIntyre

Interpretation leads in itself to a sense of better and worse, of perfective estimation. Since interpretation is everywhere in human life — there are in fact no humans and cultures without interpretation — its accompanying sense of perfection, of better and worse, can be said to be equally non-trivial. One cannot escape, so it appears, the language of perfection in one (implicit) way or another. Perfective estimation is necessary according to the intrinsic way of being of interpretation.

Beyond the language of perfection?

However, a first urgent issue to be addressed is the fact that nowadays it has become common to consider perfective language a frozen and unsympathetic language, a language contaminated by spiritual and classical suggestions, a language that may appeal to the Thomists and the Aristotelians but not to authentic cosmopolitan, internationalised persons. Donald Walhout, a contemporary perfectionist, realises all too well that the notion of perfection nowadays appears antiquated, quaint, and peculiar (1978a: 232). Some conclude that it is therefore a language that we ought not to celebrate, as it is not interesting to rise above the human condition of today. Perfection is all too angelic. Negative response to the inherent metaphysical fever of perfective language leads to the demand to eradicate perfection from our vocabularies and theories. To say, for example, that a particular tree has reached a state of perfection may be taken to carry the suggestion that there is a fundamental initiative within the tree to seek perfection. Perfective language may be seen to activate some sort of panpsychism. Furthermore, where lies the origin of our standards of perfection? What is the standard of perfection for a particular tree? Is there a Platonic ideal waiting to be fulfilled? A further problem is that, once we accept a perfective development of entities, we could be pushed into philosophically establishing a benign source to be behind it all. The existence of numerous little perfections within the world invites an ultimate source — God as grand and infinite perfection.

Should we opt for a drastic response and simply cancel perfective terminology? I think not. First of all, we must not so quickly run away from human thickness. Perhaps we have become too cautious. Being critical without larger interpretational commitment we now find ourselves more paralysed than blind (Ricoeur 1986b: 313). Today, there appears to be nothing less than a generalised incapacity for belief. Thin theory dismisses broad existential and perfective understanding because it fears the risk of interpretation — it rather enjoys the satisfactions of refined indecision (Williams 1993: 169). It is not difficult to guess why. Thick existential and perfective vision is perceived as connected to absolutist and elitist projects, which in the past have also resulted in undesirable political systems. This association, however, fails to understand that such projects are not at all involved in an adequate form of interpretation. Absolutist thinkers and politicians see themselves as having reached timeless truth beyond interpretation. Contrary to this, an authentic hermeneutic version of thick and broad existential understanding insists that one's position remain embedded in a never finalised interpretative process. The point is to learn to live constructively with the risk of interpretation (Ricoeur 1969: 27). And within the insecure context of risk one may still find benign interpretative opportunities.

Moreover, the concrete labour of interpretation may teach us that not everything within perfection is with equal intensity bound to the foundationalist framework of a classical or religious teleological metaphysics. There are human functional schemes — think particularly of the praxiological scheme described in MacIntyre (1981) — which invite perfective treatment beyond these earlier contexts. Liberal anti-perfectionism, too, endorses something like a praxiological perfectionism (Rawls 1999). There is clearly no reason why we should categorically run away from an interpretative process of distillation, a process in which we critically resist and/or affiliate ourselves with certain aspects and layers of perfective language. Without attempting to reinstall a perfective grand narrative in terms of classical perfection, we may walk toward a more relaxed and pluralist interpretation of the language of perfection — an interpretation focused on our fallible perfective lives as finite, non-angelic persons involved in numerous settings, such as those of science, art, craft, family, work, and so on.

This interpretative process of distillation with respect to the language of perfection can be placed in the context of an 'evolutionary hermeneutics' introduced by Csikszentmihalyi and Rathunde (1990). This project of evolutionary hermeneutics combines respect, critical awareness, sense of possibility, and a constructive selection of terminological responses. It is based on

> the assumption that concepts relating to the evaluation of human behaviour — such as virtue, courage, freedom, or wisdom — and that have been used for many centuries under very different social and historical conditions are likely to have adaptive value for humankind (*ibid.*: 25).

In what follows I will discern basic suggestions contained in the idea of an evolutionary hermeneutics

The wisdom of natural language

The first hermeneutical suggestion of evolutionary hermeneutics is that the varieties of natural language be received with proper philosophical respect. As John Austin has noted:

> Our common stock of words embodies all the distinctions men have found worth drawing, and the connections they have found worth making, in the life times of many generations: they surely are likely to be more numerous, more sound, since they have stood up to the long test of the survival of the fittest, and more subtle, at least in all our ordinary and reasonable practical matters, than any that you or I are likely to think up in our armchairs of an afternoon (quoted in Aschenbrenner 1971: 31).

The main issue is that the richness and the continuity of the natural languages reveal something of our nature that can never be thought up by philosophers alone.

Consequently, to gain self-knowledge we need to listen to our natural languages, which constitute nothing less than a 'depository of a whole treasure of appropriate expressions progressively formed to cope with the infinite variety of human situations' (Ricoeur 1976: 52). In our embodied interaction many concepts rise up which are far from trivial. They work pretty well. And they result from interactions tested constantly by billions of people over our history as a species (Johnson 1987: 208). Receiving natural language and its conceptual treasures with appropriate respect should, of course, not blind us to linguistically installed prejudices of common sense. Philosophy is a constructive as well as a critical enterprise. However, the critical moment does not cancel the value and internal wisdom of the natural languages. Folk psychology and the semantics of action are bound to contain undesirable reifications and deviations, but also confront us with unique human possibilities of expression — possibilities which not many are, or should be, inclined to give up in concrete existence.

One cardinal point is that giving up certain terminologies would in fact unavoidably lead to a loss of what we consider to be valuable ways of being. Linguistic elimination is not a neutral undertaking, leaving us as we were before. The fact that natural language so deeply informs our way of being turns any radical effort in reductionist purification into a dangerous experiment. We are paradoxical beings — the concepts we employ to grasp what we are become part of what we are (MacIntyre 1962: 64), people to some extent are what they believe they are. Indeed, there seems to be 'a deep tendency in human nature to become like that which we imagine ourselves to be' (Hocking 1928: 45). This means that to give a certain theory or terminology currency is bound to influence the very behaviour the theory attempts to capture.

Setting the semantics of action and folk psychology aside — the language of belief, decision, intention, freedom, end, and responsibility — immediately confronts us with certain unfortunate consequences. This is one reason why many of those who advocate eliminationism tolerate the use of the human idiom as a 'temporary device' (Margolis 1989: xiii). Cancel moral terminology and we will raise our children without or with sharply reduced moral competence. Remove all terminology suggesting freedom, initiative, and decision and we will become monotonous creatures. The elimination of these terminological possibilities is bound to produce creatures with lesser capacity. The framework of belief, desire and will is needed to be able to deliberate about ends. Without this framework no evaluative activity is possible. It can, therefore, never be a matter of indifference to accept an account of human beings in terms devoid of value, purpose, conscience, and meaning (Hocking 1928: 45). It is relevant here to underline that the ability to revise, critique, confront and transform words and concepts and theories is itself only available through the use of a rich language. More generally, linguistic complexity as such constitutes an essential dimension of our sense of ability and possibility. Language constitutes, thus, an intrinsic part of our basic rational experience. It can never be rational to give up the instruments necessary for the installation of rational competence.

I strongly suggest that we should regard a radical elimination of perfective and semi-perfective terminology as an unacceptable eradication of human evaluative experience and capacity. We need as many concepts as we find we need, no fewer (Williams 1993: 17). In my view perfection is one of those concepts we (continue to) need — in combination with a rich and thick language of perfective appraisive characterisation (Aschenbrenner 1971, 1974, 1983).

Human adaptive value

A complementary aspect of evolutionary hermeneutics is well captured in Csikszentmihalyi and Rathunde (1990). The point is to seek to understand specifically the human adaptive value of particular terminological responses.

One task is to try uncovering the meaning of concepts that seem to have stood the test of time. Such concepts can be seen as 'memes', selected and transmitted across generations, carrying instructions that seem to positively influence our survival and our human possibilities of being and expression. These concepts may be taken to represent relatively unchanging functional prerequisites of human growth and maintenance. It is clear that memes, in being transmitted, will be culturally and historically transformed and differentiated, through translation, reinterpretation, theoretical reflection (philosophy), and in interaction with new environments and demands. A supplementary task is to reintroduce neglected or marginalised concepts and problems that we ought not to cast aside. Distortion is to be cured by a recovery of those concepts and problems. We must make an effort to explicitly reintroduce old and underestimated concerns and terminologies that carry important promise — an effort that, again, involves us in a creative process of reinterpretation.

Let me offer a few illustrations.

First, while most us may not share the powers of 'wisdom' as depicted in Aristotle or Aquinas, it should be clear that a reinterpreted concept of wisdom very much deserves to survive beyond postmodernist doubts and critiques. We still (should) live with an interpretative version of wisdom, considered as 'an expert knowledge system concerning the fundamental pragmatics of life, including knowledge and judgement about the conduct and meaning of life' (Baltes & Freund 2003: 252). This knowledge system includes the recognition and management of uncertainty. Wisdom helps us to deal with the many (unavoidable) tasks of adult life: commitments, raising children, coping with illness, long-term planning, advising others, and so forth. There are wise people whom we recognise as such. The scope and depth of wisdom in today's context — its continued sense of self-transcendence and ultimate concern — is likely to involve us in 'a systemic ecological consciousness in which the consequences of events and actions are understood to be causally related to and have long-term effect for the survival of human life and for the environment that sustains it' (Csikszentmihalyi & Rathunde 1990: 32). 'Wisdom' has a functional perfective role to play besides 'intelligence', 'science', 'genius', 'talent', and so on.

Second, a related concern, which we have to bring back through reinterpretation, is a sense of existential wholeness. 'What should my life be like?' was a natural question in ancient Greece (Annas 1993: 27-46). It implied a singular kind of concern for one's life being as it should and for the kind of person one is. But today we are not accustomed to concern ourselves with questions of personal wholeness. According to MacIntyre we have nowadays entered a culture largely deprived of the vision of the whole. He insists that we must recover a larger vision, since to live in a world of fragments, which are not seen for what they are, is to live in an arbitrary and inauthentic state (see MacIntyre's 'disquieting suggestion' in 1981: 1-5). We will fail to reach proper self-knowledge and end up with emotivist manipulationism. Virtue, duty and other moral concepts need to be placed in a larger existential and communal context to be able to make rational sense. MacIntyre, in *After Virtue*, understands we cannot copy classical cosmological and eudaimonic schemes, but he still manages to propose the idea of a narratively structured existential quest for a personal and communal conception of the good life as an adequate contemporary alternative, which in different ways is still meant to be in line with certain aspects of the older demand for wholeness. The quest itself, in fact, offers something of a rational and dramatic unity to the existence of the human self.

Finally, through attentive reinterpretation we can also introduce the human adaptive value of perfection as such. Certain perfective words and schemes appear to linguistically capture something essential of what is still going on with us and with aspects of the world as received in our interpretations. In the middle of things — in which we try to get somewhere — we experience that entities, projects, developments, products, properties, aspects of being, etc., can be received according to certain standards. Appraisive language is bound to endure as long as we accept or reject (Aschenbrenner 1983: 211). Descriptive language is not sufficient. An appraisive response to the environment is part of the way we have learned to survive. Survival involves more than the mere registering of qualities; it also involves desire, aversion, satisfaction, revulsion, expectation, demand, approach and retreat (*ibid.*: 4). It is difficult to lead a human life without forming standards:

> Value and evaluation are necessary as a kind of law of human nature and being, such that we cannot help but enter the play of value, even when we would wish to withdraw from or suspend it. The necessity of value is in this sense more like the necessity of breathing than, say, the necessity of earning one's living. There are ways of continuing to exist as a human being without the latter, but not without the former (Connor 1992: 8).

Different persons may argue about which standards and ideals to follow, and some may even think that such standards are futile constructions, but perfectionism is bound to insist that disputes about standards cannot destroy the relevance of standards as such, and that persons living with the idea that standards are futile or trivial cannot themselves completely eliminate the formation and application of standards within their own existential projects and practical efforts. The stubborn presence of a sense of better and worse provides a confirmation not authentically addressed in views hostile to standards of perfection. No one can live productively, and with a sense of direction, without activating, perhaps implicitly, a scheme of worst, worse, indifferent, fair, better, good, excellent and best. Perfective and semi-perfective terminology is needed to enable us to respond to elements of striving and quality within the realities, developments, situations, and states that we find on our way.

Psychological realism

We should seek a twenty-first century version of perfectionism. The different senses, varieties and situations of perfection are meant to express and address current human properties, demands, limitations, processes, possibilities, settings, and experiences.

Evolutionary hermeneutics is bound to include the principle of a minimal psychological realism. The perfective helpful adviser (Williams 1996: 27), in aiming to show that a perfective outlook may give us a conception of a life worth living, has to consider — in close combination with the idea of human adaptive value — whether a certain vision, conception or terminology with respect to human existence is actually or potentially viable for the creatures we are in the contemporary context. The proposal in question has 'to fit in with what we are and where we are, with our actual nature and position in the order of things: otherwise it is quite irrelevant' (Geach 1979: 143). Geach's demand has been aptly reconfirmed in Flanagan (1991). It is clear that certain options, found in other times and cultures, are not real options for us, since there is for us no serious way of living them — think of the life of a Bronze Age chief or a medieval samurai (Williams 1993: 161).

Not all possibilities of other times and cultures can receive translation in our society and in our psychology, nor could samurai and Bronze Age chiefs come to live our own innermost possibilities. Besides a rational selection of different continuities and reinterpreted terminologies, we also find ourselves confronted here with unbridgeable differences of possibility as they determine selves at different times. What they are it is impossible for us to become. As John Plamenatz points out:

> We have opportunities now that our ancestors did not have in the sixteenth century, and we acquire skills, tastes and ideas unknown to them. We now develop our powers in ways that they could not do, even though they had the powers and lacked only the opportunities. But then in the sixteenth century they had opportunities that we lack, and acquired skills, tastes, and ideas that we no longer acquire (1975: 351).

The lesson to be learned is that perfective terminology may be continued on the one hand, but that we on the other hand need a perfective language that fits the way we are now and (perhaps) wish to remain.

The ironic self

According to Richard Rorty (1989) it is best for the contemporary self to hold an ironic attitude toward one's own essential set of evaluative terms. He introduces the ironic self as the most proper figure. Evolutionary hermeneutics intends to offer an alternative, which it is best to specify in direct confrontation with Rorty.

One's own essential set of evaluative terms is in Rorty described as follows:

45

All human beings carry about a set of words which they employ to justify their actions, their beliefs, and their lives. These are the words in which we formulate praise of our friends and contempt for our enemies, our long-term projects, our deepest self-doubts and our highest hopes. These are the words in which we tell the story of our lives. I shall call these words a person's final vocabulary (*ibid.*: 73).

The final vocabulary contains thin terms — such as true, good and right — as well as thicker and more parochial terms — such as kindness, decency, creativity, and professional standards. These later terms do most of the work for us. The main point for Rorty is that the ironic self, impressed by many other final vocabularies of other persons and cultures, has radical and continuing doubts about his or her own final vocabulary. There is the realisation that these doubts cannot ever be dissolved. Nor does one think that one's own vocabulary is closer to reality than that of others. Ironists are

> never quite able to take themselves seriously because always aware that the terms in which they describe themselves are subject to change, always aware of the contingency and fragility of their own final vocabularies (*ibid.*: 73-74).

Part of ironic policy is to *experiment* with other final vocabularies. Afraid to get stuck in his or her first vocabulary, the ironic self works toward a larger range of acquaintance. Diversification and novelty are therefore considered important. One's continued redescription is organised by way of comparing results with alternative possibilities of redescription. Ironist culture places its bets on ability to grasp the function of many different sets of words. Always keeping its ears open for hints about how the personal final vocabulary might be expanded or transformed, the ironic self is carried by the hope to 'make the best selves for ourselves that we can' (*ibid.*: 80).

The evolutionary hermeneutics of perfection will agree with several aspects of Rorty.

It is valid to become impressed by different final vocabularies. Through dialogue we may learn to revise parts of our own schemes. And others may learn from us. Redescription in a context of plurality also has a place in evolutionary hermeneutics. Perfectionists, too, ought not to get trapped in the vocabulary of any single book. Another point of similarity is Rorty's reference to 'best selves'. Perfectionism is interested in one becoming the best person one can become. Furthermore, diversification, novelty and richness, serving as significant standards in Rorty, have an essential position in perfectionism too, namely in the context of the issue of qualitative perfection (see chapter 6).

But beyond these similarities the difference between perfectionism/evolutionary hermeneutics and ironic selfhood is fourfold. First, Rorty, as we know from chapter 2, does not recognise the full array of goodness and perfective possibilities in interpretation. Hence, he radically underestimates rational dialogue between different vocabularies. Second, Rorty's allergic response against metaphysics seems to prevent him from fully accepting constructive distillation with respect to (very) old terminologies. He is inclined to play out the new against the old: 'An ironist hopes that by the time she has finished using old words in new senses, not to mention brand-new words, people will no longer ask questions in the old words' (*ibid.*: 78). The idea that some old vocabularies may contain terms that we ought to retain is quite foreign to the ironist stance. To be sure, there are passages where Rorty does argue in favour of a renewed reading of authors or texts from the past — he even considers the New Testament as a prime example of inspirational reading (Rorty 1999: 204) — but these references do not bring him to a fundamental constructive response to the enduring value of certain terminologies. Third, Rorty's sense of the best self is captured in an improvisationalism without a complex set of qualitative standards. The point is to redescribe oneself and to compare the results with alternative redescriptions. But how should such a comparison take place? We should experiment. Fine, but what about the outcome of those experiments? Rorty remains all too vague. Perfectionism counts on a different result, leading to the rational formulation of a set of perfective standards. Fourth, perfectionism doubts radical ironism as an enduring mental state. Human beings do not fare well in an attitude of full and continued doubt. This would result in madness. Accepting the relevance of certain terminological stabilities, it is, in fact, not necessary to live in an endless, radical movement of nervous redescription.

The intellectual temperament of evolutionary hermeneutics, so we may conclude, constitutes an alternative to ironic selfhood. It is now a matter of providing perfective content in the context of this alternative.

CHAPTER FOUR —
THE LANGUAGE OF PERFECTION — i:
PERFECTION AS POSITIVE / AS NEGATIVE

> *Flip over what is best in us and you will discover that the very capacities and abilities that enable us to be noble, admirable creatures also fund what is dangerous and ignoble in our nature.*

— Stephen Hudson

In this and the next three chapters I will be directly involved with the reception and revision of the language of perfection. This chapter deals with the tension between positive and negative perfection.

Perfection and perfective progress relate to the best and the better. Perfection is then automatically considered to be something positive. One finds such a positive view advocated, for example, in Matthew Arnold's claim that the love of perfection is the origin of human culture (1965: 91). Nowadays, however, most of us do not share Arnold's faith in perfection. We certainly cannot turn a blind eye to the increasing references to negative perfection, which pop up in different contexts. A task for evolutionary hermeneutics is to underline that the negative treatment of perfection, which is so widespread in our society, cannot cancel the continuing influence and relevance of positive perfection. The tension between negative and positive perfection should not lead to the disappearance of positive perfection. I aim to make clear that a positive interpretation of perfection can survive its negative counterpart.

One point to bear in mind is that most readings of negative perfection are themselves constructed on the basis of an (implicit) acceptance of a sense of positive perfection. This suggests there is sufficient reason to continue the language of positive perfection. Another point to bear in mind is that the survival of positive perfection should be directly combined with an adult awareness of possible perfectionist deformations, which indeed need to be criticised and neutralised.

Let us begin with perfection as negative.

Varieties of negative perfection

Resistance to the idea of perfection may be considered to emerge from perfection as frozen stability of political, psychological and technological systems (Düll 1984). Such rigid systems fully neutralise the freedom of their subparts and are radically closed to many influences from the outside. Closing itself off, as so to protect itself against any corruption, the system petrifies. The critique of closed and frozen systems associates perfection with tendencies to develop stable, invariant structures in which opportunities for alternative development have been completely banned. According to fundamental systemics, every living, human and social system is bound to exist by virtue of the selective appropriation and control of internal parts and subsystems. Development must itself insist on productive control and selection. But a frozen system is not open to any more development. An ideal state is seen to have been reached, pure and definite in form like a crystal. Hence, selection and invariance take a harsher and stricter form.

It is not difficult to find examples. Totalitarian states attempt to close themselves off from internal and external influences incompatible with the rules and intentions of the regime in question. They seek and claim a perfection of control (Morin 1991c). A sustained elimination of informational plurality is inherently totalitarian in kind. Another example is offered in David Williamson's play *The Perfectionist*, which is a study of the dangers inherent in attempting to create perfection within the context of human relationships. One could think here of the attempt to force the other to conform as well as of the attempt to create a closed and perfect system of living in response to the social chaos outside (Williamson 1986: xi). The ideological self constitutes yet another form of perfection as closure. Due to various causes such as anxiety, indoctrination and failure of education, a person's mental set can turn into a rigid cognitive system without openness, renewal, gradation or sense of variety. Such a person refuses serious dialogue with others; a wall of convictions and sedimentations will resist critical intrusion. Finally, one could think of the managerial model of Taylorism, which implies a sustained attempt to cut out deviation and initiative in individual occupational selves. Labourers are not permitted to think for themselves, but have to follow a strict scheme governing their time, space and action. Taylorism establishes a perfect division and organisation of labour with the productionist aim of enhancing effectiveness (output). Taylorism is one expression of the 'perfection of technology' (Jünger 1949) — perfection in the sense of a complete technological submission of non-technological dimensions and of a radical mechanisation completing the human technological impulse.

A second critique of perfection is available in the musical aesthetics of imperfection (Hamilton 2000), which reacts against the influential aesthetics of perfection. Perfection is here associated with the stability and organisation of a written composition. The performer is supposed to receive and perform the particular notations of a musical piece. Classical masterpieces constitute the model of perfection; something has been thought out and become timeless through notation. The aesthetics of imperfection leaves compositional preparation and fixation behind, and is focused on the freedom of improvisation. Compositional perfectionists think that improvisers are destined to produce only feeble imitations of perfection. Errors in form and execution will creep in, due to a lack of preparation and notation. In response, improvisational imperfectionists stress the event of performance, spontaneity versus deliberation, unwritten innovation and originality. Improvised virtuosity is based upon a list of recommendations — to keep ideas in a state of flux, to sometimes see error as unintentional rightness, to strive for a rough go-ahead energy, to be afraid of being uninteresting (T. C. Whitmer, quoted in Hamilton 2000: 178). It is not difficult to see similarities with the first critique of perfection as frozen system. The improvisational self embraces creativity beyond compositional closure and stability.

Criticism formulated in the context of biomedical and healthcare ethics gives us a third version of perfection as negative (Lachs 2000). Medical and genetic perfectionism is taken to imply a dangerous and arrogant project that is contrary to the basic recognition of humans as finite and limited creatures. Acting to escape the bonds of bodily contingency, certain scientists and physicians are impelled to radical and uncontrolled efforts in genetic and organic enhancement beyond the more moderated standards of curing and healing. The dangers involved are likely to be denied by those involved in the genetico-perfective enterprise who will often be driven by the conviction that we must, without reservation, try out what humanity seems to be capable of.

Critical reviews stress the fact that we do not have a philosophical clue where radical improvement should ultimately bring us. The possibility of genetic progression as such appears to have become the central goal. Another problem is that the practice of genetic revision is bound to be carried out and ordered by persons possessing only imperfect knowledge about what perfection is supposed to be. Even parents will not always agree on what constitutes a perfect child. It is fairly easy to recognise properties that we would want to avoid — think of blindness and mental illness. It is much more difficult to define properties that we would wish to stimulate. A further problem is that the genetic programming of desirable traits in children differs from the common process of socialisation in a morally relevant aspect: socialisation proceeds by virtue of communicative action, implying interaction within formative processes (Habermas 2001: 106). This is not the case in genetic enhancement. The projected child has no communicative scope. Another issue is that genetic alteration is often accompanied by transformations in other characters. In this sense, one rarely gets something for nothing in an act of genetic manipulation. Finally, perfection is likely to become an economised good. We run the danger of being pushed toward something that is a striving for nothing more than a commodity portrayed as being perfect (Keenan 1999: 105). Genetically inclined perfectionists will be the producers and buyers of perfective illusions. The absence of philosophically defined standards, emptiness of value, commercialisation, and the production of perfective simulacra strongly contribute to a negative assessment of the drive for perfection in a genetic and medical context.

A fourth critique of perfection is situated in psychological discourse (see Pacht 1984). Perfectionism is described as an undesirable and debilitating trait of personality. Selves focused on perfection are depicted as obsessive and neurotic, the likely victims of procrastination or anorexic inclination. They set themselves unrealistically high goals, and when something is successfully undertaken they are not capable of appreciating their accomplishment. Even the smallest detail that one may have missed is a source of dissatisfaction. The perfectionist 'looks so intently for defects or flaws that he lives his life as though he were an inspector at the end of a production line' (Hollender 1976: 110). Things are never good enough. The figure of the glorified self becomes the standard by which to measure the imperfections of the actual self. Perfectionists are constantly confronted with the perspective of godlike perfection (Horney 1942: 110). The quest for perfection deteriorates into an endless enterprise. Perfectionists live without satisfaction, unable to disconnect from their austere ideals, and end up with endless sadness and disappointment since the cognitive distortion that they must be perfect creates a vicious self-defeating circle of lowered self-acceptance, strengthened perfectionism and depression (Pirot 1986: 57). The real self becomes an offensive stranger to whom the ideal self happens to be chained (Horney 1942: 112). The result is hate and contempt towards the self.

A fifth important contemporary critique of perfection deserving our attention comes from the field of liberal political philosophy. One regularly hears about anti-perfectionism. The principle of perfection is taken to defend the doctrine that an objective and comprehensive account of the human good should inform policies and politics. Perfectionism in its most intense form is identified with a teleological theory that aims to direct society in a strong sense so that achievement in culture, science and art can be maximised (Rawls 1999: 286). It is the view that the state should promote a valuable conception of the good life. The anti-perfectionist movement fears political dogmatism, the loss of personal autonomy, and the elimination of freedom of thought when politics would turn into perfectionism and perfectionism into politics. Another point is that radical perfectionist selves are inclined toward elitism. They will demand and receive most of the financial and other sources. The high perfection of a set of individuals belonging to the chosen few will invite unjustly divided societal support. In this way, so political anti-perfectionists argue, the idea of fairness is betrayed. The political implementation of perfective ideals is for all those different reasons rejected.

How to assess these negative readings of the idea of perfection?

We should stress that they touch on aspects that really lie embedded in traditional positive conceptions of perfection, and hence, it cannot be argued that these critiques miss their target. We may refer to the following traditional aspects of 'classical perfection'. The idea of perfection in a more classical version connotes ideas of order, self-sufficiency, purity and definitive accomplishment. The criticism of perfection as frozen stability tunes in with these connotations. Perfection as traditionally understood also relates to an ideal conception, to be imitated in real life. This type of perfective scheme is attacked in the improvisational rejection of composition and rigid execution. Real life, according to the perspective of jazz, is not about conforming to a preconstructed idea, but about creating things in the moment. Since its conception in Greek culture perfection applies to technical production. A well-made product accurately serving the end for which it is intended is characterised as perfect. The progressivist perfectibilism of modern and industrial times radicalises and extends this connection: humanity is considered to be capable of an interminable process of perfective technical improvement of bodily, mental, social and scientific conditions. The critique of medical and genetic perfection focuses on the negative implications of perfective productionism in an organic context. The psychology of pathological perfection puts the finger on another essential aspect of perfection as classically conceived, namely the idea of highest achievement. There is no level beyond the perfective best. A perfect self is supposed to actualise everything there is to actualise, and this according to the most ambitious standard. There are no gaps or flaws. Political anti-perfectionism, finally, focuses negatively on the perfective aristocratic intentions embodied in the Greek *polis*, the ambitions of certain forms of religious perfective fundamentalism, the elitist perfectionist individualism of Nietzsche, and the perfectionist horrors of communism and fascism.

It is unwise to neglect the dangers of perfectionist deformation within official conceptions of positive perfection. The central point is to attempt to set aside the negative shades of perfection: a process of distillation is necessary. If positive perfection is to play a role today we have to articulate more benign versions of perfective being. More specifically, we have to neutralise perfectionist radicalism. This is exactly what the five negative criticisms of the language of perfection are aiming at. There is the radicality of completeness without opportunity for alternative development (frozen system), the radicality of conception without further original initiative (determined composition), the radicality of control and enhancement (genetic productionism), the radicality of striving without self-knowledge and without moderation (neurotic perfective strive), and the radicality of political vision without tolerance and equality (perfective elitism and tyranny). Systemic, compositional, genetic, psychological and political forms of fanaticism contribute to the dark side of perfective being. Imagine the *summum* of perfective darkness, an unhappy combination of several perfective radicalisations. Think of someone in power who is determined by the abnormal trait of psychological perfection while also holding on to a fundamentalist conception of the human good. Such a person will be strongly inclined to install a frozen systemic policy destined to destroy any flaw, critique and threat to stability — a policy likely to include educational as well as genetic control of the population.

But to see negative perfection as the dark side of perfective being is somehow to imply there is a bright side as well. I think this bright side is indeed there. One confirmation lies in the fact that a sense of positive perfection can already be discovered within negative readings of perfection.

Between negative and positive perfection

This is a significant point: it appears to be the case that resistance to perfection in a negative mode is, more often than not, based upon a sense of positive perfection directing or at least complementing the critical process. Let us turn again to the five critiques.

The critique of perfection as systemic closure, as established in Düll (1984), includes a small but revealing reference to something called *Vollendung*. This is an alternative word expressing a benign and comfortable sense of perfection — perfection as a balance between stability and openness. This balance allows creative and adaptive growth and freedom. We thus reach the perfection of development and openness over against the petrified perfection of stability and closure.

The aesthetics of improvisation, in certain instances at least, acknowledges its own list of virtues and thus suggests a different kind of perfectionism. To be on the brink of the unknown implies a complex practice and the presence of mental dispositions that aim to keep one from playing what has been played before. The point is to be prepared for the leap into a state of alertness. This necessarily demands particular personal qualities. It is interesting to observe explicit improvisational perfectionism being proposed in line with Stanley Cavell's Emersonian perfectionism (Day 2000). Cavell does not constitute the most common form of positive perfectionism, but the fact remains that improvisationalists in line with Cavell are concerned enough to include improvisation in an explicit perfectionist framework. Improvisational traits are proposed as perfections over against a life of conformity.

In biomedical ethics medical and genetic perfectionism is often juxtaposed with a more human and finite sense of perfection. The right realisation of one's talents, so it is stressed, should be combined with an appreciation of moderation and finitude considered to be constitutive of good human life as we know it to be. The argument is made that the struggle against misfortunes and obstacles is necessary for the development of real human virtue (Shickle 2000: 349). Effort and difficulty are also part of aretaic appreciation. Who would applaud a genetically modified runner winning every competition without the trouble of training? Suffering and confrontation with obstacles and imperfections are seen to constitute productive elements in the normal human striving for perfection. One also meets the argument that authentic perfection should be related to wisdom and self-knowledge. By now we should have learned to satisfy ourselves with the less spectacular, with bits and pieces, with little steps in the direction of perfection and improvement (Lachs 2000: 329). Perfection as such is not to be eradicated, only perfective madness. Finally, a distinction is made between genetic restoration aimed at normalising disturbed organic processes and the abnormal enhancement of capacities.

Different psychological critiques include a distinction between neurotic and normal perfectionism (Blatt 1995). There is nothing wrong with striving for perfection as long as one is able to accept failures and mistakes. The positive side of perfectionism can, for example, be seen in an athlete's authentic striving for physical fitness and performance or in the scientist's quest for a truthful understanding of nature. The remark may be made that it is not always clear whether an athlete or any other kind of striving self is related to a normal sense of perfection, but this remark can of course function in both directions. It is equally difficult to assess whether a particular perfectionist enterprise is really unhealthy. Notably researchers working in the field of education for the gifted suggest that what would be an unrealistic and unhealthy ambition for most is likely to be a fair and fruitful undertaking for the talented child (Silverman 1983). One author strictly identifies perfectionism with abnormal striving but subsequently does feel the need to underline a so-called non-perfectionist pursuit of excellence, exemplified in the accomplishments of skilled artists (Greenspan 2000). A full negative restriction of perfection forces the articulation of alternative positive words.

In relation to liberal anti-perfectionism it is clear that positive perfection still plays a role. Different authors specify a more comfortable role for perfectionist thought on an institutional level (see Arneson 2000). There is no necessary connection between perfectionism and elitism. The elitist superman version of perfection basically 'ruins a good point by drastic overstatement' (Griffin 1986: 62). On the level of personal being, liberal selves are allowed and even expected to be concerned with perfectionist views of what constitutes a good life for them. Think of the availability of an 'Aristotelian principle' in Rawlsian anti-perfectionism (Rawls 1999: 374). According to this principle human beings enjoy the exercise of their realised abilities; an increased or more complex capacity will increase one's enjoyment. A rational plan of life, a central anthropological notion in Rawls, is defined in direct reference to persons being allowed to flourish and to undertake the significant exercise of realised abilities. There is also reference to social practices that are built up through the imagination of many individuals and which increasingly demand 'a more complex array of abilities and new ways of doing things' (*ibid*.: 429; the reader may note the similarity with MacIntyre's perfective concept of a practice). The point is that perfectionism is identified here, not with a dogmatic perspective according to which others are forced to live, but with a pluralist theory of differentiated human perfections and accomplishments. The political ambition should be to provide significant and varied perfective opportunity. A hermeneutically attuned perfectionism should have no problems with Rawls's Aristotelian principle. Dogmatism is not a necessary trait of perfectionist reflection and perfectionists well understand the fallibility of their interpretative judgements (Wall 1999: 25).

The insight that we should learn from existing critiques of perfectionist deviation can now be appropriately linked with the observation that positive perfection has an implicit or even an explicit place in views on negative perfection.

It is also relevant to note one example of the presence of negative perfection in a recognised review of positive perfection. This strengthens the suggestion that, beyond the idea of a black and white conflict, perfectionist being is much more a matter of interaction between negative and positive perfection. We encounter resistance to a moral version of psychological perfectionist pathology in Christine Swanton (1997). While thematically arguing in the context of positive perfection (virtue), she terminologically proposes 'anti-perfectionism' as an important virtue working against what she calls the vice of 'perfectionism'. This vice is manifested in an insufficient reliance on one's own sense of contentment with life as it is. Each moment has to be crammed with worthwhile and perfective pursuits. Existential and moral perfectionists will take on more than they can handle. Swanton sees anti-perfectionism as 'the virtue of not being overly hard on oneself by always striving for and wanting perfection' (*ibid*.: 93). In line with human vulnerabilities, it is rational not always to opt for the strongest possible moral requirements, as otherwise one will simply become fragmented by an overpowering myriad of excessive demands. Swanton's point can be connected with the critique of moral saints (Wolf 1997). Moral sainthood is seen as psychologically unrealistic and undesirable. We need selves with interesting imperfections and non-moral perfectionist concerns. The reality of imperfection specifically contributes to a person being perfectly wonderful without being perfectly moral (*ibid*.: 95). Morally impeccable persons are likely to be boring individuals. One also comes across the argument that moral perfection needs to be avoided, not only because it turns human beings against each other in their claim for the absolute possession of the good, but also because it develops an unbearable pride in the members of an ethical clan (Foss 1946: 86). In line with Swanton one can suggest that it is not always ethical to be so ethical. The urge to be excessively moral may, in fact, lead to intolerant behaviour, directed toward less moralised persons (Olthof 2000). There can be harshness in moral demandingness.

We may conclude that positive perfectionism is ready enough to warn us against perfectionist degradations. There is a strong awareness in Swanton and others that the chief source of discomfort with perfectionism has to do with the amorphousness of the theory, the sense that it can take shapes that we would do well to shy away from (Pincoffs 1986: 114).

The interaction between negative and positive readings of perfection can teach us a lesson with respect to perfective existence. One has to be prepared to see the different shades of perfective being, the negative as well as the positive.

Balanced perfection

Only in the context of constructive and critical balance can perfection continue to be proposed as something that it is better to have than not to have. The idea of perfection as such, it turns out, is something that can be conceived in better and worse ways.

With this view of balanced perfection it is appropriate to insist that we should never feel too secure about the real nature of our perfections and perfectionist strivings. One has both to trust oneself and yet be on guard.

Normal and abnormal perfection look similar, but their basis and meaning is different in the same way that +7 and -7 are different (Horney 1942: 60). We must always be prepared to revisit the actual nature of our concrete perfective states. Perfection often arises out of less praiseworthy inclinations — think of the minority complex as sketched in Alfred Adler (1933). These inclinations are a blessing in so far as they indeed produce good perfection and push us toward an existential surplus, but they may also constitute the source of perfective neurosis. Neurotic and fanatic perfections come in numerous shades and often remain unrecognised by the fanatic self. What originally was initiated as a healthy undertaking may, bit by bit, deteriorate into a circular, pathological enterprise (and vice versa). To find a mountain path all by oneself without anyone's help, will lead to greater feelings of strength and justified pride in achievement (Horney 1942: 36). However, on the basis of these feelings of pride it may also come to be the case that we subsequently begin to seek a similar pride in every undertaking, ultimately refusing help from others on any occasion. A sense of autonomous accomplishment and pride then becomes an issue of compulsion.

Another aspect of fanatic perfective strive is noted in Paul Watzlawick (1984). He underlines that perfectionism of this negative kind has the tendency to give an opposite result in the same way that a person who tries to force herself to fall asleep is very likely to stay awake. In this case the striving for perfection entangles itself in the strange paradoxes of negation and turns out to be detrimental to perfection itself (*ibid.*: 171). Jean Starobinski (2001) offers another

57

version of this paradox of perfection. He refers to Balzac's depiction of a painter who, after trying for six years to perfect a painting of a woman, proudly shows his effort to some visitors. But whereas the painter was really convinced of having reached the ultimate point of perfection, they only see chaos of lines and colours. This is an apt illustration of how the relentless work of perfection, after a certain critical point, turns into a negative process of destruction. The advice is obvious: isn't the trick in our strivings in knowing when to stop working for perfection?

One manner by which to recognise an abnormal striving is to estimate its sense of proportion. It is one thing to attempt to prepare an important report without mistakes, another to be constantly concerned with keeping one's desk in faultless order (Horney 1942: 41). It is also a matter of not confusing possible levels of human perfection. One can perhaps obtain higher perfection in the production of a knife, but to try to reach a similar intensity of perfection in the formation of one's life story or in the creation of a community surely will lead to failure and will turn oneself and others into the regrettable victims of negative perfection. This does not mean, of course, that we should simply withdraw into miniature perfection (this may be another form of negative deviation).

Perfection is fragile, never guaranteed. There are no final perfective solutions for handling life's ambiguities and insecurities. Nor is there much room for perfective complacency: what lifts us up may bring us down. And yet, this handling of perfective ambiguity is something that can be carried out in better and worse ways. Some lessons can be learned. We may conclude that the idea of a balanced positive perfection constitutes an ongoing interpretative and existential challenge.

CHAPTER FIVE —
THE LANGUAGE OF PERFECTION — ii:
PERFECTION TODAY

> *Can we separate worse and better without*
> *a sense, initially vague perhaps, of the best?*
> *Can we know imperfection except by contrast*
> *with the fullness it lacks, namely perfection.*

— William Desmond

Having established the relevance of a balanced positive perfection, we now arrive at the task of providing a renewed interpretation of perfection. In this chapter I will describe different relevant features of 'contemporary perfection'. My aim in doing so is to prepare the reader for a plurivocal theory of perfective appraisal, which I will develop in the next chapter.

Degrees of perfection

Involved as we are — in so many contexts of life — with estimation or appraisal in terms of better and worse, in terms of imperfection and perfection, one thing to realise immediately is that earthly perfection is predominantly, if not always, a matter of perfective gradation and relative perfection. Let us begin with this issue.

The concept of perfection is directly focused on degree properties (Walhout 1978b: 30). Something can be better or worse in quality, development, striving, function, contribution, and so forth. Non-degree properties resist perfective estimation in an immediate sense. 'To be earthly' does not as such imply any degree; one is not more or less earthly. Without degree, it seems inadequate to introduce the language of perfection directly. On the other hand, there are non-trivial indirect connections. First, 'earthliness' does announce, as it were, the availability of certain perfective actualities and possibilities. Earthly creatures are destined to develop perfective qualities appropriate to life on our planet. A set of perfective attainable and attained states is implied in saying that something is characterised by earthliness. Second, in the context of certain perfective teleological schemes the earthliness of something may possess perfective value. Alien researchers from another planet, observing our globe, would be interested in capturing earthly entities for further analysis. The property of earthliness in creatures would then matter in a perfective sense (according to the perfective qualitative standard of appropriateness), in the context of a scientific teleological practice aimed at understanding earthliness and at controlling earthly creatures.

Confronted with a world of perfective gradation, we experience only relative or approximate perfection. Strictly seen, one should define perfection as 'the unsurpassability of a being relative to itself (Walhout 1978a: 5). However, in the concrete roughness of earthly and human existence much, if not all, is a matter of perfective gradation. Partial perfection is our lot (Walhout 1978b: 27). Each organism is a combination of relative perfection and relative imperfection (Goldstein 1933: 355). In concrete reality we never catch up with ultimate perfection. For us the most complete possible fulfilment will always defy and be defied by that which fulfils it. Even when we have had a perfect dinner, and even if we have psychologically experienced something as completely perfect, we cannot actually mean that nothing could be improved in the dish we ate or in the social experience we enjoyed. There is always room for improvement, however microscopically. Foss writes that in relation to confined aims and situations full perfection can in fact be reached:

> Perfection [...] is something we come across in simple affairs, in daily life. When we behave very modestly and restrict ourselves to the most simple aims, we can be sure to produce perfections in large quantities (1946: 10).

However, I would rather suggest that such a *high degree* of perfection can be reached in the fulfilment of small projects and actions that those remaining particles of imperfection and possibility for improvement will become thematically irrelevant and psychologically unnoticeable. The point remains that we cannot rise above the human condition. Clearly, no entity is capable of reaching perfection in all its relevant perfective dimensions. This is nothing less than a structural given. Furthermore, to realise one perfective option often means to repress another. Human careers, in particular, are based on the selection and elimination of possibilities. There is no way beyond this rule:

> In any multicriterial setting, absolute perfection is simply an impossibility. Perfection — the maximum realisation of every value dimension all at once — is unrealizable because of the interaction of parameters: in designing a car you cannot maximise both safety and economy of operation (Rescher 2000: 818).

Not only do we not reach fullness, but what we have perfectively accomplished may also disappear. The deterioration and destruction of perfection are an essential part of human experience and earthly reality. Skills become rusty without practice. A just person may turn hateful in later years. In the end there is the certainty of disintegration and death for each of us. Perfective states come and go.

The story of a human life is always a combination of gaining and losing, of progression in some aspects and regression in others. Sometimes we produce new personal perfections exactly in response to existing imperfections (the aretaic perfection of perseverance specifically arises in the imperfective situations of pain, sickness and hardship). In other cases a particularised increase in one ability leads to a reduction elsewhere. For example, increasing language ability in our mother tongue automatically results in a reduction of our ability to discriminate sounds from other languages (Aspinwall & Staudinger 2003: 16). The general unavoidability of relative perfection implies that we must mainly focus on a gradational perspective. Nonetheless, the custom of perfective language being what it is, one may continue to speak about a perfect car or a perfect teacher, albeit on condition that ultimately we must be prepared to translate (most of) these expressions in terms of relative perfection.

The gradational experience of perfection does not prevent conceptions of ideal perfection from playing a role as inspirational models. In the roughness of life it may be impossible to experience absolute perfection, but as interpretative attempts developed in the context of our projects and experiences, ideals of perfection provide us with directive content that is at once fictional and effective. Ideal perfection guides our concrete practice of estimating things in terms of better and worse. Moreover, it can positively influence the actual development of relative perfection (not being satisfied with what we have now, we may receive, through our ideals of perfection, sufficient stimulation and direction to go on to higher levels of fulfilment and accomplishment).

However, it is important here to note that such an ideal conception is itself something that can be established in better and worse ways. In other words, the human interpretative process of conceptualizing a particular scheme of ideal perfection is itself unavoidably played out according to the ways of relative perfection. A finalised sense of ideal perfection does not exist. There is no perfect conception of perfection. This is also an insight of balanced perfectionism. We are always interpretatively underway, even in our articulation of ideal perfection.

Perfection and reality

Having established a sense of relative perfection it is fruitful, in a second step, to deal with one connection that holds an eminent position in traditional perfectionism, namely the connection between perfection and reality. For example, for Aristotle and Aquinas a concrete house is considered more perfect than the idea of a house. It is interesting to find out whether, in some way, we can in today's context hold on to this connection. In the following I wish to underline certain possibilities. There seem to be at least four ways in which one could continue the idea of 'perfective reality'.

First, the concept of a house in itself does not mean so much. In practical life it is likely to constitute only a first step in a larger project of architectural realisation. In most cases an architect will undertake the effort to conceive a house only in order to have it built for someone. The realisation of an architectural conception therefore implies progression within the process of perfection. It is true that things can go wrong in the act of building (use of bad materials, poor workmanship), placing the architectural conception in what one may consider to be a better perfective position than its realisation. However, in most circumstances, even an imperfect material actualisation of a perfect conception of a house is to be preferred. The house as a concept, for example, will contain fewer possibilities of instrumental value. Only real houses fully contribute to our organic (and psychological) survival. The distinction between real and unreal perfection seems relevant in connection with the difference between a perfective conception of something (unreal perfection) and its realisation (real perfection).

Second, it can be said that after effort and practice I may acquire a capacity that was not available to me before. It is not an illusion to say that I then possess this capacity. And capacities are properties of real organisms. Through my capacity I may also transform parts of the world. And what has an effect in the world must be real in some sense. These transformations are in fact real. So their source, a capacity belonging to a certain organism, is something that is not an illusory property.

Third, to be striving for what we perfectively can become is to achieve a greater personal reality. We turn promise into actuality; there is realisation and fulfilment. Furthermore, possessing more perfective properties and capacities will make us feel more real and alive. To realise oneself is, in a sense, to become more real (Nozick 1990). Some people are in this regard more real than others. They are more concentrated, more integrated, more vivid, and so forth.

Finally, one can connect perfection with the systemic organisation of reality (see Laszlo 1972). Things, processes, qualities, events and actions, which we are accustomed to estimate in terms of better and worse, invite systemic treatment, directly and indirectly. They exist through the workings of systemic togetherness. First of all, each system is in a state of better and worse organisation or composition. Composition is, as we will see in chapter 6, a perfective standard. And it part of reality since it belongs to the core of actual systemic being to be properly composed. Otherwise, a system will degrade and fade away. Second, certain systems are characterised by or allow certain emergent properties to pop up. Cognitive capacity in humans emerges within a form of material systemic togetherness (brain). It is a real emergent property belonging to a concrete systemic entity. Capacities constitute another eminent kind of perfection.

These four ways suggest that it is not altogether impossible to interpretatively consider the relation between perfection and reality.

We should underline that imperfection and anti-perfection are also quite real. Think of the pollution of water. As destruction of purity and of other natural perfections, this pollution constitutes an actual process of anti-perfection. As we live in a world of relative and fragile perfection, imperfective states and processes are abundantly available in ourselves and around us. In this sense imperfection, too, can be said to exist.

Perfection, virtue, excellence

In a third step it is fruitful to clarify the language of perfection in relation to the special perfective languages of virtue and excellence.

Today, we hear about a renaissance of the virtues. Virtue ethics has become a distinguished movement in contemporary moral (and epistemological) thought. Excellence, too, is nowadays a popular word. Many organisations and firms portray themselves as striving for excellence. There seems, in fact, to be almost no institution without an acclaimed sense of excellence. Perfectionism certainly includes concern for virtue and excellence, but it is important to insist that the language of perfection is broader and more differentiated than the languages of virtues and excellence.

Not every form of perfection is aretaic, but every virtue is a form of perfection. *Areté* or virtue originally referred to a broad field of estimation, whether the praiseworthy functioning of knives, horses, eyes, or a runner's feet. In current philosophical and psychological discourse, however, virtue predominantly refers to personal dispositions (such as moral and cognitive virtues). We do not really care to think anymore about feet or eyes in terms of virtue. The contemporary interpretation of virtue, in the context of virtue ethics, makes it inappropriate to use virtue and perfection as identical concepts. Virtue plays itself out in one distinct field of perfective concern, namely that of good personal dispositions. Virtue or aretaic perfection does not occupy the totality of perfective theory.

Areté is not only translated as 'virtue' but also as 'excellence'. In philosophical discussion 'virtue' or 'excellence' is often taken to mean the same thing, but in plain speech we also use 'excellence' to refer to something more than just the contemporary understanding of 'virtue' as a good character trait. We refer, for example, to excellent wines, to an excellent performance or an excellent dinner. The idea of virtue is not specifically present in our mind when the concept of excellence is activated in this manner. Excellence recaptures something of *areté* in its earlier, much broader meaning. In its wide application excellence also comes close to the breadth of perfection. In plain speech we refer equally to a perfect or excellent dinner. In this context there seems to be no serious practical difference between both expressions. In both cases one aims to communicate one's satisfaction with and one's high estimation of a certain experience, situation, performance, accomplishment, effort or product. Philosophically, however, it is quite necessary to underline certain significant differences between excellence and perfection, and to opt for perfective discourse as our broadest language. There are several reasons for this.

First, perfective language permits a better articulation and differentiation of relevant existential aspects. For example, perfective language includes the articulation of perfection as process (think of the perfection, the perfecting of oneself) while excellence (and also virtue) as current terms relate as such much less directly to a process (we do not speak, for example, about the 'virtuing' of oneself; we also do not speak about the 'excellencing' of oneself). Furthermore, perfection seems to allow a more fluent specification of different kinds of quality. If excellence (and virtue) is taken as the basic language we shall run into certain difficulties in trying to express the perfective qualities of 'non-excellences' (and 'non-virtues').

Second, perfection manages to function as a more sympathetic term than excellence. According to its original meaning excellence directly implies a competitive comparison with others. Someone who excells is higher than others; he or she rises above the level of average accomplishment (Foss 1946: 30). Excellence means to be outstandingly better than others. In this manner we also refer to 'excellencies' — persons in high positions within the government or the church (one should note that *areté* also carries, in one of its etymological lines, a superlative association — think of the connection with *aristos*). Perfection, on the other hand, is according to its original intention not a concept that directly forces one into aggressive comparison with others. Perfective accomplishments and qualities do of course permit comparative estimation (comparisons will arise in different circumstances, notably in the context of gradational estimation), but such comparative labour is not the only, nor the main point of perfective estimation. Perfective reception is predominantly concerned, or can be made to be predominantly concerned, with the fundamental fulfilment of one's being considered in its own particular context (Tatarkiewicz 1992: 16).

Finally, since the language of excellence only refers to a very high performance or quality on the basis of comparison with others, it does not really include a varied sense of gradation. Excellence is focused on a very high level of quality and performance, not on relative states. A relative level is not what distinguishes someone from others. Perfective language, on the other hand, is capable of and indeed specialises in giving a voice to gradation and relative states. It is true that this requires a reformulation of perfective terminology. Perfection, classically conceived, refers to an absolute end-state that is the best state possible. However, processes of perfecting (which also have a position in classical perfective theory) do open up the idea of relative stages on the way toward fuller perfection. Perfective trends below the level of completion are recognised and permit the development of a language of gradational estimation. Contemporary perfectionism is bound to specialise in such estimation.

We can conclude that perfective language offers us a wider variety of expressive options.

As such, the languages of virtue and excellence do not have to be given up — far from it — but they should be seen to address specified aspects within a larger perfective context. Virtue or aretaic perfection refers to a subset of perfection, namely certain positive and stable qualities of personality. Excellence is to be employed in reference to very distinguished perfective accomplishments and qualities.

The language of giftedness

The popular language of giftedness has many obvious links with the language of perfection — giftedness refers to having a high level of perfective capacity in a certain domain and/or with showing serious promise in developing such capacity — and in this regard deserves to be included in an analysis of perfective language.

One regularly meets the language of giftedness (talent). We speak about the gifted or talented child. We say that some people have talent, while others are 'born' without considerable gifts. The extremely gifted self is defined in terms of genius. Most others, below genius, are described as talented or gifted persons. One can be more or less gifted. A person may have *some* talent. At a certain level it becomes irrelevant to refer to talent or giftedness. To say that someone has only minimal talent for something is, in fact, to say that he or she fails, and will continue to fail, to reach a reasonable perfective level. Giftedness refers to a higher level of perfective capacity and perfective promise.

Not every strong performance of a certain kind is automatically regarded as a talent or a gift. 'Giftedness' is applied on the basis of at least five criteria (Sternberg ed. 1986): excellence (perfective superiority in comparison with one's peers), rarity (a perfective competence that is rare amongst peers), productivity (real success in the development of a perfective competence), demonstrability (simply claiming to be gifted is not enough), and appreciation (a perfective competence that is highly valued in one's culture). Cultural recognition is a very important factor in the appreciation of giftedness (Csikzsentmihalyi & Robinson 1986). To memorise the content of a phone book is not likely to constitute the best way to display oneself as an intellectually gifted person. There is simply no serious cultural appreciation of a 'perfective' performance of this kind; one will rather consider such a person as someone who is wasting his time.

The theory of giftedness has nowadays transcended the confines of a strict approach in terms of IQ-testing. This is a good development, because IQ-testing has failed to address the many original forms of giftedness in different developmental domains such as music, sport, cooking, manual crafts, dancing, and so forth. An alternative multiple talent approach focuses exactly on what happens in these particular domains and practices, while IQ-testing predominantly focuses on the detection of a generalised competence in human beings in the context of a Western industrialised setting. A multiple talent approach embodies the claim that 'if dreams are the royal road to the unconscious [...] developmental domains are the superhighway to giftedness and creativity' (Feldman 2000: 10). One can easily extend this claim to perfective existence as such: developmental domains, such as the practices (MacIntyre 1981), are the best way to original human perfections.

It is, finally, perfectively important to resist one influential interpretation of giftedness. In its plain use, beyond psychology and educational theory, there is a strong tendency to portray giftedness as 'a condition that is magically bestowed on a person in much the same way that nature endows us with blue eyes, red hair, or a dark complexion' (Renzulli 1986: 60). Such a portrayal needlessly mystifies the origin of many of our perfections. It is important to cancel its claim. I offer a few suggestions.

In giftedness we first of all recognise a sense of gift. There are different ways to consider the idea of gift with respect to human existence. We come to be. One could say that our being is a primordial gift. The gift of being is itself the first good of being (Desmond 1995a: 506). We also receive the gift of different processes of spontaneous development. Our body is destined to develop in certain ways. Furthermore, we also receive in our existence cultural possibilities of development, language, skill, and so on — possibilities that are provided within familial, educational, and social contexts. Even the least gifted or talented self will have received gifts of the kinds depicted.

Giftedness as such continues to relate to a sense of receiving. One needs the gift of being, the gift of spontaneous organic development, and the numerous gifts on the level of cultural opportunity, to be able to become a gifted person. However, not everyone will do something with the basic and supplementary gifts that have been provided in this way. It is a well-known fact that in any given domain, whether it is in music or sport or art or science, only a few persons will reach the highest levels of perfective accomplishment and creativity, and only a smaller group will reach higher levels. Exactly because of this fact, there is the common tendency to understand giftedness itself as a mysterious gift, lying dormant in a particular child and waiting to pop up in a proper circumstance.

Current developmental theories of education contradict this view (Smitsman 2000). One point is that reaching a state of giftedness implies a sustained personal engagement. In childhood one may be judged on estimations of potential and giftedness, but there is no automatic rule that one's potential will ultimately flourish and turn into a full capacity. One has to work for perfection. It is rather the case that a child practising musical skills will come to perform in a talented way. States of giftedness are themselves not the products of spontaneous development. One needs to work hard to become a gifted violin player. Moreover, perfective development towards a state of real talent implies the contributive presence of different traits. Think, for example, of the plain willingness to work hard, dedication, perseverance, fascination, self-confidence, and so on. This also confirms the point that giftedness is not something that, as it were, drops out of the sky; it is a complex perfective state made possible by the hidden and not so hidden workings of a set of conditions, traits, and activities. Mozart came to perform musically with a higher level of perfection on a very early age. This could provide an argument for the presence of a mysterious talent. However, this fact should rather be taken as a confirmation that early engagement and practice in an outstanding musical familial context can produce very fine, even sublime perfective results in a comparatively short time frame. Behind every sublime performance (at whatever age) — even while its presence cannot be fully explained, or predicted, by its antecedent conditions — stands a (hidden) history of learning, understanding, experience, and practice.

The languages of goodness and value

A final point to clarify in this chapter is the relation between perfection and the languages of goodness and value.

One should recognise that there are fundamental appraisive languages besides perfectionism. Especially think of the languages of goodness (agathonism) and value (axiology). We should be interested in the togetherness of goodness, value and perfection, since only the command of a rich discourse — including perfection, goodness, and value — will contribute to evaluative intelligence (Aschenbrenner 1971: 19).

Take first the relation between goodness and value. To say that something is valuable implies that it possesses some degree of goodness or is instrumentally related to something good. And to say that something is good implies that it has a certain value, that it is considered to be valuable in one way or another. It is appropriate to accept the intimate togetherness of the languages of goodness and value. Value and goodness refer to that which is worth having, experiencing, doing or striving for in certain aspects and in certain situations.

This doesn't mean it is invalid, in particular instances, to differentiate between both languages. One could say, for example, that it is not good for someone to focus only on the value of certain confined activities and pleasures while being capable of so much more. Such a differentiation in its own way confirms that we terminologically need both goodness and value.

Accepting the togetherness of agathonist and axiological discourse we may also, without serious difficulties, integrate goodness/value within a perfectionist framework.

It is clear that most, if not all, axiological and agathonist authors working beyond and against hedonism and emotivism come close to a perfectionist sense of better and worse. In their concrete scales of value or goodness they tend to implicitly or even explicitly confirm perfectionism — think, for example, of the studies of von Wright (1963) and Werkmeister (1967). And perfectionist authors often refer to value and goodness in ways that come very close to non-hedonic and non-emotivist agathonism and axiology — see, for example, the perfective theory of Donald Walhout (1978a).

The thematic interconnections between goodness, value and perfective concepts are numerous. Let me introduce a few conceptual links. One hears about the goodness of perfection, and about perfective states and qualities being valuable ends. Precious goods and intrinsic values constitute perfective states and perfective accomplishments appreciated for their own sake (cognitive activity, artistic expression, involvement in complex enterprises). The concept of instrumental value is identical with the concept of contributive perfection. The highest possible values and goods exactly have a central place in the perfective sense of human completion (eudaimonism).

Perfectionism is bound to spontaneously make a differentiated use of agathonistic and axiological concepts. We need, for example, to be able to say that perfection is valuable or good (and not simply that perfection is perfect), that the things we value possess more or less perfective quality, or that we are perfectively striving to fulfil valuable ends. The languages of goodness and value provide perfectionism with complementary possibilities of articulation. This will in part prevent the installation of a perfective language burdened by terminological monotony.

CHAPTER SIX —
THE LANGUAGE OF PERFECTION — iii:
VARIETIES OF PERFECTIVE APPRAISAL

Human creativity in the invention of
appraisive concepts, like all creativity,
is something that should fill us with
wonder.

— Karl Aschenbrenner

We have established that the language of positive perfection manages to hold on to its own position in a contemporary context. We have also established that perfective language is affiliated with certain other languages of estimation. Since evaluative intelligence is grounded in the command of a rich vocabulary, we need in a next step to focus on perfection itself and to undertake an attempt to articulate different structural kinds of perfection. In this chapter I wish to reach a plurivocal theory of perfective appraisal.

Teleological perfection constitutes one of the most basic notions within the perfectionist frame of mind. It is therefore fruitful to begin this analysis with varieties of teleological perfective estimation.

Teleological perfections

In continuity with the recognised Latin and Greek backgrounds of perfectionist terminology (*perfectio, perficere, teleos, telos*) one can relate perfection to completion, to something that is brought to its end. Perfection as a final state implies an earlier developmental process of perfecting. It suggests a 'going through', a going from the beginning to the end of something. A thing is called perfect when the perfecting process arrives at its ultimate stage, beyond which there is no further possibility of perfecting for the kind of being in question. There is actuation until perfection is reached, and then the process is terminated. End also means termination. However, the end of perfection implies a more positive conception of end — something that is good to reach, not just neutrally so (Blanchette 1992: 48). Perfection is beneficial. It is pleasing and provides satisfaction (Christian Wolf, quoted in Schneewind 1998: 438). It is something that is better to have than not to have. Teleological perfection tunes in with the temporal and developmental side of perfection as it takes time to approach an end in a progressive way, since one has to pass through relative stages of perfection and imperfection. Teleological perfection refers to living creatures essentially involved in development and action, and usually capable of reaching different stages of perfection.

Passmore (1970) confines teleological perfectionism to an organism that reaches its natural end, but it is fruitful to seek a much broader or more varied definition. An organism reaching its natural end (or its most appropriate end, in the case of humans) is involved in a very obvious type of teleological perfection, but everything that in one way or another concerns the reaching of an end invites interpretation and estimation in terms of teleological perfection. Human enterprises and actions aimed at wrong or trivial ends are also to be interpreted in teleological terms. Criminal projects are teleological enterprises. A successful robbery is the fulfilment of a certain end. Of course, perfectionism, while accepting the idea of negative teleology in a formal sense, will insist that it is not valuable or good for human beings to be involved in such projects. There are good as well as bad or evil teleologies. Authentic perfectionism is focused on the fulfilment of good or worthy, valuable ends, and wishes to stay away from 'destructive perfection' (Walhout 1978b: 30).

Some may perhaps insist that it is better to portray human life without reference to teleological perfection. Perhaps humans should just drift along without a sense of orientation, development, existential striving. Perhaps we rather reach our best state as soon as we are born — the rest is downhill. This option, however, does not resonate with common human experience. It is impossible to understand human life without reference to constructive development and to the positive reaching of certain ends. This is, in part, what makes us human. To act, in however minimal a form, is already to establish purposive behaviour (Nuttin 1967). Without developments, processes and progressive actions humans could not sustain themselves. We experience lack and are destined to reach beyond such lack: ends penetrate the course of desire from within (Desmond 1987: 19). Desire needs mental organisation, a system of better and worse, hence a hierarchy of ends to be reached and fulfilled. We are, in fact, doomed to be teleological — there is no escape from ends!

Different forms of teleological perfection can be proposed.

Existential teleological perfection

Existential teleological perfection constitutes the most comprehensive and dramatic version of teleological perfection (other versions of teleological perfection focus on more confined fields of developing, striving and doing; in ideal circumstances these confined or partial fields will contribute to, or at least not fundamentally disturb, existential teleological fulfilment). The issue of existential teleological perfection refers to the question, what constitutes the best possible life for me? A perfective response will observe that we are destined to estimate the worth of our lives by the goods that define our spiritual orientation (Taylor 1989: 42). It is in fact not possible to make real sense of our lives without the availability of evaluative discrimination one way or another. Lives can be estimated as better or worse according to different perfective standards.

On the one hand, there will be many things which we cannot control — when and where we are born, where we are raised, when and where we will die, specific bodily properties, opportunities that have appeared through sheer luck, certain unfortunate experiences (sickness, accidents, suffering, violent actions undertaken by others), and so forth. We do not fully control meaning, happiness, flourishing or fulfilment. On the other hand, most of us have significant possibilities to control and work towards what we consider to be a better life. The variety of control finds its source in personal and societal limitations and openings. To be able to work towards significant existential improvement and fulfilment it is necessary to become oneself sufficiently conscious of the elements addressed in existential teleological perfection. One needs to address the idea of a 'best life' while being alive — from younger adulthood onwards, and perhaps even earlier (in a more playful manner). It is likely that in our complex society (in which numerous existential options present themselves) confrontation with this idea is a constituent part of the actual process towards existential teleological fulfilment. This confrontation, clearly, can be undertaken in better and worse ways.

Different contemporary perfective authors tend to set aside the question of existential teleological perfection. They fear a return to Aristotle or Aquinas. These fears are not justified. We must in particular resist aretaic functionalism à la Edmund Pincoffs (1986) and its argument that we should not seek the perspective of a captain concerned with the ship's direction, but only that of an engineer focused on the smooth operation of its engine and working parts — wherever the ship sails to. From this perspective virtues have to do only with our working well in social gatherings, nothing more. The important thing is that we are creatures of organisation and live in each other's lives — there is no place for a deeper and larger teleological account of the virtues in Pincoffs. But aretaic functionalism is based on a false metaphorics, inadequately confining us to the position of engineer by way of a confrontation with another inadequate position. Typically, a captain possesses final knowledge about the true destination of his or her ship and is involved in tackling problems of how to get there. Aretaic functionalism is quick to argue that in real life we never obtain this type of (dogmatic) certainty. There can be no eudaimonic captains (hence, there is also no role for the virtues on this existential level). Now, we must of course agree that there are no eudaimonic captains. But why could we not propose another figure, less secure perhaps but certainly more real? The figure of an existential explorer comes to mind — a figure involved in an interpretationally complex existential project characterised by ambiguities, uncertainties, tensions, possibilities and qualitative developments. Perhaps some explorers may in their lives discover or significantly approach an authentic perfective goal adequate to what they are and can become. Others will be less fortunate or less capable. However, the point remains that such explorations and quests do exist (in real life we find people involved in such quests), and may be interpreted and acted upon in better and worse ways. Think of a person who 'devotes himself entirely to trivial pursuits such as stamp-collecting when capable of far more than this' (MacIntyre 1960: 83). This example already suggests an opening for an appropriate eudaimonic search focused on a deeper existential fulfilment beyond the collecting of stamps.

Existential teleological perfection refers to everything that is a positive part of the process of fulfilling one's life as best as possible, of fulfilling one's best and most valuable possibilities. While permitting a plurality of existential scenarios, perfectionism does remain concerned with defending one's central sense of existential promise. A best possible life is most intensely connected with, even if not completely reducible to, the 'fulfillment of the promise of the self' (Maslow 1971: 128). We can here also refer to Heidegger's description of 'die perfectio des Menschen' in terms of 'das Werden zu dem, was er in seinem Freisein für seine eigensten Möglichkeiten sein kann' (1963: 264). Perfective existential promise refers to the process of actualising one's inherent potentialities and one's most worthy possibilities, to fulfilling one's proper and, in part, unique functions, qualities, and capacities (Gewirth 2001).

We do not automatically have to understand human existential fulfilment as co-extensive with pure contemplation and spiritual perfection. Some may continue to consider contemplation — or rather the interpretational practice of contemplation — as their own ultimate concern, but there are so many other worthy goods and existential teleological options. The quest for a personal and general conception of existential fulfilment, in relation to a plurality of fundamental goods is still possible today. Beyond the actualisation of basic capacities and organic structures, and beyond a certain level of cultivation and education, we are confronted with an exciting variety of perfective existential teleologies. Thomas Hurka notes:

> A person need not be skilled at science to achieve perfection, and the more alternatives she has to science, the more likely it is that she is suited to at least one. The more routes there are to perfection, the better chance each has to be able to travel by one (1993: 167).

Spontaneous teleological perfection

It is relevant to propose spontaneous teleological perfection as another significant form of teleological perfection. Spontaneous teleological perfection refers to natural processes of development (organic growth). Eyesight, the capacity to move, and fertility are results of such processes as is the organic capacity to restore. In this regard one can refer to the body as 'the artist of its own healing' (Pellegrino & Thomasma 1981: 79), or to the 'self-doctoring of the body' (Desmond 1990: 246). This sense of perfection is based on original powers of development and quality in living entities. Development is spontaneous in the sense that no direct action or effort is needed. One does not have to exercise or to learn anything to become fertile, and no special action is required to be able to see as such. Fertility and eyesight are organic gifts of being.

It is true, however, that in most cases we will be confronted with states based on an inimitable combination of spontaneous and acquired perfection. Acquired perfection refers to qualities developed through explicit action, effort and practice — skills and virtues, for example, are learned and demand practice. Most organically established capacities and qualities do somehow need regular activation, otherwise they will deteriorate. In turn, explicit instances of acquired perfection are always based, directly or indirectly, on qualities and possibilities opened up by earlier and continuing processes of spontaneous perfection — think of athletic performances. The way of being of plants may be largely determined by spontaneous organic perfection, but the way of being of humans is opened up by virtue of species-specific processes of spontaneous perfection and deeply complexified and particularised by the workings of acquired perfection.

It should be noted that the current revolution in genetic engineering drastically disturbs the distinction between spontaneous and acquired perfection. One aim of genetic engineering is in fact to set up revised or new processes of spontaneous organic perfection. But spontaneous perfection is then initiated by explicit action, and this means it becomes a form of acquired perfection. It remains to be seen how perfectionism should respond to this issue. Genetic engineering announces a new era of perfective possibility *and* pathology.

Hedonic teleological perfection

Let us turn to a next form of teleological perfection.

Perhaps with some care, one can propose the idea of hedonic teleological perfection. Hedonism and perfectionism are in one sense opposed — immediate and simple pleasure versus a human life of complex quality beyond simple pleasure, of accomplishment connected with existential teleological hierarchy. However, there is pleasure and enjoyment in perfective experience, and there is perfective goodness in pleasurable experience (on hedonic goodness, see von Wright 1963). One can discern different kinds of pleasure, many of which connect with organic needs and enjoyments, others that relate to higher perfective achievements. There are the enjoyments of a chocolate eater, but also the satisfactions of a concert pianist. Pleasure and satisfaction is often a complementary product of perfective striving aimed at certain states and accomplishments. The hedonic dimension is then part of non-hedonic teleology. But it is also possible to explicitly strive for certain pleasures. It is proper to define striving in terms of hedonic teleological perfection when it is straightforwardly directed toward pleasurable states. The process of drinking wine and eating chocolate is in many cases a teleological process aimed at original hedonistic goodness. We do not eat chocolate and, then, also experience pleasure; but we aim to experience a certain kind of pleasure, and therefore eat chocolate. Hedonic goals exist and may constitute authentic ends within a normal perfectionism. In itself, pleasure is a good. There is also a complex hedonic experience, notably in the context of our aesthetic receptions and appreciations. The experience of complexity and richness may itself be an aesthetic pleasurable experience. The effort to appreciate a certain landscape, for example, can in certain circumstances, namely when we are explicitly focused on experiencing the pleasure that accompanies the perfection of a landscape, be defined as an enriched form of hedonic teleological perfection.

Teleological perfection in roles and projects

Perfection also applies to human functioning within social roles and other project settings (tasks, domains, practices). This leads to a fourth and fifth sense of teleological perfection. Processes of perfection aimed at the fulfilment of one's role as a parent, teacher or police officer invite the idea of teleological perfection in roles. Everything needed to fulfil the regional demands of a role belongs to the field of this kind of perfection. In a role one is confronted with a project setting consisting of numerous practical challenges. The teleological perfection of a role is always a matter of the perfection of a project, since a role is defined in terms of one or several functional project(s). But not all instances of teleological perfection in projects take place in the context of roles. Going for a swim, a practical context involving different physical challenges, is part of a role performance in the case of a professional swimmer and in the case of a parent teaching his or her child to swim, but it can also be undertaken for one's own pleasure beyond the demands of any role. Perfection in projects can thus be proposed as in part a distinct form of teleological perfection. It refers to the process of fulfilling ends within practical and domain settings outside the realm of role.

The teleological perfection of roles and projects allows a higher level of estimative clarity and certainty. It is in fact easier to see which ends are characteristic of functional roles, and to establish whether a physician or a police officer adequately works according to the worthy ends of medicine or police work. The same is true for project settings outside role. The ends to be fulfilled in swimming are not esoteric or far-fetched (relaxation, exercise, health, bodily enjoyment). The perfective contents of the story of a human life are far less clear and secure. A sense of perfective limitation appears. Only in confined or regional spheres, so it appears, do we have the prospect of experiencing a very high intensity of perfection. The virtue of a limited challenge of perfection lies exactly in its rate of accomplishment. This leads to regional moments of happiness and relative perfective confirmation (Bollnow 1968: 201-205). Those regional and temporal moments constitute 'islands of perfection' in a sea of dense and complicated perfective endeavour.

However, even when scenarios of perfection become less secure and definite beyond a role or a project setting, it remains valid to support wider existential issues of perfective judgement. We continue to need larger existential perfective interpretation and estimation in confrontation with particular roles and practical perfections. Roles and project settings without larger existential confrontation are likely to turn into absolute fields without critical awareness. The demands and habits involved in the teleological perfection of roles and projects may come into conflict with the challenges of existential perfection. Furthermore, a broader existential perspective on our actions and less extended efforts will tell us more rapidly whether some of those settings and roles are not trivial (or evil). Some roles, for example, deserve to be characterised according to Balthasar Gracian's remark that 'to be eminent in a humble profession is to be great in little, is to be something in nothing' (quoted in Hafter 1966: 136). In the more fruitful cases human selves will find a significant part of their larger existential fulfilment in specific roles and settings.

It should be underlined that it is best to set the idea of teleological perfection aside — at least in a direct, psychological sense — in the settings of organisation, community, culture, world history, earth, cosmos, and God.

Persons embedded in organisations, communities and cultures are themselves involved in teleological scenarios, which give content and structure to those organisations, communities and cultures. And these personal teleologies are influenced by the specific contexts of organisational, communal and cultural immersion. But we cannot say that organisations, communities and cultures themselves are systemic realities psychologically striving for certain aims. Only humans (and other organisms) are teleologically involved in a direct manner. To be sure, it is impossible to grasp the point and purpose of these larger systemic realities without central reference to ends, but these ends are conceived and fulfilled by human selves. The same is true for roles and practices/domains.

Nor are world history, earth and cosmos directly teleological. Human history, beyond personal life stories, refers to the actions and developments of a vast plurality of human selves, combined with events beyond humanity. But there is no distinct and separate historical teleological force. This is also true for earth and cosmos. Material reality below the level of organic being is not teleologically organised (panpsychism is not generally considered to be a relevant option). Of course, parts of inanimate reality play contributive roles within animate teleology. In a secondary sense these parts are teleologically relevant. Furthermore, humans and other organisms remould parts of inanimate nature, which thereby receive teleological imprint. Again, this underlines an indirect connection with teleology.

Finally, within the framework of a secular complex perfectionism there is no reference to God and infinite perfection. In life and action we are obliged to stop at the limits of our projects, but in abstract thought we can endlessly go on in extending and applying the idea of perfection (Foss 1946: 13). We may finally end up with an ultimate metaphysics of perfection in God. Perfection subsequently loses the adequate meaning it once had in the context of roles, functions and particular lives. The idea of infinite perfection seriously complicates the language of perfection. A *secular* perfectionism is destined to place its bets predominantly on concrete and finite perfection, on the perfections of human and non-human creatures, on the perfections of earthly systemic being. Beyond a secular perfectionism, obviously, the question of the perfection of God remains a central issue.

Teleological perfection of miniature action

The next type of teleological perfection concerns that of action. Every time we undertake a simple or miniature action, including cognitive and linguistic action, we already allow judgement in terms of better and worse. When something is undertaken a sense of failure and success is automatically invited. Teleological perfection of miniature action plays itself out in (very) small units. Walking up the stairs is already a matter of perfection: it can be done in better and worse ways according to certain ends and standards. According to Kurt Goldstein the urge to perfection is very much a part of the developmental stages in childhood. The need to complete incomplete actions explains many of the activities of the child:

> As long as the child's walking is imperfect, he tends to walk and walk, often with no other goal than walking. After he has perfected the walking, he uses it in order to reach a special point which attracts his attention — that is, to complete another performance, and so on (Goldstein 1966: 147).

The relevance of teleological perfection in miniature actions indeed becomes very visible in the context of training, when even the movement of one finger may be a matter of explicit consideration. In most instances beyond training and earlier development, however, human beings do not commonly concern themselves with the perfection of such miniature actions, but direct themselves mainly towards larger aims, settings, projects and narratives. Chains and clusters of miniature actions form the content of the processes of teleological perfection in roles and projects, but, of course, not all collections of miniature actions are embedded in significant practical settings. Endlessly walking up and down the stairs, which possibly involves a chain of perfected miniature actions, may be part of nothing much.

Productional teleological perfection

We transform and make material things with an eye on ends. This suggests what can be called a productional sense of perfection.

Productional teleological perfection is a highly important version of practical perfection and often constitutes a central part of what is at hand in roles, projects and occupations. It refers to the process of successful making or creating of a product of whatever kind (chair, text, building, tool, etc.), according to an end conceived by an author or a producer. Productional teleological perfection touches a basic meaning of perfection in its traditional conception. Perfection, by way of the Latin term *perficere*, is linked with the sense of something 'thoroughly made' (*per* relates to 'thoroughly', *facere* means 'to make') (Blanchette 1992: 43).

A radical stress on productional perfection is, for example, found in René Magritte. He writes: 'Une maison, une lentille d'objectif, une bille de billard ou tout autre produit de l'activité humaine doit être parfaite, pour qu'elle remplisse bien sa mission essentielle' (1994: 15).

Although the 'thoroughly made' refers in the first place to the product as such, it is implied that a good product is likely to be created in line with the intention of a producer. The perfection of products finds its origin in a successful effort to create according to ends and confirms a process of productional teleological perfection, since productional perfection normally leads to products that are thoroughly made. There are only two exceptions that in concrete instances cut the link between perfect product and productional teleological perfection. One may intend to make a flawed product. Then, there is productional teleological perfection without a perfect product. Or one may arrive at a perfected product without intending a process of productional perfection, by virtue of sheer luck and coincidence. Then, there is a perfect product without proper teleological striving.

Contributive perfection

Besides teleological perfection there are other forms of perfection. These forms remain connected with what happens in teleological perfection, but also present new aspects of perfective language.

We only exist through instrumental otherness, through the help and contribution of many things beyond ourselves. Our systemic being as such is a combination of elements that interact and contribute. Contribution is everywhere. This is a fundamental fact that deserves to be honoured by another sense of perfection, namely contributive perfection. I will clarify this in a new segment.

Contributive perfection may be applied in different ways. Let me offer a few possibilities. An entity or an object or an aspect of being can be perfectively judged in so far it helps to fulfil the ends of living others. A horse is considered perfect when it fully responds to the demands and ends of a farmer. It contributes to and is hereby part of the teleological perfective project of farming. This brings estimation in terms of contributive perfection into play. The idea of contributive perfection can also be applied to processes within organisms. A stomach, for example, contributes to the general nutritional state of an organism, and our immune system protects us against bacteriological and viral invaders. The stomach and immune system contribute then to the organism of which they are an essential part. An organism itself constitutes a systemic togetherness of contributing factors. Furthermore, what happens earlier may contribute to what comes later. Some of my childhood experiences and accomplishments positively contribute to what I have now become, and certain persons have helped me to become what I am. These earlier moments and persons invite estimation in terms of contributive perfection (it must be admitted, however, that in most cases it will be very difficult to specify accurately the contributive role of an earlier moment and person — we may possess only vague recognition). Contributive perfection can also be applied to aspects of being contributing to the formation of inanimate objects. The natural formation of a diamond, for example, is only possible on the basis of specific mineral elements and tectonic pressures. Hence, these elements and pressures have contributed to the systemic being of a diamond. It is not that a diamond can evaluate its own value or the contributive values of its internal parts and external formative environment. But *we* value the presence of diamonds, and therefore can acknowledge the contributive values which have led to the formation of a diamond.

There are no independent perfections then; contribution is everywhere. Organisms live by virtue of 'affordances' (Gibson 1982). No living entity can come to exist and strive for perfection without the contributions of other entities and elements. We are what we are not only by ourselves:

> One would not be freed into the fullness of one's own powers without this person or that, my parents, this teacher, that teacher, none ever really knowing how much they have given; this childhood friend; this stranger whose unsolicited smile on a dark stretch of life made it possible for me to rise in the morning and continue; those whose gift is their simply being there, a mute reminder of the mystery of the

gift […] Because of the gift of the others, the help of the helpers, there is no heroism alone (Desmond 2001: 330).

The idea of contributive perfection invites a more general consideration of the togetherness of entities, events and systems. There is a pervasive earthly interconnection:

> A thing, anything: this chair, that man, the tree in the yard, the goose overhead, the wish which is father to the thought, the plankton helpless in the sea, and the stitch which in time saves nine — each is what it is in virtue of other things being what they are. We live in a world community of things on which we are helplessly dependent (Feibleman 1952: 290).

Each contributive other constitutes a *perficiens* — a contributing factor in the perfection or perfectionist striving of a *perficiendum* (Walhout 1978a: 16). Many aspects of being serve as *perficiens* — think of objects and tools, but also of air, wind, sunlight and water. Living creatures specifically appropriate aspects of the environment in order to mature and to multiply their functions (Weiss 1967a: 267). They often force things into contribution. Grass contributes to the cow's fulfilment, but only by way of a direct elimination of the being of grass by the cow's efforts (Walhout 1978a: 164). Perfection as contribution may thus conflict with the original perfective teleology of a contributing entity. A horse, for example, needs to be trained so as to bring out its own original teleological inclinations. This problem does not arise (any more) in the case of non-living tools and objects. A dead organism does not have teleology, only the worms that eventually penetrate it and the humans that eat its meat.

The clash between original teleology and contributive submission introduces the question of destruction and immorality. We use and cannot fail to use, but the temptation of use is dominion, subjection, and slavery (Desmond 2001: 420). The reality of contributive perfection is such that violence between organisms is ineradicably a part of nature:

> Nature is such that one living thing lives by destroying and consuming other life, and of course this is one of the things that make all men call nature a dirty old toad or the like. But if someone decided to be a conscientious objector to this arrangement, he would soon have to choose whether to endure the pangs of conscience or of hunger. If this objection went so far as stopping the phagocytes in his blood from destroying alien life, he would die quickly and nastily (Geach 1979: 19).

Contributive effects can be stronger or weaker and, hence, more or less relevant to a receiving or appropriating organism. For example, the rain is as contributive factor strongly relevant to the growth of wheat, while the growth of wheat is only minimally relevant to the rain (Buchler 1966: 197). Often we do not notice significant contributors to our perfective existence. One reason for humans polluting the environmental gifts of water and air is that we take them for granted, failing to understand their unique contribution to the fundamental organic and human quality of life.

Another issue to note is that certain events have contributive effects precisely in their destructive workings. For example, the flood that drowns may also cleanse (Desmond 1995a: 517). Fire may play a positive role in the ecology of the forest. To understand the paradoxical play of contribution it is relevant to refer to the idea of obstacle/organ (Jankélévitch 1977). Death, for example, offers existential structure, direction and vitality exactly by setting an ultimate limit. That which implies the end of life creates the possibility of meaningful life. Life without an end, in which initiative may always be postponed, would mean a kind of mental death. The paradoxical nature of certain contributive effects challenges a simplistic conception of contributive perfection. It also challenges the idea of a world without limit, suffering and destruction. The world is not built as an absolute harmony. Chaos plays a productive and essential role.

Contributive perfection expresses a perfective dimension less explicitly addressed in teleological perfection. It is subsequently a matter of allowing creative interaction between both kinds of perfection. We then arrive at an enlarged perfective discourse. Let me offer a few possibilities of interaction between teleological and contributive perfection.

Different instances of teleological perfection directly invite articulation in terms of contributive perfection. In the context of the teleological perfection of products, contributive perfection becomes an explicit part of what one aims at. The production of a perfect tool or a perfect table implies the production of something that is contributively perfect (tools and and use-objects are meant to have instrumental value for humans). In the context of teleological perfection within a role occupations focused on service immediately come to mind. A butler is defined by a dominant concern for contributive perfection.

Contributive perfection is connected to teleological perfection in a larger sense. Everything that happens in a human life may play a contributing role in an existential teleological endeavour. For example, spontaneous teleological perfections can be estimated in terms of their higher or lower contributive value for the process of existential fulfilment. The same is true for the broader contributive effects of perfections in the context of action, role, and production. The idea of contributive perfection stimulates a deeper exploration of what is at hand in teleological processes. And teleological perfection offers a thematic setting in which contributive perfection is often destined to function.

Qualitative perfection

In another step we must deal with qualitative perfection (perfective quality), which also constitutes a very significant variety of perfection.

This kind of perfection can be taken to refer to, or to be concerned with the value of many existing properties of systems, objects, entities, organisms, humans, and so forth. Humans may evaluate these properties according to (a combination of) perfective qualitative standards. Gradations of better and worse are connected with these standards being more or less fulfilled. If a property fulfils a perfective qualitative standard it constitutes an instance of qualitative perfection. Teleological perfection is concerned with development, striving, with the effort to reach a certain perfective state or property, whereas qualitative perfection is concerned with the actual (gradational) presence of such states or properties.

It should be underlined that qualitative perfections deal with features actually found in items that leave a certain impression on the person judging those items (in the same way, teleological and contributive perfective appraisals are meant to be concerned with developmental stages and instrumental values that are *really* there). Those impressions may at times be wrong — for example, I may receive an impression of someone as being courageous, while the individual in question is not courageous at all, but rather someone who completely lacks a sense of danger and risk — but the point is then to enter a process of interpretative and evaluative revision until a rational qualitative estimation has been reached.

I shall propose different sets of perfective quality. It should be noted that the link with existing aspects in items is in certain cases indirect, perhaps even vague. However, also in these cases appraisal in terms of qualitative perfection is to be brought back to aspects that are expected to be there.

Perfective qualitative standards

Among the perfective qualities that seem to be valid in a more general way one finds completeness, composition, and purity. One reason for the generalised value of these standards is their affiliation with systemic being. Adequate systems in the world cannot exist without a (very) substantial approximation of these qualities.

Completeness — A system that is complete lacks nothing in the requisite parts, properties or functions. This distinct perfective standard implies estimation or evaluation in terms of structural totality. Things that are complete are positively received because it is likely that something that is not (sufficiently) complete will not function properly or will function below standard or will disintegrate and cease to exist. Human beings as organic systems cannot exist without the functional organic parts of heart or liver. Completeness of a certain kind is available in a car with all its parts and in a physician with all the relevant professional qualities. We are not functionally interested in cars without wheels and in physicians lacking diagnostic skill.

Composition — Systems can only exist on the basis of sound composition. Composition makes a being a concrete organisation of the power to be. Proper systemic structure implies functional togetherness. Parts should be situated in their proper position, possess whatever it is they need to possess, and interact in proper ways with other parts. Composition is present in an organism with all the elements having their right position, balance, and function. In the wake of composition, one may also refer to affiliated or synonymous perfective qualities such as harmony, structure, coherence, and unity.

Purity — Having no foreign, disturbing elements suggests a third perfective qualitative standard. Purity is present, for example, in an altruistic effort not contaminated by (hidden) self-interests, and in an army not infiltrated by enemy individuals. Lack of sufficient purity can be medically dangerous for an organism. Purity is systemically important. Organic diseases are often caused by the infiltration of foreign bacterial organisms.

A second set of qualitative perfections with generalised validity includes the qualities of richness, continuity, and scope.

Richness — A traveller having many memories and experiences can be said to possess interpretative and emotional richness. Richness means multi-dimensionality, complexity, variation, and plurality. We naturally appreciate forms of richness. Complexity of competence and varied experience help us to sustain our lives. We admire persons with moral and existential richness. Depth, in one of its meanings, can also be considered a form of richness. We speak, for example, of the hidden depth of a person, thereby referring to the availability of unexpected richness. One could also mention versatility as a standard of richness. A versatile self is good at doing different things.

Continuity — The perfective standard of continuity refers to a system that maintains itself or continues to be, to properties that stay or endure. We are ourselves interested in staying alive, in keeping our qualities and competences for a longer time. The positive role of continuity is beyond doubt. Each living organism is an effort in continuation. Beings are striving to perpetuate themselves. Some systems or entities continue by way of stability, others by way of flexibility and transformation. Strength is one other perfective standard connected with continuity. To last for a long while without breaking down, hence to have continuity, is a form of strength.

Scope — A dictionary containing all the words of a language has maximum scope. Scope refers to extension, in relation to membership as well as to breadth of influence. The English language encompasses many more native speakers and a much larger geographical area than the Dutch language. It has monumental scope, enormous influence and domination. In many instances scope functions as a positive property for the systems possessing it. Most of us are involved in attempts to enlarge our personal scope. Scope may come close to richness (obviously, a dictionary containing all the words of a language is also a rich dictionary), but this is not necessarily the case. Imagine a postage stamp collector whose collection consists of a vast number of stamps of one and the same kind. The scope of this collection is surely large, but one can hardly speak of richness.

A third set of generalised perfective qualitative standards deals with effectiveness, economy, and appropriateness. These standards tell us something more about the concrete value of certain capacities, qualities, properties, objects, and so forth. As evaluative terms, they often seem to function in an indirect manner. They estimate, then, not the presence of a certain quality within an object, but a further value of this quality — namely its effectiveness, the economic manner in which it reaches an effect, and its relevance in a particular context.

Effectiveness — This standard focuses on the degree to which something has a certain effect or reaches a certain result. In many cases the issue of effectiveness belongs to the world of action and capacity (see sub-section on capacities), but not always. An elemental quality (green colour in a plant, for example) may be very effective in calming down human nerves, but it is hardly proper to see a colour as an active entity like an animal or a human.

Economy — To adequately produce something, fast and with minimal loss of energy, is to work according to the standard of economy. This standard is, for example, displayed in an experienced runner who manages to run fast for a longer time with minimal waste of energy. But economy, too, finds application beyond the realm of active organisms. To have a proper medical effect, a herbal tea is often best served with a minimal concentration of its ingredients in a cup of hot water. One may thus claim that herbal tea has a positive effect with minimal loss of energy (no high doses needed). This is exactly what the standard of economy is about.

Appropriateness — This standard is exemplified in a police officer displaying his particular role perfections while at work but not while dealing with his children at home (unless these particular role perfections happen to be relevant in the context of family). A sound qualitative property activated in an inappropriate context automatically diminishes in value. It may even become a disvalue. The standard of appropriateness or relevance underlines the importance of context as an element in accurate appraisal.

A final set of quite general perfective standards introduces the issues of rarity and abundance. Again, these standards function more indirectly. Properties, qualities and objects that are rare or unique often are even more strongly appreciated exactly because of this. For many other properties and objects, however, it is important that they are abundantly available. The question of a smaller or larger number or amount contributes to the concrete appreciation of perfective qualities and, therefore, become part of their appraisive characterisation.

Rarity — A landscape may possess a rare constellation of positively received features. Rarity contributes then to our perfective appreciation of the qualities

83

of such a landscape. In the wake of rarity, uniqueness constitutes a more intense standard. Uniqueness is a radical instance of rarity. This standard is, for example, displayed in the invention of a new scientific theory. An innovation stands alone, and is unique in its accomplishment.

Abundance — Most basic goods should be abundantly available. It has no value to aim at the elimination of a basic product, such as bread, in order to make it perfectively more valuable. That would be perfectively perverse! On the other hand, unique performances in music or art will in principle never become abundant. It is invalid to have expectations in this direction.

Capacities as perfective qualitative properties

Besides the standards mentioned, capacities (functional responses, abilities, powers) constitute a new structural type of perfective qualitative properties.

Perfectionist theory is intensely involved with the appraisal and characterisation of different kinds of capacity. Capacities allow us to survive in the world, to sustain and enhance the quality of life and community. They give expression to what we are and can become. A capacity is a successful response by an organism to a challenge. Existential perfective striving, focused on becoming a certain kind of person, is in large part concerned with the acquisition, development and maintenance of capacities. Capacity is typically exemplified in the skilful and complicated actions of an acrobat, in the cognitive performance of a scientist, and in the virtuous behaviour of a member of a profession.

Many capacities have a universal or general validity. They are appreciated (or ought to be appreciated) in every human culture in one way or another. But other capacities are far less general, due to their particularity, specialisation and complexity. A capacity, or a level of capacity, may even be unique and belong to only one individual (think of Mozart again). However, in relation to particular and complex capacity, there is the general (perfective) expectation that each culture implies (or ought to imply) opportunities for the particularity and complexity of capacities — a culture only involving its members in general and basic capacity does not exist.

There are different divisions according to which varieties of capacity can be defined (forcing me to bother the reader with one more extended list).

General/special capacities — The capacity to see is general. We are expected to be able to see. General capacities come close to or are even part of spontaneous perfection. Lack of visual capacity is considered to be deeply regrettable. The capacity to play chess is, in comparison with vision, much more special in the sense of being far less universal. We do not expect everyone to be able to play chess. It is also not tragic not to know chess (it is perhaps more tragic not to be capable of learning how to play chess, but this is then connected with one's lack of general cognitive skill).

84

Non-combined/combined capacities — In a strict sense each capacity implies the presence of other capacities, but, clearly, there are capacities where this is more intrinsically the case. The general capacity to see is rather a non-combined capacity, while the capacity to draw or to make paintings is much more immediately a combined form of capacity, based on the close togetherness of distinct ingredients — vision, motor skills, aesthetic sense, and so forth.

Basic/complex capacities — Basic capacities do not contain much human challenge; they lack plurivocity, richness and innovation. Most human selves can undertake basic capacities without much learning. Complex capacities, on the other hand, need to be taught and specifically include the field of 'intelligences' as defined in Gardner (1993). The capacity to write novels or to interpret and perform a classical musical piece are highly complex capacities, while the capacity to walk to work is a less complex matter.

Creative/non-creative capacities — The capacity to conceive and produce something new and significant in one's field of concern can be called a creative capacity. If valuable innovation (newness, surprise, originality) is not part of one's competence in any serious way we are confronted with the functioning of capacity on a non-creative level. Obviously, not all capacities and settings invite or permit creative behaviour. In certain basic fields there may be nothing to invent.

Division of capacities according to fundamental human layers — We may characterise and distinguish capacities according to the principal human functional and psychological layers. Nonetheless, they can each be appreciated for its own, dominant exemplification of a distinct aspect of human organisms. Let me provide a schematic list: a) bodily capacities connected with bodily strength, agility, speed; b) emotional capacities connected with affectivity, relation, emotional intelligence, and empathy; c) communicational capacities connected with the expression of messages, rhetorical capacities; d) technical capacities connected with making tools and other products; e) perceptual capacities connected with our auditive and optical functions (music, photography); f) cognitive capacities connected with the intellect, sound reasoning; g) practical capacities connected with knowing-how in concrete, practical contexts, with non-propositional knowledge (reflective practitioners); h) aesthetic capacities displayed in drawing, decorating, designing; i) moral capacities dealing with doing one's duty, respecting rights of others, caring for others; and j) aretaic capacities connected with having certain positive character traits.

Division of capacities in connection with particular objects/roles/projects — We can, finally, mention the breadth and variety of the specified capacities in direct relation to particular objects, roles and projects. Bicycling is defined as a capacity in relation to the object of a bicycle. Nursing is a capacity defined in relation to a specified role. Doing mathematics is defined in relation to a specific project or practice. And so forth. We need perfective articulation in those concrete settings. This is an essential way in which we are used, in daily life, to speak about persons and their abilities.

These distinctions (and it is likely that there are other distinctions) allow us to describe and to perfectively appreciate the varied realm of capacity. The thematic interaction between the different kinds of capacity is significant, because it contributes to a sharper analysis of the world of capacity. It will, for example, be possible to see one personal quality as combined/complex/bodily capacity, or as particular/ creative/emotional capacity.

Positively received properties

All the perfective qualities mentioned before are, in fact, positively received properties, but there is a group of positively received properties that has not yet found a place in our appraisive system. For reasons of conceptual demarcation my suggestion is to use 'positively received properties' explicitly for this new set.

Human and other organisms receive different features in the world as positive properties — notably in highly specific situations that determine one's appreciation of something as perfective quality. Think of the clarity of a text, the brightness of a painting, the sharpness of a knife, the warmth of sunlight, the freshness of water, and so on. When positively received by an organism in a non-trivial sense these features become perfective qualities. Positively received properties include many aesthetic qualities.

Note the difference between capacities of organisms (humans) and positively received properties as here defined. One does not really say of a text that it has the capacity to be clear but rather that it is a clear text, whereas it is appropriate to say of a writer that he possesses the communicational and cognitive capacity to write clear texts.

Note, also, the difference between positively received properties and the more generally valid qualities of composition, completeness, purity, and so forth. For example, sharpness is not always an appreciated quality. One can think of numerous contexts in which the sharpness of an object is received as a negative quality. One would not want to sit in a chair with very sharp sides (as this would cause unfortunate injuries). This brings us to the fact that perfective reception is many instances a matter of evaluation in a specified context according to special perspectives, experiences, and aims.

Extended list of perfective qualities

Why this quite extended list of perfective qualities divided into the different sets of general perfective qualitative standards, capacities, and positively received features?

The principal aim is to develop — in combination with teleological, contributive and other versions of perfection — a language that permits us to develop adequate and differentiated estimation in terms of better and worse. With such a language we should manage, or aim to manage, to estimate everything we find on our way. Leaving out one of the proposed perfective standards may introduce gaps of estimation, since we can only make evaluative discrimination on the basis of evaluative concepts (Aschenbrenner 1971: 19). Estimation in terms of better and worse, it turns out, is itself carried out in better and worse ways. We speak about what we estimate, and we estimate things because we have a functional language at our disposal.

We are, thus, destined to apply perfective standards to the process of selecting perfective standards itself. The perfective standard of richness tells us to include as many different standards as possible, the perfective standard of appropriateness tells us only to include adequate standards, the perfective standard of economy tells us not to include more standards than it is terminologically necessary to do, and so forth.

It is not clear whether, and how many, more perfective qualitative standards could or should be included. It is prudent not to consider the list of perfective standards as definitely closed.

The different perfective standards unavoidably imply certain interconnections. For example, the completeness of a system is likely to confirm or to lead to systemic stability and vice versa; human capacities are likely to serve as the source of actions that will lead to certain positive features in products such as paintings and texts (textual clarity goes back, in most cases, to the human cognitive capability of clear thinking and writing); and so on.

Interconnection, however, does not mean that some of the proposed perfective standards are redundant and should simply be taken as ingredients of another standard. There are, in fact, a sufficient number of situations where a perfective standard will refer to a distinct aspect without (deep) interconnection. As mentioned before, there can be textual clarity of a text (positive feature) that is not caused by human capability (sheer luck, coincidence). Something can be stable without completeness or complete without much stability. Efficiency can be inappropriate (it is not socially and morally appropriate to be an efficient thief).

There are situations where one perfective qualitative standard will cancel out another perfective standard. A zoo containing all animals is perfect in scope, but is bound to score low in composition (loss of an appropriate eco-systemic structure and of normal interaction between animals) (Weiss 1967a: 199). A monochromatically painted canvas will possess unity, but lacks richness of colour (Nozick 1990: 167). In reality as we know it not all perfective standards will flourish equally. Concrete perfective evaluation will have to focus on different perfective standards with varying concern. Each perfective reality must be judged according to suitable perfective ends and standards.

It is good, therefore, to insist on a distinction between relevant and irrelevant applications of perfective standards. This distinction applies the perfective standard of relevance or appropriateness to the practice of appraisal itself. For example, the perfection aimed at in art has traditionally been associated with the expression of order, purity and harmony, but today we live with other artistic goals. Hence, it is important not to judge new schools of art according to an earlier model of perfection. The perfective dimension of visual compositional harmony has nowadays lost its cardinal position in art. The question of relevance and irrelevance also arises in the concrete ways in which we approach an object in terms of perfective estimation. Often, we estimate something according to a specific angle. In job interviews applicants are reviewed with respect to a selected set of properties and competences. Perhaps, only philosophy and certain other theoretical disciplines are focused on more complete reviews and forms of appraisal. In practical life, where most of the appraisive work is done, we especially act and evaluate in line with very specific angles and concerns.

Qualitative perfection in relation to teleological and contributive perfection

Teleological and qualitative perfective estimation are interconnected. Qualitative perfection aims at the synchronic description of what is here and now perfectively available in a particular creature, object, reality, product, or system. Teleological perfection focuses on developmental processes. In this way each addresses perfection from a different angle: from the side of qualitative perfection we say that someone possesses a certain quality up to a certain level; from the side of teleological perfection we will say that someone has reached a certain stage on the way toward fulfilment. But these qualitative and teleological interpretations and appreciations logically come together. Proper estimation in terms of qualitative and teleological perfection is destined to arrive at an identical conclusion about one and the same object. A watch fulfilling the end for which it is built, which is to show the right time, must have the quality of harmonious togetherness of its mechanical parts (composition), since only a watch without compositional conflict can properly fulfil its end. From the perspective of teleological perfection one should insist that a watch fulfil its end properly. Hence, its composition cannot be wrong in any structural manner. From the perspective of qualitative perfection one insists that a watch has proper composition. Hence, it will then also not be the case that it fails to fulfil its function.

The perspective of teleological perfection often directly refers to the dimension of quality, that is, to the development of qualities and to the fulfilment of ends characterised by quality. Furthermore, teleological striving is only possible when certain qualities are present. Qualitative perfection in turn implicitly includes reference to lower, average and higher stages of a certain qualitative state. To say that something has only average stability, for example, means that one is aware of a higher level of stability — a higher level that invites the idea of further teleological striving. Moreover, standards of capacity are connected with teleology directly. A capacity means being able to do something, and doing is a teleological process.

There are — as one could expect — also strong relations between contributive and qualitative perfection. Entities contribute to others exactly because of their qualities (someone with weak capacity will simply be able to contribute less in most circumstances). An army with a larger scope will be able to contribute more to the defence of a country. And many qualities are, at least in part, considered qualities exactly because of their contributive consequences. Think of a physician with completeness in competence and skill. Obviously we like this quality in doctors because it will drastically improve our chance to get the right medicine prescribed (contributive effect).

We may conclude that qualitative perfection directs estimation in terms of better and worse in a way that is thematically complementary to teleological and contributive perfection. In concrete perfective judgement the different senses of perfection are destined to play a role.

The groundwork of perfectionist drama

In this chapter I have provided a basic list of perfective concepts and distinctions. Some will continue to doubt whether we need such a prolonged list. The risk of scholastic exaggeration is certainly there; however, we must also avoid a univocal reading of perfection. In my view we cannot avoid these concepts and distinctions. They conceptually address significant evaluations in terms of better and worse.

The basic perfective list aims to tune in with *recognisable* aspects of human and earthly reality, that is, to make contact with the groundwork of perfectionist drama. Neglect of essential distinctions would cause us to miss out on significant aspects of perfective being. If we bother to look around we will observe that indeed, we are makers of tools and objects (productional perfection), that we are connected to contributive factors and are ourselves contributive factors in the perfection of others, that we are embedded in roles and practical settings in which we are striving toward things, that we try — or at least have the possibility — to make something of our life as a whole in terms of perfective accomplishment (existential teleological perfection), that we estimate aspects of being in terms of qualitative standards, and so on. Only by means of a differentiated scheme can one articulate the concrete interaction of varieties of perfection.

In an ideal setting everything is supposed to run smoothly, in line with the more important perfective ends. In actual settings things are destined to run much less fluently. But perfective conflicts, too, only find appropriate expression in a rich and broad language of perfection. We need a varied list precisely to be able to discern the tensions between perfective kinds.

CHAPTER SEVEN —
THE LANGUAGE OF PERFECTION — iv:
ARETAIC PERFECTION

> *Die Tugend ist nicht ohne Kampf; sie*
> *ist vielmehr der höchste, vollendete*
> *Kampf.*
>
> — Hegel

Virtue or aretaic perfection without a doubt constitutes the most popular issue within contemporary perfectionist thought. As human functional responses to demands and challenges in the world and in one's personal being, the virtues belong to the already established field of perfective quality. Virtues, as I have mentioned in chapter 6, are perfective capacities. This chapter aims, thus, to extend one distinct element of the perfective scheme of capacity. I will offer insight into different aspects of an aretaic personology for fallible selves.

Let us begin by addressing the psychological issue of traits in general. Exactly this issue will, after a while, bring us to the psychological position of the virtues — virtues constitute an important subfield of traits.

Traits

Psychologists and ordinary people alike refer to the personality or character of someone. According to Allport (1961: 32), character is evaluated on the basis of personality while personality refers to description without evaluation. I assume he wishes to express the difference between moral and non-moral traits. We find a similar distinction in Brandt (1970: 23), who speaks about character traits (courage, truthfulness, generosity), which have moral implications, and traits of personality (talkativeness, warmth, calmness), which do not have (serious) moral implications.

My suggestion is, however, not to follow the logic of this division.

Character and personality can in principle be taken to refer to the same issue, namely that of stable and extended psychological dispositions of an individual self. These dispositions can be called traits. Let us define character or personality as 'a relatively stable configuration of deeply entrenched and widely ramified traits and dispositions of perception, cognition, emotion, motivation, and behaviour' (Rorty 1992: 40). Traits have to do with dispositional continuity in the way we act, desire, strive, think, feel, respond, and communicate. Parts of a character or the personality of adult persons may change over the years, but this change is normally not so rapid and extensive. A sudden and drastic transformation would rather lead us to say that someone is hardly the same person (Kupperman 1991: 16). We expect a level of sameness in people and furthermore expect narrative coherence within personal history.

Many traits automatically suggest a negative or positive moral estimation, while others are morally neutral. However, there is also a negative and positive reception of traits beyond moral being. It is, in fact, hard to find 'characterisms' (Aschenbrenner 1971) that do not embody negative or positive appreciation. Trait interpretations basically arise in the context of reviewing and estimating others. The language of traits, especially the language of aretaic traits, flourishes in our concerned reception of persons. A loss of the language of traits would automatically result in a loss of personal, practical, moral, and social orientation. An appraisal of the qualities of character or personality must be seen against the general background of a world in which we must choose between people (Pincoffs 1986: 165). Trait interpretation also permits us to make predictions about behaviour.

One difference between moral and non-moral traits is that moral traits are, or ought to be, considered good (it is immoral not to positively appreciate moral properties), while many non-moral ones are negatively or positively received only with an eye on particular activities and settings. Talkativeness is a good trait to have in social functions, but constitutes an obstacle in activities where silence emerges as a higher value — think of religious meditative practice. Some will argue that it is also not good to possess the moral trait of compassion in business settings, but a non-trivial perfectionism does of course not allow for this option — it can never be good to be involved in activities in which the lack of compassion is *systematically* considered as a good.

Not every relatively permanent feature of a human person is a trait.

Habits, for example, are narrow and limited determining tendencies in a person (Allport 1961: 345). One important aspect of a trait is that it often takes a while before it can be established that a person authentically possesses such a trait. But habits are typically determinate. Think of the habit of brushing one's teeth each night and morning. A person may develop such that these confined habits after some time find their way into a larger system of habits concerned with personal hygiene. There may come a moment where through interaction between similar habits one acquires the trait of personal cleanliness. Habits are much less general than traits and more easily definable, whereas traits are expressed in differentiated ways. Allport offers politeness as an illustration:

> Politeness is more than a mere congeries of habits. A truly polite person will vary his behavior even to the extent of breaking his polite habits to maintain his trait of

politeness. Ordinarily at dinner table it is not polite to drink out of one's finger bowl; but the story is told of the Washington hostess who did so in order to reassure her Oriental guest, who had already drunk from his. She violated her habit but maintained her trait (*ibid.*: 346).

Attitudes, too, are different from traits (*ibid.*: 347). They refer to a very specific object. One is for or against something. Being kind to one's dog constitutes a positive attitude. If this attitude would come to be embedded in a larger sympathetic concern for animals and humans then we come closer to a trait — namely the trait of kindliness.

Another problem is that certain ascriptions are sometimes assumed to function as traits in one way or another, while they are not traits in a proper sense. We may, for example, say that someone is in love, angry, absorbed, tired, admirable, acceptable, or has a fox-like appearance. But these kinds of ascription cannot qualify as authenticated psychological traits (Allport 1955: 309). Let us specify why this is so.

Some ascriptions refer to temporal states that lack the typical stability and continuity of traits — we are not constantly in love, angry, or absorbed. In normal circumstances these emotive, organic and practical states appear in particular moments only. Second, other ascriptions refer to temporal organic properties. One will become tired after a day of hard work or one may even feel chronically exhausted in the case of bodily illness. But this is not itself a psychological disposition. Third, to say that someone is admirable or acceptable is to express social judgement without mentioning intrinsic traits. Admirability and acceptability are not in themselves psychological dispositions (the personal drive to be found admirable and acceptable may, of course, constitute a trait), Finally, to state that someone looks like a fox is to express one's perception of visual structure, which is not a psychological trait. Traits and virtues are not there like material objects: 'Character belongs to a person, but not like his nose, his car, or even his height [...] character endures over time, but it is not a thing' (Sabini & Silver 1982: 156).

Non-trait states and properties can, of course, be connected with the presence of certain traits, and this in different ways.

Appropriate forms of being in love and being angry could be taken as signs that certain virtues are present. Chronic tiredness may constitute a source for, or an obstacle to, certain traits and virtues. While it is not possible to admire someone for his or her admirability, a person can be rightfully admired for the traits he or she possesses. A relation between traits and visual appearance also seems to exist in different ways (see Zebrowitz 1998). Traits and appearance may have a common genetic source or may arise from living in a certain environment. People with a violent temperament will tense certain facial muscles and thereby influence their visual appearance. Those with an unappealing face may receive more negative response and thereby develop negative personalities.

In many aspects, however, it will remain imprudent, and unfair, to expect a direct relation between the presence of traits and visual characteristics. To directly connect someone's facial structure with the presence of traits is to ignore traits and virtues having histories — they can develop and be transformed, even while our visual characteristics remain as they are. To have a trait and to be self-conscious about it is already to be confronted with the possibilities of modifying, abolishing or developing that trait (MacIntyre 1972: 232). It is therefore best to qualify the physiognomic dimension of the theory of traits. Perhaps certain persons will at the age of fifty indeed have acquired the face they in fact deserve (George Orwell, quoted in Zebrowitz 1997: 53), but many others will rather have acquired a face they did not really deserve. The Dorian Gray effect is a principle with only limited validity.

Traits can be common or personal (Allport 1961).

Common traits are those aspects of personality according to which most people in a culture can be fruitfully compared:

> A common trait is a category for classifying functionally equivalent forms of behavior in a general population of people. Though influenced by nominal and artifactual considerations, a common trait to some extent reflects veridical and comparable dispositions in many personalities who, because of a common human nature and common culture, develop similar modes of adjusting to their environments, though to varying degrees (*ibid.*: 349).

Single trait words embody common standards.

Very occasionally a person is so typical of his culture that common traits seem fully adequate, but in most cases concrete description of a person will involve reference to personal traits. Common traits are categories into which an individual is somehow forced, while personal traits offer more authentic expression to one's personal being. Personal traits, like common traits, refer to broad determining tendencies, but it makes no sense to speak of a normal distribution of personal traits among a population. Each personal trait is more or less unique to one person. Several words are therefore needed to express this uniqueness. One will, for example, speak of a 'peculiar anxious helpfulness' (*ibid.*: 359). Personal traits give expression to the fact that, ultimately, character is unique:

> It is the thisness of the self, known in the singular, idiosyncratic savour of its deeds [...] My deeds are exactly the same as yours, but they are never exactly the same as yours, for your deeds are yours, and mine are mine. Such uniqueness has everything to do with character as my own — never a general character, always a this (Desmond 2001: 257).

Principal aspects of aretaic being

Let us now turn to the virtues as such. I will discern several principal aspects of aretaic being. Traits function as real virtues if the following conditions and specifications are satisfied.

Aretaic continuity

In line with traits in general it can be underlined that the virtues have adequate psychological continuity. They are dispositional. A reasonable degree of stability over time is an essential condition. There can be no pointillistic sense of virtue (although, one must perhaps admit certain virtues which may only rarely become active — think of physical courage in dangerous situations; this is not something that will arise on a regular basis in civil life). Hurka (2001: 42) is quite wrong in insisting upon a strongly atomistic definition of virtue in terms of occasional desire, action and feeling. The perfective standard of continuity seems an essential part of the logic of virtue. A sporadic right act does not make a virtue. Persistence is a necessary sign of aretaic being (Dewey 1978: 363). As Zagzebski puts it, virtues are in 'the category of the more enduring of a person's qualities, and they come closer to defining who a person is than any other category of qualities' (1996: 135). Of course, strength and continuity of character in itself does not embody goodness. Wicked persons may have very stable characters. Vices are often stubborn and also belong to the category of the more enduring of a person's qualities. Dispositional continuity is then a necessary but not a sufficient condition for aretaic perfection.

Good traits to have

Virtues are by definition good traits to have. Human beings do not get on well without them (Foot 1978: 2). Virtues contain an essential positive normative component (Heil 1985: 29). One author writes: 'The possession of the virtues, and the absence of the vices, creates a social atmosphere in which everyone can thrive and flourish' (Bond 1996: 159). One may, in line with this, conclude that society itself is a work of virtue. Elsewhere, we read that

> in order for a trait to be a virtue, it must tend to foster good human life in extensive and fundamental ways. It must be the perfection of a tendency or capacity that connects and interlocks with a variety of human goods in such a way that its removal from our lives would endanger the whole structure (Wallace 1978: 153).

It may be too dramatic to suggest that the loss of the virtues of politeness or friendliness would endanger the whole structure (however, the general disappearance of politeness and friendliness would perhaps not annihilate togetherness, but it would certainly introduce a serious and highly regrettable deterioration in the quality of human relation), but, whatever our more particular opinions about life, it is clear that human togetherness, notably our working together in a variety of consensual and worthy projects such as building houses or running hospitals, needs the cardinal virtues in one form or another:

> We need prudence or practical wisdom for any large-scale planning. We need justice to secure cooperation and mutual trust among men, without which our lives would be nasty, brutish, and short. We need temperance in order not to be deflected from our long-term and large-scale goals by seeking short-term satisfactions. And we need courage to persevere in face of setbacks, weariness, difficulties, and dangers (Geach 1979: 16).

Right responses

Virtues are good to have because they embody right responses to demands in the world and/or in oneself, demands which have to be met (Swanton 2003). The important virtues are connected with human grounding experiences, and have to do with appropriate functioning in each of these principal human spheres (Nussbaum 1988). Virtues are about what is difficult for humans, about temptations to be resisted and deficiencies to be made good. Virtues are involved with corrective work (Foot 1978: 8). Temperance is a corrective response to bodily pleasures, and to items in the world that produce such pleasures. Justice is a corrective response to our inclinations toward self-concern and partiality and to the needs and rights of others. Without relevant response to these unavoidable demands human life will not remain as it is and as we would like it to continue. Aretaic responses include action, abstinence, promotion, appreciation, honouring, receptiveness, love, respect, creation, and so forth (Swanton 2003). Depending on the demands that have to be addressed, differentiation of response will arise. One promotes justice and appreciates a painting; one loves one's children and is properly receptive to the needs of distant others; one respects proper authority.

Depending on the responses and demands at hand, one person getting involved in a street fight to save another person will show courage while another may not need to activate courage at all. A professional boxer is likely not to be confronted with fear (he knows he will impress and win easily) and, therefore, does not need the corrective work of courage. Most others almost certainly will need courage. The necessity of virtue depends on who and what we are in particular. A claustrophobic person needs courage to do certain things while for others it is not a sign of courage to step into a small lift (Foot 1978: 12). The life of virtue in person x is not the life of virtue in person y. The necessity of virtue also depends on what human beings in general are — for example, beings who do not want to be hurt or endangered. Hence, it is the case that 'people who could never regard their safety as a good, who could not see injury to themselves as something to be avoided, would have no use for the principles of courage and could not be brave' (Hunt 1997:28).

A tendency to a proper degree

A virtue is, thus, a tendency to a proper degree — not too much or too little, applied at the right moment in the right situation, and toward the right target. If a virtue could lead to an excess of virtue (it is sometimes argued that generosity is such a virtue), then a virtue could be at fault. This is paradoxical, since it would mean that a virtue may be a bad trait to have. Hence, it is important to include the standard of appropriate activation as an essential ingredient of virtue. As functional responses to demands in oneself and in the world, virtues constitute a distinct field of capacities. Virtues are enabling and effective traits. Aretaic being is a continued existential accomplishment aimed at functioning well as a perfective human person in the world as we know it to be.

Certain traits are particularly difficult to turn into, or to keep as, dependable virtues since they lend themselves all too readily to spontaneous excess. This appears to be the case with loyalty, which is traditionally taken to be a virtue (Ewin 1992). We spontaneously grow into loyalty. Furthermore, loyalty seems exactly characterised by setting aside good judgement. One unconditionally sticks with a group or an organisation, or with one's country. If loyalty is a virtue it certainly constitutes one of the more risky traits of character.

Depth and complexity of the virtues

Adult or real virtue always involves different principal layers of existential being. Persons are complex interior entities. A virtue is not a simple property, like a minor skill lying at the periphery of one's personality.

Aretaic being is bound to inhere in the specific ways we act, feel, desire, interpret, think, and so forth. These ways — in combination with the range of situations and aspects of being toward which a virtue is specifically directed — define the psychological content of aretaic perfection. Virtue is a combined and rich capacity. We should note the perfective quality of intra-aretaic composition, this is, relevant interaction, structuration of, and interaction between layers and ingredients of personality (this standard, like other standards, will never receive complete fulfilment, but in real virtue we must significantly approach a state of completeness). It is possible that a person will possess a good trait in certain dimensions but not, or not sufficiently, in other dimensions of selfhood. A good trait is then not yet good enough. Real virtue must be properly organised in one's person and authentically express 'fine inner states' (Swanton 2003: 26). A virtue organised only as a superficial technique — for example, in a social worker simply using friendliness as a method (MacIntyre 1975: 106) — fails to express such states. A virtue is based on interest that is entire and wholehearted (Dewey 1978: 363). Otherwise, we are confronted with traits below the level of virtue. The following treatment of virtue (courage) must therefore be resisted:

> When we hold that a man is courageous we do not attribute any particular motive to him; his courage may be due to ambition, to emulation, or even to a fear of certain forms of opprobrium, yet his action may be justly called courageous (Maurice Mandelbaum, quoted in Brandt 1970: 32).

Besides intra-aretaic composition, there is also inter-aretaic interaction. Without such interaction it is difficult, if not impossible, to keep any virtue in good order. A virtue can only be properly present if certain connections with other virtues are available. The virtues hunt in packs (Rorty 1988). Without the workings of the virtue of autonomy, for example, the virtue of social consciousness is bound to deteriorate and turn into passive conformity (Helwig 1957). In turn, the virtue of autonomy without a complementary sense of social and communal orientation will soon come to lean towards individualism.
As Yves Simon points out:

> Thus in order to be temperate, a man can certainly use the modality supplied by justice, as well as the modality supplied by fortitude. A man wants, and needs, to be temperate with justice and courage, and vice versa. Can one be truly courageous without moderation? How do we tell the difference between courage and recklessness? Being without fear does not of itself define courage. But not being reckless clearly involves a modality procured by temperance. Any virtue may degenerate, so to speak, if it becomes intemperate (1986: 128).

Aretaic interconnection does not confirm a strong thesis about the unity and totality of the virtues. There are literally hundreds of aretaic ascriptive terms — each of these terms is directed towards a specific demand and target. It would be totally absurd to expect someone to adequately respond to all these demands and targets. No one is able to aretaically satisfy the perfective standard of inter-aretaic completeness, since there is no closed system of the virtues (Bollnow 1958: 26). Furthermore, the interdependence of the virtues does not require all virtues to be present to the same degree. A person possessing the virtue of justice may possess the virtue of temperance in a much weaker form, but in a sufficient state still for the virtue of justice to continue most of its work (Simon 1986: 129). Nonetheless, a reasonably virtuous person will have to satisfy aretaic interconnection to a significant degree.

98

Natural and adult virtue

Natural virtues are not yet real or adult virtues (Ramsay 1998). They are the results of natural inheritance (and basic social embeddedness) rather than of a deliberate development (acquired perfection). In natural virtue we miss deliberate cultivation for some purpose and intelligent practice (habituation). Aretaic perfection is a disposition resulting from explicit development. In its adult form a virtue is more than a spontaneous capacity. Of course, some of the more simple virtues, such as temperance and friendliness, may succeed for a longer time in spontaneous, unreflective form. They will in this regard tend to remain successful. But the more complex virtues, such as justice and integrity, are bound to demand reflective development much more quickly, certainly in our shifting and complicated times. Adult virtue is a disposition with a certain (implicit) cognitive, axiological and practical history — it is a disposition inhering in all the relevant quarters of selfhood, not just in the conative or affective realm. This is not a plea for an intellectualised sense of virtue, but it is a plea against blind virtue. Ultimately, even the more spontaneous virtues, such as generosity and friendliness, need to be applied with interpretative finesse and with a cognitive concern for larger context. They, too, involve the agent's exercise of judgement. A real virtue is an intelligent disposition (Williams 1993: 36). For example, the virtue of parental love does include affectionate spontaneous response, but also less spontaneous deliberate action (Swanton 2003: 131). It is not so difficult to be a loving parent, but it is much more complex to be a good loving parent.

The presence of real virtue is such that it is highly unlikely (and psychologically unrealistic) that one will not (or would not come to) identify with the point and purpose of a virtue, that is, with the good of a virtue itself (the goodness of a perfective capacitational accomplishment) and with the goods that a virtue aims to protect, respect, produce or enhance. Virtue thus becomes in part an intrinsic good in the mind of the aretaic self. This identification will in some selves be explicit and conscious; in others it will remain very implicit and dormant. However, in actual discussion persons without earlier conscious aretaic identification should come to reach an approval of and identification with the dignity of a certain virtue. Note, however, that not everyone who consciously confirms aretaic dignity possesses real virtue — think of the akratic self. But the point remains that real virtues do require implicit or explicit identification. Traits can have goodness without such identification, but then they are not yet aretaic traits in the full sense of the word.

Beyond radical consequentialism

It is important to stress that a purely consequentialist definition of virtue runs contrary to the psychological depth of aretaic being. In defence of a pure consequentialism of the virtues, Julia Driver (1996: 120) offers the following story about 'extra-terrestrial mutors'. Mutors have adapted to their harsh environment by toughening their offspring. Beating a child in a certain period will lead to a rise of life expectancy. Hence, there is a need to develop intense pleasure in bringing up a child like this. They therefore develop a special trait — the disposition to beat children who are at a certain age. Doing good for the children as such is not part of their intention, but what they are doing can be described as good, even though they are not doing it because it is good. It is a virtue because others would value it and because it produces significant social benefit. It may be true that human beings — unlike mutors — do need good intentions and proper identification, due to their particular psychological make-up. But, so Driver insists, in principle this is not necessary for virtue in relation to *other* types of creature. A virtue is a character trait which — generally speaking — produces good consequences for others (*ibid.*: 122). This is what centrally matters.

Driver's consequentialist reception of virtue does not convince. Mutors are indeed not human persons, and we only care and know about the virtues in relation to humans. The rest is fiction. It is difficult, impossible even, to accept as a virtue the confined acts undertaken by those mutors. It is rather an instrumental ritual, to be activated within a particular and limited period. Moreover, the human person's reliability with regard to actions and consequences is strongly connected with deeper aretaic identification and habituation. Virtue is a success term (Zagzebski 1998: 136), and only selves with aretaic content are regularly successful. Reliability is connected with regularity and effectivity. Virtuous selves are the more reliable producers of virtuous actions, more reliable than consequentialist selves without psychological and aretaic thickness and fullness. Effectiveness undeniably implies that consequences are important, but the point is that consequences are better served by persons in good aretaic shape (if one's courage or justice fails to deliver the proper consequences most of the time, it is best to wonder whether courage or justice is actually present).

The fact that aretaic identification is consequentially better has led some utilitarians to combine an explanatory focus on consequences with a pragmatic focus on aretaic being. Crisp (1992) proposes a utilitarianism of the virtues. This results in a concrete defence of aretaic selfhood beyond direct attention for consequences. Real virtues are in fact the most likely means to maximise utility. Kilcullen (1983), too, points out that virtues offer better consequentialist guarantees. This is something that utilitarianism is bound to appreciate. One problem, however, that seems to haunt a utilitarianism of the virtues is the schizophrenic distinction between theoretical utilitarian justification and psychological aretaic motive. One aims to create non-utilitarian aretaic selves because this gives the best results according to the theoretic standard of utilitarian maximalism.

Two further important differences between utilitarianism and aretaic perfectionism concern the rejection of extreme maximisation and the presence of a plurality of values. Utilitarian maximisation is an example of fanatic perfection and seems not to pass the principle of minimal psychological realism (Flanagan 1991). Moreover, the full range of our responses to what we value (see Anderson 1993) — responses of desire, love, admiration, respect, etc. — testifies to the many different values, perfections, scales, and states which we appreciate. Real axiological experience contradicts a monotonous utilitarian definition of value. Concrete value characterisation (Aschenbrenner 1983), so we may conclude, cannot be reduced to utilitarian estimation.

Virtue's ambition and scope

An ambitious theory of virtue will consider several fundamental contexts as necessary references for authentic aretaic being. It directly invests in the perfective standard of scope. This implies, for example, that justice is only considered a moral virtue when it includes a fair reception of the rights and needs of persons beyond one's own circle or community. A more ambitious theory of virtue will extend aretaic concern in justice to the realm of humanity as such, while a more minimal theory of virtue will only look at being and behaviour in particular roles and domains. A strongly individualised perspective on virtue — trait egoism (Frankena 1973: 64) — will focus only on traits that benefit the quality of one's own existence. The goal of the egoistic stance is only a person's own reality (Nozick 1990: 152).

Which theory to choose?

It is obvious that we are deeply involved in networks of partiality (Cottingham 1996: 59). Without partiality and particularity we would be nobody and be quite unable to obtain serious aretaic content. On the other hand, partiality and particularity do imply certain risks of disproportionate confinement. It is therefore of vital importance, in line with MacIntyre (1981), to insist that aretaic ambition of a more robust kind is to be considered an essential aspect of real virtue. Everything below a certain level of ambition or scope does, then, not constitute a virtue. MacIntyre aptly defines virtues as qualities necessary to achieve goods internal to practices, qualities contributing to the good of a whole life (life stories), and qualities needed to sustain communities and social traditions (MacIntyre 1984: 273). However, one should slightly temper the ambition of his threefold definition of virtue. For him a trait is a virtue *only* if it positively functions in each of the three established levels of human concern, but it is seems more realistic to consider a trait as a virtue if it functions positively on at least one level and does not constitute an obstacle for proper functioning on the two other levels. This leads to a more relaxed and livable sense of virtue, without giving up aretaic ambition and scope. In such a still ambitious perspective, courage is not operating as a virtue when someone (a murderer) turns his courage to bad communal ends (Foot 1978: 16). And perseverance is not a virtue in a good piano player who in his practicing regularly disturbs people in their sleep at night (Simon 1986: 21). In these situations courage and perseverance unambiguously fail on the level of local or general community. They constitute traits below the level of virtue or even vices. It should be noted, though, that an authentic virtue may in fact be dysfunctional in the context of certain communities (MacIntyre 1988b), namely in those communities which themselves contradict the life of virtue (virtuous selves should contradict the goods of a dictatorial regime).

One problem concerning the issue of aretaic ambition lies in the field of occupational praxiology. Take, for example, the trait of toughness as it functions in political occupations (Galston 1991). The need for toughness arises from certain unpleasant but unavoidable facts about politics — the attainment of the worthiest ends at times demands the use of distasteful means (*ibid.*: 175). Toughness will, for example, bring political leaders to selectively use the element of fear with regard to those who cannot be rationally persuaded, and this with the aim of accomplishing authentically valuable and necessary aims. In doing this they will seriously recognise the moral costs involved. According to Galston, toughness only functions as a virtue when used with reluctance. One must always preserve a lively sense of the disagreeableness of what one is required to do. Aretaic toughness 'allows the agent to contemplate the performance of intrinsically distasteful and objectionable acts, but only at the right time and in the right manner' (*ibid.*: 182). Political toughness, as defined in Galston, clearly differs from the situation in which someone plays the piano at night, causing negative consequences for others. It is in fact not necessary or unavoidable to play the piano at night, certainly not in a regular fashion, while political toughness is presented by Galston as unavoidable. Toughness is essential to be able to function well in the occupational practice of politics (the issue of role perfection), even while involving negative consequences for others. Could we, therefore, conclude, as Galston does, that toughness is a virtue?

On the one hand, Galston's sense of toughness does not seem to contradict an ambitious definition of virtue. While having a productive function within political occupation (practice), political toughness does not automatically have to disturb the workings of a life story and social life at large. Toughness will not be abundantly applied, except in cases where it is really necessary to fulfil good political ends. It is not a matter of seeking a tough stance in most other contexts, because that would imply lack of proportion and appropriateness.

On the other hand, there are certain complications concerning toughness as virtue in an occupational setting. It could be argued that virtues normally possess internal beauty, while toughness (as defined in Galston) is a trait with a direct negative and ugly content. And the fact that one ought to be aware of the disagreeableness of what one is about to do seems to constitute another non-aretaic aspect of toughness. Virtues involve identification with the goodness of what one is about to do. Disagreeableness will, of course, also arise within certain other virtues but not so intensely. If toughness is a virtue, it rather seems a cryptic virtue — a virtue that does not elicit enthusiasm. Another issue is that one may get psychologically used to doing things in such a tough manner (it is quite an effective trait, something well-known to circles of organised crime). There may be a hidden attraction in toughness, which, after a while, is bound to bring one to use toughness all too regularly, far beyond a proper context. In becoming a trait that is exercised with a certain enthusiasm it loses its fragile status as virtue, if it is one, and turns into a vice.

The many complications that inhere in toughness teach us a central lesson, namely that identification with an occupational role might be ethically danger-ous (Lebacqz 1985: 35). The paradox is that socially useful roles may require the development of traits below virtue, of cryptic virtues that easily turn into vices, perhaps even of vices. Good professionals will then become less good or even bad persons precisely by being psychologically well adjusted to their occupational tasks (Applbaum 1999: 66). The idea that toughness is a virtue in politics is not without reason (it is not irrational to claim that if politics is some-thing we need, and if toughness is needed in politics, then we ought to some-how celebrate it as a virtue — at least when it can be organised in such a way that our life stories and our larger community will not be negatively affected), but the problems that we have noted bring to light that it is also an idea full of paradoxes and difficulties. Since demands within particular practices — includ-ing the occupations— could always involve us in traits that are dangerous, con-tinuous aretaic vigilance will remain necessary.

A further issue concerning aretaic ambition lies on the level of life stories. What about a courageous act that results in sacrificing one's life? This, obvi-ously, endangers the continuation of one's existence and therefore appears to fail on the basic aretaic level of life stories. Nonetheless, in such a case we are not really inclined to see courage as non-virtue or vice. On the contrary, we would speak of heroic or sublime virtue. A (theoretical) solution could be found, perhaps, in considering sacrifice as a tragic but consequent existential under-taking for particular individuals in particular contexts. The meaning and value of our life stories is deeply entangled with the lives of others, notably the lives of those who are close to us — family, friends, colleagues, fellow citizens. Attempting to protect one's family through courageous action is then not an act against the deeper logic of one's personal life story. On the contrary, such an act may deeply express one's concrete identity. Obviously, we should not portray those rather desperate experiences as glorious instances of perfective joy and fulfilment. The point is, simply, that in our imperfect world a trait such as courage can be a virtue even when in certain situations it is not beneficial to the possessor (Swanton 2003: 20). Nonetheless, the existential value of virtues must here be seen to remain in place. As Geach states:

> Men need virtues as bees need stings. An individual bee may perish by stinging, all the same bees need stings; an individual man may perish by being brave or just, all the same men need courage and justice (1979: 17).

One further point concerning aretaic ambition, which it is interesting to introduce (beyond MacIntyre's scheme in *After Virtue*), is the question of ecological virtue. Indeed, why stop at the level of human community? With respect to an ecological dimension of virtues it may now be valid, in today's context of ecological catastrophe, to include concern for nature as a cardinal aretaic target besides practices, life stories, and human community. Most current definitions of virtue still fail to consider this step. Fortunately, the current rise of environmental virtue ethics is likely to change things drastically. One now hears about the 'land virtues' (Shaw 1997), and about the virtues of 'environmental stewards' (Welchman 1999). The ecologisation of aretaic being would imply that a trait ceases to be a genuine virtue if it, for no adequate reason, disturbs or destroys the good workings of nature (ecosystems) and of natural entities. Louke van Wensveen (2001) makes a very good point when she writes that authentic virtue must at least imply the wish to sustain the conditions for the prolongation of virtue. It is clear that ecosystemic being is an essential condition for the survival of humans and, consequently, for the human virtues. Cleanliness is not a virtue, therefore, if it involves using certain household chemicals destined to undermine ecosystem sustainability on a collective scale. The introduction of ecological being as a fourth layer of authentic virtue is perhaps not without tension. Due to unavoidable conflicts between nature and humanity, it will not be easy to arrive at a unified conception of environmental virtue. A trait with strong ecological direction would cease to be a virtue if it embodies inadequate consequences for human practice, existence and community, but it is not always clear what is adequate and what is not. For example, should we not come to withdraw from certain quarters of the earth and let these quarters be for the benefit of nature itself? Much may depend on how many of our so-called rights of expansion we are prepared to give up. Most of us will fail to consider this issue in an open way, accustomed as we are to focus on the pleasures and advantages for humanity without taking non-human others into serious consideration.

Virtue and freedom

Let us turn to the following problem in aretaics, namely the connection between virtue and freedom.

As cultivated dispositions, virtues sometimes appear to turn into automatic responses beyond our responsibility. According to Pincoffs we should not

confine virtues to qualities for which a person is responsible: 'We can and do pre-
fer and avoid people on account of qualities they have when we have not the
least idea whether they may justly be held responsible for these qualities' (1986:
88). However, this may be true for naturally good inclinations, but not for adult
virtue. The reference to freedom is essential in real virtue:

> My past choices have built up a disposition to be honest, but my present decision
> is not just a reflex determined by that disposition — it is my endorsement of that
> disposition. The disposition is not a causal force, making me choose; it is the way
> I have made myself the way I have chosen to be, and in deciding in accordance
> with it, I endorse the way I have become (Annas 1993: 51).

On the other hand, we are not free to become generous and virtuous now (*ibid.*:
56). Aretaic being requires longer habituation. One must work to become
virtuous. This takes more than the sudden free decision to become generous.
One cannot simply choose to have a certain state of character; all one can do
is try to develop that state of character (Bond 1996: 140). Furthermore, due
to one's psychological history, or perhaps due to the presence of unconscious
drives, one may work very hard to become virtuous but never really succeed.
Certain personal conditions must be right — there is something like 'aretaic luck'
beyond our control. We may therefore, to some extent, appreciate the following
insight:

> Tugenden werden nicht fabriziert, Tugenden kann man nicht besitzen, Tugenden
> 'hat' man nicht [...], sondern im Gegenteil, Tugenden haben uns. Wer daher eine
> Tugend bei sich selbst entdeckt und dies nicht als Überraschung erfährt, der hat
> keine Tugend bei sich selbst entdeckt (Mieth 1984: 31).

Many aretaic perfective states may, indeed, come unnoticed (Bollnow 1958: 24).

In line with the earlier distinction between common and personal traits, it is
again fruitful to add that concrete selves always possess the virtues in a particularised manner. My courage is not identical to yours. There is no uniform
sense of virtue. Moreover, behind each aretaic self stands a different psychological, moral and perfective history. Each of us is involved in inimitable development. With each person we sense a different history of interaction: in person x
friendliness may have contributed to a later development of tolerance; in person y courage may have helped to attain justice. Qualities, skills, capacities,
virtues, fallibilities and vices interact in unique ways, depending on the situations
we have gone through and on the challenges we have faced.

Virtue and skill

Virtue, like skill, is a perfective capacity. Virtue equally constitutes a functional
response to aspects of being in oneself and/or in the world. However, for the
rest virtue is different from skill and other non-aretaic capacities. In this sense

there can never be aretaic and moral whiz-kids like there are, for example, mathematical whiz-kids.

Virtues are psychological traits, whereas skills are non-trait capacities. Like habit and attitude a personal skill possesses continuity. It endures in a person as the learned ability to bring about predetermined results with maximum certainty, often with the minimum outlay of time or energy or both. But whereas virtues are characterised by a pervasive personal presence and large existential relevance, skills are attributed to a person in special activities and without the necessity of existential and moral identification. The skill of making pots, for example, is not applicable to playing the piano, but a virtue, such as justice, is not confined in this way (von Wright 1963: 139). Confined justice is in fact not justice at all. Virtue has a broad range of application and is therefore more important in the formation of personality (Zagzebski 1998: 115).

Furthermore, if someone deliberately makes a spelling mistake this does not count against his or her skill as a speller (Foot 1978: 8). If a skilled dancer performs poorly because he or she is explicitly not trying, we do not say he or she is not a skilled dancer (Wallace 1978: 51). Indeed, greater expertise makes one a better candidate for acting contrary to one's skills: 'a grammarian is excellently qualified to make grammatical mistakes if he or she pleases, and a highly skilled chemical engineer is the logical candidate for sabotaging a chemical factory' (Simon 1991: 10). Contrary to this, explicitly doing something contrary to courage or temperance does constitute a strong sign of non-virtue. Virtues are characterised by a depth of personal involvement, scope of application, and continuity of aretaic engagement. Virtue includes existential readiness. A person with justice, for example, will not deliberately waste his or her virtue —while a person with skill may decide to remain inactive and thereby still be skilful, a just person, on the other hand, cannot postpone his or her justice (Simon 1986: 72). Finally, it should be noted that certain skills, such as the particular skill of torturing, are not worth having, while virtues are always worth having (Wallace 1978: 43). Virtues embody an essential tendency toward good human use. They make a human person not only competent, but also good.

Could a skill become a virtue?

Some capacities appear to allow both technical and aretaic versions. Clarity in writing texts is a matter of skill (technique), but, when embedded in a broader and more intense disposition to be clear in one's communication to others, clarity turns into an aretaic perfection. Many other, more particularised skills do not seem to include the possibility of aretaic extension and intensification. It is difficult, for example, to see how the skill of riding a bicycle could receive straightforward aretaic extension. It is likely that skills allowing aretaic extension are in fact skills that already hold an important position within the life of virtue. Virtues are themselves not skills but always do include aspects of skill — skill and virtue are interconnected (Zagzebski 1998: 115). Skills serve virtues by allowing a person to act or respond effectively, and effectiveness — as we know — is a basic ingredient of virtue. The skill of compassion, for example, can include knowing what to say, the skill of fairness can mean knowing how to evaluate student papers, and the skills of courage knowing how to stand up to a tormentor (*ibid.*: 113). Virtues include the presence of skill, whereas skill can exist without the virtues (however, it is of course true that complex skills need to be learned, and serious learning is only possible when certain virtues are present to some extent — think of the virtues of openess, perseverance, and so forth).

Varieties of virtue

There are different kinds of virtue, which can be established according to different interpretational keys. It is in the context of aretaic division important not to consider a human person as a segmented creature to be sliced up. To possess temperance and tolerance is not like having legs and arms. Virtues are not organic parts. However, a person in his or her way of being does permit aretaic judgement in direct relation to different situations and with an eye on different capacities and aspects of personality. Our responses to items in the world and in ourselves invite aretaic differentiation.

Let us consider several aretaic distinctions.

Basic and non-basic virtues — Life around us changes — clothing, the names we give to our children, also our virtues (Bollnow 1958). Many virtues and interpretations of virtue come and go. A change in the organisation of common life will in part lead to a transformation of what counts as virtue and vice (Pincoffs 1986: 7). The human sense of aretaic ascription evolves throughout history. We are not interested in chastity anymore. However, it is likely there is a basic aretaics, an elemental ethos, which does not (or ought not to) change drastically (Bollnow 1968: 23). The basic virtues normally do their silent work. MacIntyre speaks about the central invariant virtues (1975: 104). According to Nussbaum (1988) these essential virtues refer to grounding fields of human experience, among which are fear of important damages, bodily appetites, distribution of limited resources, and so forth. The basic virtues are necessary in each human society. If not available in actual cultural or historical situations, then this is to be deeply regretted. Basic virtues do receive a different content in different cultures and historical periods, but only from the perspective of somehow belonging to the same functional type of virtue.

Self-regarding and other-regarding virtues — Self-regarding virtues are meant, in principle at least, to be directly beneficial to the person possessing these virtues. Think of courage and temperance. Of course, a real and concrete virtue will work on more than one level of concern — we want courage also to properly work in moral context, and we do not wish personal courage to have destructive consequences for other persons and communities. Nonetheless, it is relevant to define the primordial role of courage or temperance in terms of self-maintenance and self-development. There are other virtues that never directly function in a self-regarding context — think of justice and generosity. These basically function as other-regarding virtues and are primarily meant to benefit others beyond oneself (it is here assumed that one is automatically good toward oneself; in this regard one does not need the corrective work of justice and generosity).

Temporally evasive and continuous virtues — The varied temporality of the virtues leads to a further aretaic distinction. Courage in a physical and deadly context (war) is likely to be activated at most only once or a few times in someone's life story (professional soldiers and police officers excluded). Only exceptional circumstances reveal the physically courageous self. Other virtues are relevant almost every day. Think of temperance and tolerance, which are regularly or even continuously activated in common existence. Certain virtues are temporally evasive. Justice and integrity involve many different tasks and challenges, stretching out over a longer period of time. Others, like temperance, are easily recognisable and temporally direct. One is or one is not properly moderate, but it is much more difficult to determine one's degree of justice and integrity. Perhaps we can here distinguish between complicated and simple virtues.

Primary active and secondary active virtues — Virtues can also be divided into primary active and secondary active virtues (Trianosky 1987). Many virtues are directly connected with action. Generosity and kindness involve certain behaviours. One cannot be generous without doing anything. Other virtues are not bound to action in such a direct manner. Empathy is rather a reactive trait, not an active one; it is an auxiliary virtue which enables us to better carry through our good motives. As secondary active virtues they are traits that enable the other virtues of action to carry through their aims.

Aretaic subfields — Within the context of virtuous existence a set of aretaic subfields is available. This gives rise to the next set of aretaic kinds. We ascribe virtues to others in line with certain aspects of personality (intellect, emotion, expression, self-concern, etc.). Cognitive virtues (clarity of thinking, practical finesse, logicality, cognitive creativity, openness, intellectual tolerance) predominantly focus on matters of cognition, argumentation, reasoning, and interpretation. Not all traits are equally relevant for 'critical thinking'. One certainly needs a willingness to follow an argument where it leads, a disposition to demand evidence for candidate beliefs, and a frank acknowledgement of cognitive fallibility (Siegel 1997: 59), but one may very well lack justice or temperance and still do well in one's scientific projects. Affective virtues are concerned with emotional reception and identification (empathy, compassion, care; many of the affective virtues belong to the field of moral virtues). The virtues of communication (directness, a freshness in expression, clarity of writing and speaking) predominantly deal with expression, semiosis, and communication. Existential virtues (courage, temperance, perseverance, hope) contribute to the quality, sustenance and development of one's existence (in this sense, many cognitive virtues also belong to the field of existential virtue). Social virtues (politeness, more formal and casual versions of friendliness, tactfulness, and helpfulness) are fundamentally other-regarding, but in a much less intense and engaged manner. They function in official and informal social settings (being polite to one's client, being tactful to a student). Moral virtues (justice, care, honesty, generosity, tolerance) are other-regarding in an intense, engaged and systematic manner. Much more is at stake beyond formal concern. We enter the field of moral seriousness, oughtness, and the supererogatory.

Moral virtues, in particular, must be situated in a wider descriptive context. Moral being connects with other ingredïents — notably duties and rights (and, of course, also consequences). Similar to an organism that cannot survive with one of its essential organs missing, virtuous morality without a distinct recognition of rights or duties or consequences would dismantle authentic moral experience. This insight cancels the idea of a radical virtue ethics. Some virtues will rather function as deontic virtues. Honesty, for example, includes a fixed disposition to avoid certain acts that violate moral rules. The presence of rules is also a source for aretaic learning. Rules constitute an essential part of aretaic pedagogy. Furthermore, knowing that we are fallible creatures, creatures with vices, it is obvious that civilised existence begs for the firm workings of a deontic morality. We need an ethics of deontic limitation and a language of obligation, wrongness, and the permissible (Bond 1996: 187). This insight should, in turn, equally lead us to cancel a univocal language of duties and rights without a larger anthropological, perfective and aretaic framework. The work of duty in its best form is to be undertaken exactly by virtuous selves.

It may be interesting to extend the list of aretaic subfields further, notably in relation to certain realms of practical concern. However, these other subfields seem in large part connected with a particular and specialised activation of virtues in more general fashion already belonging to fields mentioned before. The political realm clearly engages numerous cognitive, existential, social and moral virtues. This is also true for the artistic, economic, sportive, occupational, and ecological realms. However, virtues or complexes of virtue which perhaps could be proposed as having an original presence in these supplementary realms are, to name but a few, aesthetic sense (artistic virtue), a sense of democracy (political virtue), thrift (economic virtue), sportsmanship (sport), professionalism (occupational virtue), and a sense of natural conservation (ecological virtue).

In a secular framework one may decide to translate religious virtues (hope, faith, and charity) into existential or moral virtues. Consider hope. It appears that we need a virtue in view of the fact that chief ends generally are possible but arduously difficult. In other words, it is necessary to possess

> a virtue that preserves us alike from fatuous presumption that blinds us to the difficulties and dangers of the path, and from despair that would make us give up, lie down, and miserably perish' (Geach 1979: 18).

Religious selves, of course, will continue to experience faith, hope and charity as belonging to the distinct realm of religious being.

There is no Berlin Wall between kinds of virtue. As we have seen, virtues and kinds of virtue interact (aretaic interconnection). The different kinds of virtue are also involved in what could be called 'migrational movements'. The migration of virtues prevents a strict demarcation and recognises the fact that one and the same person can function in different contexts and, consequently, will be aretaically judged according to different standards and dimensions. A scholar strongly attached to scientific or philosophical truth may show signs of courage (resisting institutional pressure), which, due to the particular setting, are best taken as signs of intellectual courage (courage aimed at the protection of an intellectual good). But courage functions also in moral contexts beyond the world of the intellect, as well as in other aretaic contexts.

It will regularly be the case that someone possesses an aretaically relevant capacity in only one realm and not in another. We function better in one setting, and less well in others. This is typical for our society, characterised as it is by a radical plurality of specialised roles, contexts and domains. Scientific, intellectual honesty does not always translate into extended moral honesty. Justice in the context of one's family or group may not translate into larger societal justice. Real virtue, as we have seen, will function in all the relevant fields. Justice with relation to one's family is better than nothing, but does not constitute an authentic form of aretaic being. It is a trait below virtue, even if already a trait with some goodness. Existential courage without social and moral extension, too, is a trait below virtue. Courage is an existential virtue (since its very first essential function is to maintain our existence against threats), but to be a real virtue it must also play a role in the other principal fields. As clarified earlier, aretaic ambition and scope are essential in the life of virtue as such.

The complicated issue of aretaic segmentation announces in one sense another issue, namely the problematics of situationism versus aretaics. In a next segment, we need to address the situationist critique of aretaic being.

Virtue and situationism

Situationism doubts the language of traits and virtues. It is claimed that our aretaic ascriptions are not backed up by real traits. Should we therefore leave the language of virtue? I think not, Let us reconfirm aretaic being.

It is first of all clear that 'no trait theory can be sound unless it allows for, and accounts for, the variability of a person's conduct' (Allport 1961: 333). Obviously, not all our traits are equally strong and consistent. And we often oversimplify in our interpretation and evaluation of others, whereas we should better recognise that 'no one is as simple and firmly structured as our labels imply' (*ibid.*: 336). Furthermore, it has become more difficult today to find out whether a person possesses certain virtues. Classical virtue ethics was based on the idea of a smaller community 'where people know each other since birth, where there are fixed role-models together with their imputed virtues, where life is short, where people know roughly what to expect from one another' (Heller 1991: 90). In contemporary aretaics, however, we simply have to accept that many persons have in substantial part turned into interpretational puzzles. Moreover, flexible capitalism has led to a certain corrosion of character: it has certainly become more difficult to possess stable traits: we are in many contexts asked to be able to change on short notice (Sennett 1998). This means that the lessons of situationism have to be heard.

Situationism concludes that different situations, with their specific demands and obstacles, largely determine what we will do or not do. This implies that a virtue as stable disposition makes no sense. Our aretaic ascriptions are illusionary. To an uncomfortable extent, we are all chameleon-like. Situationism opts therefore for an alternative assessment:

> If we took situationism to heart in our ethical practice, we would revise certain habits of moral assessment — we would hesitate to evaluate persons by reference to robust traits or evaluatively consistent personality structures on the grounds that these are unreasonable standards to expect actual persons to approximate (Doris 1998: 514).

In real life, however, the truth seems to lie in a variable middle. Situationism is right in pointing out the availability of persons who act without continuity and coherence in different situations. As Iris Murdoch (1997) notes: 'The good artist is not necessarily wise at home, the concentration guard can be a kindly father' (*ibid.*: 113). On the other hand, it is not automatically the case that we are all chameleon-like with equal intensity. Situations do not automatically eliminate traits. On the contrary,

> major traits are often remarkable stable over time, and it is difficult to detect patterns of systematic change. Traits typically appear to have a resilience in the face of the normal events of a life [...] In adulthood, it may take major events such as mental illness to induce substantial trait change (Matthews & Deary 1998: 69).

We do know people who are almost always neat or tactful (Allport 1956: 250). Our character is influenced by the many roles we find on our way — and roles do alter character — but we also integrate information, attitudes, identifications, and so forth, into our personal system. We seem to be capable of possessing an integrity that cannot be completely eliminated by roles and other situations (Weissman 2000: 121).

Integrity, itself a complex virtue, is a part of each real virtue. It is a virtue without which the other virtues cannot be possessed (MacIntyre 1999: 317). This is a central issue at stake in the debate between aretaics and situationism. A person of integrity is able to resist external pressure and inner temptation. And each virtue, being characterised by such resistance, logically implies a sense of integrity. This aspect is exactly put aside in situationism. For the situationist, integrity is an illusionary construct.

Situationism is not, as is sometimes suggested, a matter of realistic psychology versus aretaic theoretical philosophy, but rather leads to a clash between different competing psychological schools (for example, Gordon W. Allport's personology versus situationism). The principle of minimal psychological realism, as formulated in Owen Flanagan (1991: 32), is not necessarily lost for the aretaic side of the argument — virtue, if properly defined, may still be relevant for creatures like us. The following remarks aim to establish a middle between trait and situation — a middle informed by empirical concern without giving up on the virtues (on empirical aretaics and ethics, see Musschenga 2004).

One main issue underlying the point and purpose of situationism is that we never observe virtues and other traits directly and in a complete interpretative context. We only observe and interpret acts and expressions in a confined set of situations. We are confronted with what can be called a *sittlichen Auslegungskunst* (Meier 1996: 94). When we are not around, people may behave differently, due to different personal and environmental factors. Furthermore, it is clear that no act or expression is the product of only one trait. When one writes a letter, different determining factors will play a role (Allport 1961: 334) — a sense of duty, opportunity, the presence of memories, and so forth. Traits are only one of the factors that determine a present act. Hence, situation and outside factors do matter. But this is not new for virtue ethics, which is typically focused on the fact that virtues — beyond closed theoretical principles — deal with changing contexts, demands, opportunities, feelings, and so forth. Without changeable contexts and demands there would be much less aretaic challenge to begin with. Virtues are perfective traits exactly because they offer adequate response to situational tribulation. The debate between situationism and aretaics is not a debate between recognition and non-recognition of situational factors. It is rather a debate between distrusting and trusting the quality of aretaic interpretation as well as the quality of aretaic being itself.

Let us consider these two aspects.

The quality of aretaic interpretation

Aretaics counts on the ability of human persons to develop subtle, complex and sometimes relaxed aretaic interpretations and appreciations of others. Most of us are experienced enough to know what situations can do to a character, but also how persons can withstand pressures and obstacles. Aretaic interpretation itself can be undertaken in better and worse ways. One needs virtues to be able to detect the virtues. A good judge of people possesses certain qualities — insight, intelligence, experience, and complexity (Allport 1956: 513-16). He will counter the danger of oversimplification by realising 'that he himself is too complex to be briefly accounted for' (*ibid*.: 520). The good judge should also be initially prepared to expect others to possess virtues (in line with the demands of benevolent interpretation), while equally prepared, in due course, to critically discern signs of anti-aretaic being. One aspect of human selfhood concerns the impression of one's personal characteristics that one person makes on another. Realising this, people may involve themselves in a politics of impression. One may act as if one is virtuous (aretaic Machiavellianism). Ethics and aretaics may turn into etiquette and impression-fabrication as described in Goffman (Bovone 1993). This is important. We may be confronted with 'counterfeit virtues' (MacIntyre 1991). We are sometimes too quick in ascribing virtues on the basis of a limited set of actions and situations. Misreading a novel will normally not cause significant social and personal harm, but a misreading of the qualities of others carries more direct risks and potential for harm.

We especially need to be aware of the right questions, perhaps in the back of our mind. What in future behaviour would constitute a reason to cancel or change our aretaic interpretation? What is the type of reason behind one's action? What exactly is it in a situation or an action that pleased or pained someone? Certain actions and expressions would bring us to change our interpretation and perhaps lead to the conclusion that someone does not possess a virtue. It cannot be simply be a matter of visibly doing what the virtuous person would do. The reason why an action was performed must also matter in our aretaic assessments of a person.

For example, the difference between gluttons and temperate people is not only a matter of behaving in a certain way, but also a matter of inner axiological identification (Hunt 1997: 31 -32). A skilled glutton is quite likely to show self-restraint because this will in the long run lead to better and longer enjoyment of food and alcohol. Placing a very high value on the pleasures of eating and drinking may thus result in what looks like temperate behaviour. But authentic temperance has to do with placing a certain limit on the value of basic pleasures of consumption. The concerns that absorb the attention of the intemperate person will play only a subordinate role in a person with real temperance — other (perfective) goods will hold a much more central role (personal self-fulfilment, practical accomplishment, well-being of others, natural conservation, etc.).

An aretaic hermeneutic circle comes to surface. Observing parts of a personality in confined situations we interpret someone as being honest in a global sense. This global aretaic sense of honesty will influence our further interpretations of aspects and actions of a person, and so forth. We may come to discover contradictions and deviations. These newly discovered aspects and actions could cause us to revise or even to overturn our aretaic judgement. We may perhaps arrive at the conclusion that we can trust someone's honesty to a certain limit but no more than that. Real and rough aretaic interpretation is not a matter of everything or nothing. In a world of relative perfection we must accept some kind of appropriate compromise.

Balanced situationalism is an essential ingredient of aretaic interpretation. However, balance can lead to different outcomes. Situationism suggests only one non-aretaic outcome, while contemporary aretaics remains open to a less pessimistic scenario: we are often much better and more continuous in our virtues than radical situationism portrays us to be. At least, it is not impossible that this is the case for a significant number of persons.

The quality of aretaic being

This brings us to the second point, namely the quality of aretaic being.
Yves R. Simon writes:

> Think of an honest man who is honest only as long as he is not exposed to great temptations. He will not steal fifty dollars from anybody, but if he had a chance to steal fifty thousand, without much risk of being caught, he might do it. Likewise, it is not so rare for people to be truthful as long as they are free from pressure. But put under pressure, many will break their word and tell lies (1986: 1).

Simon offers here one insight into aretaic psychological realism, rather in line with situationism. But it is not difficult to discern other realistic aretaic possibilities. For example, think of someone who would definitely not steal fifty thousand, even if no risks were involved. This same person, rather, would be likely to keep a fifty-dollar bill found on the street, but would feel much less morally at ease with three thousand dollars found in a wallet with an address included. This example is already less negative in aretaic terms. The insight to be grasped, perhaps, is that aretaic being knows many inimitable varieties and combinations. Relative aretaic being can in some people come close to higher perfection, while others will barely manage to live in line with shades of virtue. All is possible according to the nature of the human creature.

It is good to make an explicit distinction between virtue as an instance of relative perfection and virtue as the ideal of absolute perfection. In human life we are only confronted with the realities of relative or approximate virtue. Edgar Morin writes, for example, about the virtue of sincerity: 'La sincérité ne peut être pure qu'à un moment particulier de combustion entre les gaz qui la nourissent et la fumée qui s'en dégage' (1975: 155). Aretaic purity is an ideal. There are many limitations on the concrete possession of virtues:

> A virtue is not something that one either has all or none of: a fairly long story usually needs to be told to explain the way in which and the extent to which an imperfect being possesses virtues (Ewin 1992: 414).

Responsiveness and quality have to be good enough to be an instance of aretaic being — virtue is a threshold concept (Swanton 2003: 24). It is difficult to determine sharply where a sense of real virtue is approached and where trait below virtue begins, but one clear condition is that a sense of real virtue must be active in all the principal fields in which a person works. 1f there is significant incompletion in this regard then we may perhaps say a person is on his way toward possessing a virtue, but that he is not yet at the aretaic threshold. If there are only much smaller failures, due to unavoidable complexities and fallibilities, while one's virtue is somehow active in all principal fields, then it can be claimed that one possesses virtue as relative perfection. My suggestion is to consider relative aretaic perfection of this robust and positive kind as a version of real, although not perfect virtue. 1f one defines virtue only as absolute virtue, then we shall end up with no one being capable of virtue. The principle of minimal psychological realism forces us, it must be admitted, to lower the level of aretaic demandingness.

Aretaic references within situationism

In a world of relative virtue it can subsequently be argued that situationism offers different lessons about life. But, in its own way, these lessons carry positive aretaic opportunity. Situationism, in this regard, is likely to be able to contribute to the development of better virtuous states. This is something that we cannot simply set aside. In fact, situationism seems to contain its own set of aretaic references.

Confidence in one's character is precisely what puts us at risk in morally dangerous settings, and situationism effectively reminds us of this (Doris 1998: 516). We are fragile and vulnerable selves. This insight invites self-knowledge. In the words of John Kekes:

> The implication of the general proposition that all human projects are vulnerable is that the same is true of our own projects. It is easy to assent to the general proposition but exempt ourselves as being somehow special, protected, or immune. Reflection on our vulnerability makes us see ourselves as one among many, with the same liabilities as everyone else (1990: 206).

The situationist self will come to realise that it is much better not to have dinner with a former girlfriend when one's wife is elsewhere. Such self-knowledge about one's weaknesses does in itself resemble something of an aretaic trait. Being aware of the situational threats helps us to be responsible selves (Doris

2002: 153). Consistently avoiding situations destined to bring out one's moral fragility — which is exactly the advice offered by situationism — suggests nothing less than the relevance of the virtues of practical wisdom and carefulness. Situationism finds itself in a position similar to that of postmodernist constructionist thought. Criticising the classical virtues, postmodern authors often end up proposing their own virtues for example, the existential virtues of flexibility and irony. Situationism, too, can be seen to propose its own version of the virtue of self-knowledge.

In insisting that a better understanding of the agent's situation and its contribution to the action will lead to a greater understanding of others (Harman 1999: 329), situationism also suggests its own version of tolerance. We know that aretaic demands will never be fully met and will therefore more easily forgive others. It is especially good to realise the at times tragic character of human existence, in which one can simply lose one's virtue and perfection. For example:

> A person's courage can be exhausted by having faced too many dangers or too serious ones, and it may be broken by a devastating defeat or extreme physical injury. People who live through such shocks may lose their ability to respond to any dangers, real or imagined, with any courage at all (Hunt 1997: 29).

In clarifying that we are never independent from relation and context — that, indeed, relations are essential to us — situationism furthermore introduces relatedness as another virtue versus the vices of arrogant independence (the idea that one can autonomously shine in full glory without contributive connection to others) and bad faith:

> It is an expression of bad faith, or wishful thinking, just to hold out a blank ideal of perfect stability, without also offering a realistic account of how it could come about. When we do begin to develop such an account, we will find it very rare indeed for virtuous qualities to become so firmly fixed in individual character as to be impervious to climates of social expectation (Merritt 2000: 381).

Aretaic progression

Besides suggesting situationist virtues, the situationist argument logically opens up the possibility of aretaic progression. This is not something that can be structurally canceled as a possibility. Situational factors may indeed distort our virtuous stabilities, but we can become conscious of this and, in our new awareness, try to perform better next time. We may acquire a desire to do something about it exactly through our reflective concern for our weakness (Simon 1986: 130). In this manner we work our way towards virtue. Today, virtue is a matter of life-long learning — certainly with regard to the more complex virtues. Aretaic complacency is not an adequate reaction with regard to the shifting obstacles and complicated situations confronting us nowadays. We live in a world of gradual perfection. There can be no quick perfective conversion and transformation.

We may claim that aretaic language remains all in all sufficiently intact. The words of Christine Swanton suit our finding. She insists that: 'Situationist personality psychology has much to offer a psychologically realistic account of the nature of character: it has not removed virtue ethics from the moral-theoretic landscape' (2003: 33). The quality of aretaic ascription, situation, relative virtue, and progressive aretaic development are important factors in a realistic theory of the virtues.

Virtue as absolute, harmonious perfection would imply a completed struggle, a full victory. This is an aretaic ideal that we can still take to our hearts in some sense, namely in the form of hope. This is a necessary condition for aretaic being. About this hope Rosalind Hursthouse writes:

> We manifest it when we try to incalculate the virtues in our children. We manifest it when we try to make ourselves (we think) better people and try to improve our own and other people's ethical views. We manifest it when we try to bring about social change (1999: 264).

Aretaic necessity, aretaic innovation

We may conclude that there is a life of the virtues in a contemporary setting. Undoubtedly, in times to come, it will be important to develop new virtues adequate to living in the twenty-first century. Some earlier virtues are bound to receive a transformed content, notably in connection with an ecological extension. Alternative virtues will appear, perhaps in dialogue with other cultures or new practices. Aretaic imagination is bound to respond to fresh, unexpected, and unavoidable demands that we shall come to find on our way. One can suggest that necessity, being the mother of invention, is also the mother of virtue (Solomon 1996: 98).

CHAPTER EIGHT —
HUMAN PERFECTIVE EXISTENCE — i:
PERFECTIVE NATURALISM

The trouble is that the human species
is the only species which finds it hard
to be a species.

— Abraham Maslow

Now that we have learned something more about the content and the variety of perfection it is appropriate to turn more closely to a *rational* defence of perfective existence itself.

The main drive behind perfectionism is to let us function up to standard, but why are the selected perfective dimensions and qualities so important? How exactly do we know which standards are relevant? It is one thing to formulate a list of perfections — to talk about qualitative, teleological, contributive perfection, about virtue, and so forth — but it is quite another to defend its specific human existential relevance. In connection with this issue I shall in this chapter develop a perfective naturalism. Perfective naturalism constitutes a basic step in the direction of a rational understanding of the life of perfection of the human species.

Before we reach a perfective naturalism for humans we must first deal with the goodness of being, as well as with a perfective naturalism for plants and animals. This will place us in a better position to specify the relation between perfection and human nature.

The goodness of being

The goodness of being constitutes, I believe, the most elemental valuational principle of perfectionism. This elemental principle is well evoked in the thought of William Desmond (1995a). The fundamental fact that there is a reality, that there is an earth, that there are beings, is good. The gift of being is itself the first good of being. As Desmond writes: 'The good of being is not for the sake of anything in particular; to be is to be good; the good of being is to be, and to be is good' (*ibid.*: 505). To be sure, the celebration of being as good can always be doubted if one intellectually wishes to do so, but the critic's own explicit effort of being unavoidably testifies to another truth, namely that it is good that we are. It is good that there are plants, animals, rivers, mountains, and numerous other integrities of being. According to Desmond the idea that goodness is but a human construction imposed on worthless being only results in an unfruitful axiological anemia. In the end this will destroy our own value. As he points out:

> For if the creation is valueless in itself then the human being as a participant in creation is also ontologically valueless, so likewise his human construction is also ultimately valueless, Every effort to construct values out of himself will be subject to the same deeper, primitive, ultimate valuelessness. Human values collapse ultimately into nothing, if there is no ground of value in the integrity of being itself (*ibid.*: 509).

If the goodness of being is not accepted as such, perfective naturalism cannot really make a start.

Perfective naturalism for plants and animals

Accepting the goodness of being, we arrive at the next step: the goodness of specific living beings. We enter, thus, a perfective philosophy of life.

Certain properties, developments, capacities and accomplishments — being properties of life — are seen to be immediately valuable with an eye on survival and on the original quality of life of members of a species. If one is not interested in survival and quality of life, in the goodness of beings, these values automatically fall away. Perfective naturalism insists upon the elemental goodness of being alive in a particular manner — each being is a yes to being, by simply being (*ibid.*: 513).

We are in this context brought to a perfective naturalism for plants and animals. A comparison with plants and animals is strongly educational because there is, one could argue, a conceptual connection between life and good in the case of human beings as in that of animals and even plants. In each case life comes up to some standard of normality and precisely this standard will rationally determine relevant aspects of goodness and perfection. Each living creature is an effort-to-be of a specific kind. For each species one can somehow come to determine what counts as an advantage and what does not. Life intrinsically implies a set of values or goods, since each and every effort-to-be embodies a negative and positive reception of aspects and elements in the world. As humans we have some idea what counts as a plus or minus for ourselves and for other species. Advantage is, to say the least, not an alien notion. Mary Midgley notes:

> Saying that seals are well adapted to cut through water commits us, not just to a view about what is good and bad water-cutting, but also to saying that cutting through water is an advantage, something that can be worthwhile for creatures to

do. We do not speak of animals as being well adjusted to fall over cliffs, or get stuck in holes, or even to neglect their young (1978: 74).

These are facts of natural goodness (Foot 2001: 26). Plants and animals have a reasonably firm nature that has been well tested, and everything that contributes to and fulfils this nature is good or valuable. Consequently, varieties of perfection are to be articulated in line with a specific nature and its relevant fulfilment.

We should define the intrinsically desirable organic life of a certain kind of plant or animal in terms of properties that make an organism a certain, successful earthly form of life. Perfection for lions is something other than perfection for ants or spiders. The particular identities and teleological schemes of plants and animals embody a scheme of perfective demands and accomplishments. It is necessary for plants to have water, for birds to build nests, and for lionesses to teach their cubs to kill. Otherwise, they cannot survive as the creatures that they are. The noise made by the rustling of the leaves is in this respect irrelevant, but the development of roots is not (*ibid.*: 33). These necessities simply belong to the basic way of being of plants, birds and lionesses. This is what it is for members of a particular species to be as they should be and to do what they should do.

Fulfilment of these necessities is a positive thing and directly invites perfective treatment (estimation in terms of better and worse). To be able to survive in the world certain capacities, qualities, developments, contributive elements, and so forth are needed. Different species are equipped in a variety of ways. Each organic nature gives expression to a successful way of earthly being. We may therefore assume that no species, no plant or animal, would like to miss out on vital accomplishments and actualisations which make it possible to properly sustain organic being. Animals and plants are recognisable entities with necessary, productive properties. In order to have a proper life as a flourishing member of a species, recognisable demands must be met and different qualities and capacities must be available.

It is the clarity of vegetal and animal nature that makes it such a clear-cut illustration of how perfective naturalism argues from fact to value. The interpretation of plants and animals permits the articulation of certain schemes of perfection. We can determine which things are instrumental (contributive perfection), which processes of spontaneous perfection need to take place, which skills need to be learned in certain animals (acquired perfection). We can discern perfective qualities. Each animal and plant has typical demands of completeness, composition, purity, and so forth. There are the animal capacities. Some animals are involved in productional perfection (building of nests). There are the activities of hunting and finding a mate (project teleological perfection). All these varieties of perfection are to be applied on basis of a conception of a specific organic nature.

Perfective naturalism for plants and animals: critiques and responses

Perfective naturalism for plants and animals has received criticism from different sides. It is important to offer a response to these points of critique before entering a perfective naturalism for humans.

Creatures of change

Evolutionary theory and genetic science show plants and animals to be creatures of change. Organic kinds could have been different, and perhaps will transform in later times through genetic manipulation, mutation, or changes in the environment. If transformation presents itself as a realistic option then the question arises why it is so good for an animal to be as it is *now*.

It is true that organisms can change and will change. However, it is equally true that a typical organism remains what it is for a longer time. Evolution toward another successful organism would again involve endurance and lead to another reasonably stable scheme of perfection. Organisms are not so protean as to lack a generic essence altogether (Attfield 1987: 45). Biological transformation does not take place overnight. The time frame implied in evolutionary theory offers sufficient space for a robust perfective interpretation. One must stress that perfectionism does not intend to transcend the human organic and earthly realm in the direction of godlike eternity. It is a perspective that attempts to appreciate organisms at a given historical time (Foot 2001: 29).

Genetic engineering seems captured by a spirit of radical change to transform organisms into something other and better. But it is valid to suggest that perfectionism qualifies genetic engineering rather than the other way around. It is in fact improbable that drastic genetic engineering will reach the same natural kind of wisdom, quality, and effectiveness that seems to define processes of natural evolution within the eco-systemic context. Genetic experimentation is likely to constitute a risky adventure. The fact that we can artificially change organisms does not make trivial the value, integrity, and dignity of what naturally existing organisms are here and now. This is a matter of deep moral concern that remains all too unrecognised within genetic industry.

Imperfect nature

Evolutionary theory brings up the critical point that survival does not mean that some organisms are completely formed in terms adequate to their environment. There are, for example, species that now possess organs and characteristics that simply have lost their use. This means that there are cases where there is not a perfect fit between organism and environment. The perfective standards of effectiveness and appropriateness are then not fully met. Hence, it cannot be said that organic nature is always the best source for determining the best possible way of being for a certain species (perfection). One prime example of imperfect nature is the presence of the dodo:

> It has wings, but they are too short and too weak to propel it into the air; it has a tail but this tail is disproportionate and in the wrong place. You would think it was a tortoise which was dressed up with the cast-off skin of a bird' (Buffon, quoted in Shanahan 2004: 96).

This is perhaps true, but perfectionism has no problems with such facts. It does certainly not demand absolute perfection, focused as it is on relative and approximate perfection. Species that survive can be assumed to do so on the basis of relative adaptation — a perfective adaptation that is somehow sufficient, otherwise survival could not have been the result. The environment may drastically change, and this implies that earlier relative perfective fits between animal and the rest of nature may come under stress or simply disappear. The earth gives and takes, and there is nothing that guarantees that a perfective state will always accurately apply to the state of an environment. Hence, the fact of evolution itself.

Anti-teleology

Classical perfectionism is based on teleological metaphysics, but contemporary theories of animate nature do not see evolution as a teleologically directed process. Through mutation and a non-directed step by step selective process, whereby certain genes and gene combinations are favoured (creatures with less appropriate gene combinations are likely to disappear), specific creatures and organs arise. The fact that non-teleological processes have determined organisms and organs may bring one to the conclusion that living creatures are nothing much — only symptoms of anonymous processes without a perfective director.

Evolution, indeed, is not in itself a teleological enterprise. We are confronted with the undeniable fact that through non-teleological evolution teleological creatures have appeared on earth. The only thing we can do, frankly, is to note this fact and live with it. But in this case, it still continues to be possible to consider organisms as successful living entities, which in a variety of adaptive ways do properly respond to the world. These teleologically functional responses and qualities are there, whatever the non-teleological cause of their being. We should recognise this (moreover, why could we not consider non-teleological evolution itself as something mysteriously magnificent?). Some will perhaps insist that it cannot be possible that teleology arises out of non-teleology. Hence, a secret designer must have been at work. Peirce, for example, refers to a cosmic sheriff. Others will insist that organic teleological systems are meaningless bubbles in a sea of blind processes. No significance can arise out of insignificance. But these two positions are not necessary. A perfective approach to nature can simply decide to focus on accepting current organisms with perfective quality, without further religious speculation or reductive inclination.

Channels of fertility

While perfectionism is directly concerned with the well-being of individual organisms, evolutionary theory rather deals with fitness in terms of the likelihood of leaving offspring (Williams 1993: 44). Organisms become pure channels of fertility. This is the only contributive standard that matters.

Perfectionism does not deny the contributive role of organisms in the production of new organisms, but it is also not blind for the many properties and perfections of organisms beyond the likelihood of leaving offspring. There is no reason not to be concerned with organisms and their inherent qualities according to other perfective concerns and standards. Animal organisms do more than leaving offspring (otherwise there would have been no work for ethologists), and what animals do more should be perfectively received.

No essential properties

One can argue that it is problematic to decide about a set of essential properties and perfections of organisms. One critical argument is that determining which normal organic properties fit the environment is itself determined by the fact that the idea of a normal environment is already influenced by a conception of certain functions as normal (especially see Kitcher 1999). Hence, we do not have a rational, non-circular ground for deciding what is a normal organism and what is not. There is the general suspicion that essences are being tied to a particular small subset of organic properties picked out in advance as especially pertinent for considering the organic good of a certain kind. The main point is that the idea of an essential nature and its perfections fails in accuracy, definitiveness and rational underpinning. We cannot reach a clear and reasonable set of properties and perfections.

The critique that picking out properties is an arbitrary undertaking is invalid. We need to distinguish between a) properties by which we can recognise a living organism of a certain kind — some of these properties are necessary; b) properties that we expect a normally functioning organism of a certain kind to exemplify (particular individuals that lack these aspects will not lose their recognisable organic membership); and c) properties that an organism could lose without damaging its recognisable membership nor its normal perfective status. Let me elaborate on these three types of property.

A sufficient number of typical properties must be available to be able to recognise a living organic individual of a certain kind. A living dog without legs is still a living dog. A dog without a heart can, for obvious reasons, not be recognised as a living creature. As long as an organism is alive, one may expect a sufficient amount of recognisable properties to be available. Of course, one could mutilate an organism in such a way that, while it remains alive, it would become very difficult to recognise its specific organic kind (genetic screening would then become necessary). But this is not a normal (nor a moral) situation. Everything that serves as a clue for deciding the specific organic nature of something as a living creature is a relevant property. Some properties are essential — think of breathing or digesting in dogs — but no one property is sufficient on its own: living creatures do not remain alive by virtue of one property alone. In fact, this situation makes the task of recognition easier rather than more difficult. Biologists and ethologists, in most cases, do not seem to have difficulties with recognising properties that, precisely in their complex togetherness, offer sufficient confirmation about an organic nature. It is impossible to cancel all fuzziness, to be sure, but a reasonable sense of organic recognition seems to be available.

The inability to move, blindness, brain damage, and so forth are deeply regrettable, but missing these properties or ingredients does not bring us to insist, for example, that a fox terrier is not to be recognised as an organism of a certain kind. However, we have then a terrier with a significant and fundamental lack, unable to perform perfective functions which a terrier normally manages and is accustomed to perform — functions that allow it to successfully make its way in the world. It is obvious that these perfective properties (capacities, qualities, fulfilments, teleologies) are defined on the basis of a connection between organism and environment — how else to define earthly perfections? However, I do not see why it would be irrational to note that wings and the activity of flying are essential perfective elements in the life of an eagle. The environment is as it is for a longer while, and organisms are evolutionary responses to this environment. If the environment changes, there will be new evolutionary responses. Consequently, new properties and perfective standards will arise. Some properties may look rather futile — think of sweating or shivering in the cold — but once we realise the role of these functions in allowing many organic kinds to properly respond to earthly situations (looking for shelter against sun or cold), their perfective degree should be honoured. The more a property is needed for survival (of individuals and/or species) and/or quality of existence as a specific organism, the higher its perfective role. Accepting the goodness of being a certain organism, we must accept also the goodness of relevant perfective properties. Capacities, for example, involve us and other animals in properties that it is better to accept than not to accept. It is simply good to see, to be able to walk, to use legs and hands. Resistance to these capacities is highly unlikely. To voluntarily close our eyes and never to look at the world again would result in the degradation of the capacity of vision as such. This is an option without serious appeal. It does not have appeal because an organism can be assumed to wish to keep its perfections and the accompanying possibilities of performance, on the basis of which it defends its kind as a good kind (Rolston 1994: 172). Two cardinal perfective rules present themselves — it is better to continue than not to continue actual and successful qualities of perfection, and it is better to live with more than with less robust perfective possibilities. These two rules protect the perfective essence of organisms, an essence that is based on actual organic composition.

One can name, finally, different properties the lack of which does not lead to perfective degradation or to difficulties of recognition. Think of a cat missing a small part of its ear or missing one tooth. There may be some perfective damage, but not much. The baldness of human persons is perfectively not highly significant (with, perhaps, the possible exception of aesthetic considerations).

No necessary development

A last critical argument is focused on the difference between discerning perfective properties and essential nature on the one hand, and the necessity to develop and continue these properties. For example, the fact that an egg has the inner destiny to become a chicken does not imply that it should become one. It is not wrong to make an omelette (Scheffler 1985: 43). Or take an acorn. This is not only the seed of an oak, with implied perfective possibility, but also a morsel prized by squirrels. It can never be decided, so the argument goes, which property takes an overriding position. To discern basic properties and perfective qualities does not imply that we may not eliminate or disregard these properties and qualities in favour of other properties and qualities. Perfective naturalism subsequently loses its moral relevance.

I think it is fair to assume that an egg and an acorn are genetically organised to try to become a chicken and an oak tree. This is their primary spontaneous teleology, engraved in their respective genetic codes. The genetic set functions in a sense as a normative set (Rolston 1994: 173). It proposes a scenario for further development. In ecosystemic context it turns out that eggs and acorns also play a contributive role in the life of other organic kinds. It is therefore not wrong to make an omelette for humans, and it is also good that squirrels have found things like acorns to survive on. Nonetheless it would be wrong to reduce the way of being of eggs to contributive perfection and not to understand that acorns embody a teleological scheme beyond being food for squirrels. The fact that possibilities get destroyed or prevented does not destroy the principal developmental scheme of seeds and eggs.

Perfective naturalism for humans

The different responses have, I hope, offered something of a robust response to the criticism. Debate is sure to go on for a longer while, but, for the moment, there is reason enough to accept the rationality of the project of perfective naturalism. From the reality of plants and animals we may turn to a perfective naturalism for humans.

There is no reason to consider a study of human perfection based upon the nature of human life as less adequate than the study of other living creatures (Wallace 1978: 16). One should, of course, note that it will be more difficult in the case of humans to formulate a common concept of human nature — difficult but not altogether impossible. In relation to humans there will be a

> great increase in the number of respects in which evaluation is possible, if only because human lives contain so many and such diverse activities: because human beings do so many different kinds of things (Foot 2001: 39).

The cultural and conventional aspects of human existence ensure that more intense interpretative labour will have to be undertaken in order to arrive at a basic list of human properties and perfections. Nonetheless, we will still be able to come up with estimations and interpretations of human will and action that continue to share a conceptual structure with estimations and interpretations of states, processes and operations in nonhuman living things. In both cases, so perfective naturalism points out, we are confronted with facts about a feature of a certain kind of organism. These facts concern 'Aristotelian necessities' — that which is necessary because and insofar as good hangs on it (Elisabeth Anscombe, quoted in *ibid.*: 15).

What is good for human beings is the development of human nature. There is an acquired outlook from which perfective naturalists speak (Hursthouse 1999: 193). They think that it is fundamentally good to develop one's nature as a human, and that it is good to survive, and so forth. Perfectionism speaks, thus, from a positive philosophy of human life. We cannot ourselves fail to be interested in staying alive. From our particular experience as human beings, we have the fundamental idea that our kind of life is good. The fact that perfectionism tunes in with a primordial appreciation of human life's goodness makes it a stronger theory, not a weaker one.

Our properties and perfections can be discerned and defined according to the scheme established in the previous section on perfective naturalism for plants and animals. A large part of human nature and its perfections is contained in our organic way of being. Above the animal way of being we also possess kinds of properties that are not found in other animals — although we should here not fail to observe capacities and properties in animal beings deserving treatment according to certain concepts normally reserved to humans (think of narrative being, for example).

A relevant method to establish a list of essential human properties and perfections is to start from the negative idea of human deprivation (Foot 2001: 43). Our theoretical and practical way of being includes interpretative, argumentative, imaginative, semiotic, narrative, and communicative capacities. Without these things we are deprived. Not every human will possess each of these essential traits, but the issue is that this will always be a source for deep regret. It may not be a tragedy for a vegetable to be a vegetable, but it undoubtedly is a tragedy for a human to be a vegetable (Rolston 1988: 68). For example, take away narrative competence and we end up with a creature that we do not really wish to be. It is clear that normal human beings are defined by a fair sense of narrative skill. There will be a minimum level of narrative competence below which one does not function as a good human. Moral competence is one distinct form of practical perfection the lack of which makes it impossible for us to sustain ourselves as the humans that we fundamentally are and wish to remain. Moral defect, too, is for humans a kind of 'natural' defect (Foot 2001: 51). Role perfection constitutes yet another form of practical perfection. Human communities, which are needed for developing human selves, cannot do without a division of tasks and roles. Failure to fulfil a role consequently constitutes a defect in a human being. These kinds of defects are to be taken in the same sense in which we may say that 'a dog that is incapable of perception or a plant that is incapable of nourishing itself is defective' (Wallace 1978: 34).

According to Thomas Hurka a being who never plans for the future, and lacks that competence, is not a human (1993: 42). He writes further:

> It is not sufficient for a human to exist, that the material of a human body be present. This material must be organised in the right way, instantiating the properties and performing the activities of a full-fledged human (*ibid.*: 47).

I think this claim is too sharp. Hurka fortunately softens the blow by making a distinction between being a human in a narrow and broader sense. The narrow sense refers to a human with a sense of normal perfective capacity. The broad sense refers to a human as an organism connected to the human species. In other words, persons with serious perfective lack can still be recognised as humans, but not as humans in a normal perfective situation.

Bernard Williams (1996: 34) doubts whether we can work toward a deeper structure of humanity, but I see no reason why it would be completely impossible — through logical implication and essential interconnection of properties — to end up with a network of human competences and properties linking the concept of human nature with certain 'provisionally nonnegotiable points' (Nussbaum 2000: 120). Obviously, only an open-ended list is viable since, in Nussbaum's words,

> we want to allow the possibility that some as yet unimagined transformation in our natural options will alter the constitutive factors, subtracting some and adding

others. We also want to leave open the possibility that we will learn from our encounters with other human societies to revise certain elements in our own standing account of humanness, recognizing, perhaps, that some features we regarded as essential are actually more parochial that that (1990: 219).

However, even while much interpretational labour lies ahead, this should not prevent us from appreciating the idea of a common humanity. Features of common humanity lead us to recognise others as humans, however distant their location and their particular forms of life:

> When one sits down at a table with people from other parts of the world and debates with them concerning hunger or just distribution or in general the quality of human life, one does find, in spite of evident conceptual differences, that it is possible to proceed as if we are all talking about the same human problem; and it is usually only in a context in which one or more of the parties is intellectually committed to a theoretical relativist position that this discourse proves impossible to sustain (Nussbaum 1988: 47).

For Nussbaum constitutive elements of human existence — however differently exemplified in different persons and cultures — include facing death, bodily constitution, organic needs, bodily qualities and capacities, capacity for pleasure and pain, consciousness and self-consciousness, emotion, reason, development, striving, need for education, perception and interpretation, mobility and action, moral capacity, aesthetic sensitivity, play, creativity and imagination, individuality, sociality, culture, relation to nature and the cosmos. Again, persons and cultures may lack some elements, but this is then something to regret. It is good to possess these experiences and capacities in some or other way (even facing death is necessary for humans, as without it we would experience endless 'death' while being alive).

The list of perfective distinctions and concepts (including the virtues) — formulated in chapters five to seven — tunes in with constitutive elements of humanity. Being what we are, we are normally involved in teleological, contributive, qualitative and aretaic perfection. Different human cultures are likely to be differently involved with teleology, contribution, quality, and virtue, but the general structure of striving, of contributing and receiving contributive effects, of possessing, appreciating, and obtaining perfective qualities constitutes a shared human experience (or, at least, an experience which in large part ought to become universally shared).

Perfective naturalism for humans: critiques and responses

Perfective naturalism for humans has received its own set of critical responses (often in combination with critiques on perfective naturalism for plants and animals). In the following I will deal with and respond to critiques of human perfective nature.

Irrational and immoral tendencies

A first argument is situated within perfectionism itself. Some perfectionists warn us not to use the concept of human nature without discrimination. Everything human comes out of human nature, but not everything fulfils human nature in us (Walhout 1980: 290). The problem is as follows:

> If good lives depended on the realisation of common human potentialities, then perfectionism would involve us in the development of many irrational and immoral tendencies. From the fact that human nature potentially is in certain ways it does not follow that it ought to be in those ways. In fact, trying to live good lives must include repressing some human potentialities. The question of which parts of our complex nature we should curb or foster is crucially relevant to good lives, but it cannot be settled by reference to human nature, for it is our nature that prompts the question (Kekes 1988: 172).

There is indeed a radical difference between vegetal/animal and human nature. Vegetal and animal kinds are what they are. They are not burdened by the possibility or the obligation of changing or limiting parts of their nature. Vegetal and animal perfection and flourishing can be attached to their nature as it actually is. The question of morality does not play for them. But this is not fully the case with humans. Otherwise we could logically come to defend human activities such as murder, torture and rape. One intense aspect of the typically human way of being is that we can decide to invest in certain properties rather than others. We live with the blessing and burden of radical choice. This leads to the difficulty that humans are the only species that is bound to find it hard to be a species. We cannot simply be content to be. Complication, misdirection, and ambiguity are common obstacles in our lives. This is not the case for other organisms:

> For a cat there seems to be no problem about being a cat. It's easy; cats seem to have no complexes or ambivalences or conflicts, and show no signs of yearning to be dogs instead. Their instincts are very clear. But we have no such unequivocal animal instincts (Maslow 1971: 186).

This all means that we have to come to a rational decision about the perfective value of many of our properties. One of our perfective capacities is the capacity of self-knowledge and revision. This is also a typical part of our being a complex entity. Activities and properties unsettling the construction of community, for example, cannot be part of our best perfective essence. Rape, torture and murder come out of human nature, but are not a part of our perfective centre as we generally would like it to be or to become. Through cognitive effort, emotional refinement, socialisation and enculturation we *normally* become beings with a developed moral competence. We could perhaps decide to destroy this competence. However, that would be irrational for humans to do. It would be all too damaging for the human species. Much of our other perfective capacities would then disappear, since, clearly, we need a context of morality to be capable of establishing many of our higher perfective states (in turn, we need numerous other perfective states and qualities, such as rationality, to be able to continue and enhance our morality).

Destructive species

Perfectionism (in response to the first critique) tends to present a positive story about perfecting ourselves as moral and perfective creatures. However, a second critique focuses on a darker side, which necessarily stays with and in us.

According to Feibleman (1970) mankind is a destructive and aggressive species. This is an essential and typical ingredient of human nature and is not something than can be cancelled. We have to cope with the fact that we are makers and destroyers, helpers and hurters. In war we quickly destroy what was patiently and creatively constructed during peacetime. Perfectionism tells only half and too beautiful a story. How have we arrived at a state of generalised aggression? Our original sense of aggression is connected with an organic response to obstacles and with the drive to install need-reduction. The more generalised human version of aggression is connected with the fact that we have learned to go beyond simple drive-reduction. We store more food than is necessary, for example. We seek security through aggrandisement. Such behaviour implies larger circles of aggressive response (expansion of our territory) and larger opportunities for aggressive response (effective instruments, technology). Subsequently, we find ourselves driven into a sedentary life, with an accompanying frustration of the need for aggression. Frustration boil up and leads to destructive acts in which we try to recover something of our primal experience with resistances. Underneath our civilised being, aggression will continue to ramify.

The ubiquity of war, massacre, and so forth prevents the formulation of an easy response. However, Feibleman himself is quite interested in a moral outcome. First of all, it is necessary to underline the constructive and destructive aspects of aggression: 'Leave out the aggressiveness, then expect no achievement; leave in the aggressiveness, then count on more destruction' (*ibid.*: 121). Furthermore, the moralisation of mankind should be intensified by the development of constructive substitutes for our negative aggressive needs. As Russell once suggested (quoted in *ibid.*: 122), one should provide rivers with rocky and dangerous rapids near to large cities, so that our need for challenge can be satisfied. The fact remains, thus, that as humans it is better to have communal and positive creation in a moral context, rather than to passively permit destructive drives — drives that will not disappear — to direct most of our destiny. Peace is better and more functional than war. The fact that we as yet cannot fully live up to this functional ideal does not invalidate the ideal as such.

Feibleman's narrative includes the significant possibility of moralising mankind; we need, as much as possible, to redirect our aggressive inclinations (Freud's sense of sublimation comes to mind). Redirection is a form of perfecting our nature as it now is. Hurka makes a complementary point (1993: 48-49). Humans have emerged from natural selection. To succeed in surviving a species must be aggressive. Hence, one could argue that perfective naturalism should come to celebrate our aggression. But for Hurka the origin of a species, its evolutionary explanation (which includes reference to aggression), is never a confirmation of its present behaviour (furthermore, organisms also survive through other things than attack or aggression — for example, through blending in the environment). Humans have other options than those included in its earlier organic past.

The issue of redirection — of revising ourselves in some of our urges — leads to a perhaps paradoxical version of perfective naturalism, Part of human nature, its underlying aggression, is to be redirected on the basis of other parts of our human nature, namely our capacities for revision, rationality and morality.

No basic list of properties

One could bring up the point that the list of perfective capacities and performances in humans is too large to be able to arrive at a fair list of nontrivial properties. In athletics bodily powers are realised to the full. Fine, but it is not clear whether abilities to slide and dribble are serious expressions of essential human physiological systems (see Kitcher 1999). Think about those who are able to eat vast amounts of food. Do they thereby perhaps confirm the efficiency of their digestive systems? What then should be included and what not?

It is important to distinguish between general properties and qualities, and particular actions and performances. It is clear that particular athletic and sportive skills, such as the ability to dribble, do not belong to essential human nature. One can be fully human without playing soccer. These particular capacities are situated on the cultural level of human practices. Nonetheless, it is so that skills of many different kinds are positive expressions of important and essential human physiological properties and capacities. Sport celebrates our bodily and practical way of being. Something physically splendid occurs (Hurka 1993: 39). Dribbling as such is not an essential perfective function for human beings, but being involved in bodily skills (dribbling or playing soccer being a fine example of such involvement) on the basis of our organic constitution is definitely part of what we normally are and wish to be. Eating vast amounts of food (unless in response to very hard physical labour) is never a positive expression of the powers of our digestive system. It rather implies a process of physical and perhaps psychological perfective degradation. Our bodily powers are not realised in a proper way, but are stretched to unnecessary limits. Particular capacities should be included in perfective naturalism only if productive for our survival and quality of human life, and they should be included as worthwhile options, not as obligatory demands (unless we are confronted with more fundamental capacities — they straightforwardly have a position within perfective naturalism's essential content)

Monotonous proposal

There is a worry that perfective naturalism tends to propose too determinate a specification of what it is to be a good human being (Hursthouse 1999: 211). This does not cohere with the fact that each person is in some way 'an apparent violation of the syntax of the species' (Allport 1955: 19). We are not perfective copies of each other. This critique addresses the monotonous drive behind classical perfectionism.

Perfective naturalism for humans in contemporary fashion does not in any way suggest a monotonous portrayal of human life — far from it. Cultural and personal differentiation and particularisation is itself a basic human property. Perfectionism, as Donald Walhout points out,

> maintains unambiguously that there is a meaning and standard of good applicable to everyone, but that the content of the good in concrete existence varies with every individual according to his unique capacities, so that while there may be many common aspects in the good, it may also be radically diverse' (1978a: 13).

Each human life embodies to some degree an individual perfective scenario. It is clear that human persons do not lead a general human existence. The basic content of perfective naturalism does not prevent a constructive response to the more individualised question of personal fulfilment. Possibilities of human nature depicted in perfective naturalism can be satisfied in many valid ways.

No human invariances

Another critical argument against perfective naturalism focuses on the historico-cultural dimensions of human existence. Joseph Margolis claims that 'human beings have no essential nature, are only what they are historically formed to be or to be capable of making of themselves' (1996: 191). Changeably constituted by our changing cultural history we must conclude, so Margolis argues, that there are no proper human invariances:

The deeper point is that we guess at those invariances we believe to be the best candidates for genuine invariances; and we invariably settle for those that, in some limited span of the flux, manage to remain reasonably intact (1989: xxii).

In this view, our perfections and human properties are only interpretative fictions. Changeability and plurality prevent the idea of a stable human perfective nature.

Joseph Margolis himself, however, suggests something of another reading concerning the continued desirability of certain human properties when he writes:

> Persons are the primary agents who use and make and affect changes in language, art, history, and the like — they are the primary bearers of culture; in fact, they function as such agents because they have, possess, understand, and learn how to use language, traditions, practices, institutions that, as the agents they are, they do not actually make or institute from a condition originally deprived of such resources. They are and function as cultural agents because they are the bearers of cultural powers (*ibid.*: 201).

These cultural powers, thus, are quite important. Margolis underestimates the perfective implications of his reference to such powers in persons. It is not the point that rationality and other robust competences cannot be taken away from us (history gives and takes, so to speak), but rather that, when these powers would indeed disappear, it can still be argued that it would be far better to have been able to keep than not to keep those powers. It is far better to be able to write than not to write. This is an embedded, situated claim, but nonetheless a reasonable one belonging to the framework of an evolutionary hermeneutics. What is 'invariant', then, is not the continued actual presence of a power (although many powers are with the human race for quite a long time, beyond 'some limited span of the flux'), but rather the continued positive perfective estimation of certain powers and properties.

A rational perspective

We may conclude that our response to critical arguments against perfective naturalism for humans confirms a substantial number of general and individual properties and perfective qualities, which can be picked out in a nontrivial way. In this way perfectionism can be presented as a rational anthropological perspective. The language of perfection does not drop in from nowhere, but is grounded in the history of the human organism.

CHAPTER NINE —
HUMAN PERFECTIVE EXISTENCE — ii:
PERSONAL PERFECTION

> *Il ne nous est pas donné de vivre une*
> *première vie, à l'essai, pour apprendre*
> *comment vivre. Pour chacun de nous*
> *l'apprentissage de l'existence se confond*
> *avec l'existence*
>
> — René Le Senne

Perfective naturalism installs a *general* scenario for the interpretation and formation of human lives. It plays a fundamental role in underlining the positive role of different perfective capacities and developmental possibilities. However, as concrete selves we do not live in a general way. We are not perfective copies of each other. The question of personal perfection or personal perfective existence lies embedded in that of perfective naturalism but requests explicit attention. As John Kekes points out, the idea of human nature sets necessary requirements that any reasonable conception of a good perfective human life must meet, but meeting them is not sufficient for reaching an actual form of the good life (1995: 18).

In this chapter I will, briefly, list a few aspects of personal perfective existence. I do not aim to provide a systematic exploration (the concrete formation of human life stories is a very complicated issue to handle), however I do hope my remarks will shed some light on human perfection as something that is essentially played out on the level of individual being.

Particularity

It is obvious that each human self is born in a particular place and culture. This immediately sets each of us on a particular path of perfection and imperfection. The general conception of human nature itself includes reference to the fact that it is exactly a universal rule of being human that one is born in a particular setting (on cultural particularity, see Geertz 1973). As particular cultural beings we are bound to predominantly invest our energy in the available stock of perfective possibilities. Some selves may enter into dialogue with other cultures — through travel, personal contacts, scholarly study, and so on — and thereby meet opportunities for transforming and transcending one's stock of

available perfective options. The enlargement or transformation of human perfective possibility constitutes an individual variable too — some are capable of
it, others are not. It depends, not only on the culture and family in which one
is born and in which one lives, but also on underlying inclinations and traits as
well as on coincidental and unforeseen events that happen to pass by.

Freedom

Freedom is an essential aspect of human existence as depicted in perfective
naturalism. A comparison with other organisms reveals that human beings
have a wider set of options concerning alternative direction and creative
response. We can confront a plurality of values and perspectives, and develop
in innovative ways. Our confrontations, alternatives, innovations, and developments suggest the presence of an optionalist surplus. We have deeper capacities
of detachment, anticipation, revision, and rational decision. These capacities
contribute to a principal sense of human freedom.

The issue of freedom introduces individual behaviour and perfection in two ways.

First, it turns out that we can be more and less free. The relative freedom of
self-perfection is an acquired freedom. As Gordon Allport stresses:

> A person who harbours many determining tendencies in his neuropsychic system
> is freer than a person who harbours few. Thus a person having only one skill,
> knowing only one solution, has only one degree of freedom. On the other hand, a
> person widely experienced and knowing many courses of conduct has many more
> degrees of freedom (1955: 85).

Human variability in the degree of freedom may be considered a main factor
in human perfective existence. My personal quality of freedom is not exactly
like yours.

Second, the freedom to select and to choose implies that I will opt for one
thing and that you might opt for something quite different. The relative freedom of decision steers our personal perfective (and non-perfective) life course.
Present and future stages in our existence are to a more than substantial degree
determined by the free decisions we have taken in earlier stages.

Individualisation, level differentiation, and specialisation
of perfective capacities

Many of our perfective properties and capacities, not only freedom, are destined
to personally differ in terms of individualisation, level of performance, and specialisation.

136

A very simple skill will perhaps be similar in most of us, but the more complex capacities — think of the virtues — will show significant variation of personal content, due to our individual histories of being and experience. The experience and development of courage, for example, is likely to be perfectively individualised in at least a few particles of our affective, mental or active system. We all carry our own aretaic colours. My courage will not be the same as yours. There is an aretaic *idios*, an irreducible singularity of aretaic selfhood (on idiotic singularity, see Desmond 1995b: 55-101). Personal virtue is, thus, a matter of individualisation of a generally available capacity. We expect members of our society to possess the virtue of honesty, but we do not expect them to possess honesty in exactly the same manner.

Besides individualisation, perfective capacities are also personalised or differentiated in the degree or level of performance. As is the case with freedom, we do not reach perfective states on one and the same level. Some are really gifted, while others will only pass a test of competence with minimal scope. One person possesses a skill to a fair degree, while another will possess the same skill on a good or an excellent level. Western thought often speaks in terms of black and white, of having or not having, but with regard to perfective states and capacities it is clear that we must rather install a fuzzy logic capable of addressing the many gradational states between possessing and not possessing a perfective competence.

Finally, we should also refer to the personal implications of specialised perfection. A person may, for example, possess the perfection of musicality. However, this perfection will not be one of a so-called general musicality but one of concrete musical ability, directed towards classical music or jazz or both or towards some other musical disciplines, but not to every possibility at once. It is very likely that there will be further specialisation — musicality applied to certain composers or to particular musical schools. Musicality typically functions as specialised perfection. This is the case with most, if not all, forms of cultural perfection. Without specialisation one would never becomes a master in anything. The issue of specialisation constitutes a distinct source of personalised perfective behaviour and performance.

The objective and the subjective view

The contemporary self lives with two perspectives, which cannot be brought into a coherent togetherness, the objective and the subjective view. The tension between these views constitutes a further distinct personal challenge.

The objective view is 'a standpoint so removed from the perspective of human life that all we can do is to observe, nothing having value of the kind it appears to have from the inside' (Nagel 1986: 209). Indeed, 'from far enough outside my birth seems accidental, my life pointless, and my death insignificant' (*ibid.*: 209). In fact, there is no reason why human beings and their form of life should ever have existed. Each of us (potentially) has the capacity to realise that he or she is only a tiny, coincidental point in an infinitely vast universe. Simply looking at the stars at night may be enough to realise this capacity.

In itself the objective view cancels the issue of human perfection. Stories of human and personal perfection do not matter in an infinite cosmos that does not care about our little involvements.

However, humans are also unavoidably focused on the subjective view. It lies in the nature of the human organism to be concerned with its own existence, quality, and survival. In the subjective view, from the inside, 'my never having been born seems nearly unimaginable, my life monstrously important, and my death catastrophic' (*ibid.*: 209). Our life history, what we have experienced, what we do and have accomplished, is highly significant for us. We cannot help experiencing pleasure, satisfaction, happiness, and self-fulfilment. Simply being who we are is enough to have a deep subjective experience of self-mattering. Clearly, the idea of perfective striving and performance only makes sense in the context of a subjective view.

But the real point here is not so much to highlight the link between personal perfective experience and the subjective view — this is a very visible link — but to specifically underline the personal implications of the thematic tension between the objective and subjective view.

According to Thomas Nagel we should indeed realise that both the subjective and objective views have a positive existential and perfective role to play. Each is a vital part of us. A concern with only one view will lead to a pathological state of being. Exactly their difficult pairing produces a psychological ground for a balanced form of humility between nihilistic objective detachment and blind subjective self-importance (*ibid.*: 222). One could add that we also find a ground for a balanced form of personal ambition — an ambition softened by the insight that there is a vast universe beyond our little personal space; an ambition strengthened by the insight that, no matter how vast and anonymous the universe, we cannot escape the challenge to creatively respond to our self-concern.

It can be expected that each person will have to deal with the difficult togetherness of the objective and subjective view in a particular manner. There is no rule to follow, besides the basic point that both views should somehow be given their due. At certain moments in time, surely, the activation of the objective view will have a sobering effect on how we care to lead our life, focused as we often are on little and even futile concerns. At other moments we may feel gloriously happy that we are embedded in a specified perfective enterprise. This may help us to get through life in a meaningful way, thereby providing a fortunate axiological shelter from the impersonal cosmos in which all efforts seem so useless from the start.

A life worth living

In our times we do not anymore play according to rule that there is an ultimate and fixed state for all. Agnes Heller writes:

> The modern person does not receive the destination, the telos, of his or her life at the moment of birth as happened in pre-modern times. We enter the world as a cluster of possibilities without telos (1998: 5).

Existential teleological perfection (see chapter 6) is not predetermined; it is in part a matter of 'existentialist' decision, imagination, and effort. The complexity of our nature, as established in the argument of perfective naturalism, makes it possible for us to prize a variety of goods and perfections and to order them in different ways, and this opens the way for substantial variety. We nowadays accept many valid conceptions of a good life. Numerous teleological directions and worthy opportunities propose themselves, notably in the context of practices (see chapter 10).

This means that no one can, without inflicting existential damage to oneself, turn a blind eye to the question: What kind of life is worth living for me? Not that we should all become systematic psychologists or philosophers of existence, but it seems highly unlikely in our time — with its ambiguities, conflicts, complications, and possibilities — that human existence without any degree of reflection on, and concern with, perfective value and direction could produce a very satisfying way of being.

The question of a worthy life, and our response to it, is a deeply personal issue.

First, each human self is likely to experience a gradational movement from existential coincidence towards personal necessity. In response to particular possibilities, experiences, situations, relations, and events there will be for each of us a relevant conception, or a smaller set of relevant conceptions, of 'a life that succeeds' (Bühler 1969). We select and opt for certain directions and projects. Doing so, we ultimately give up numerous possibilities. One could say that 'every decision is like a murder, and our match forward is over the stillborn bodies of all our possible selves that will never be' (R. Dubos, quoted in Koestler 1975: 708). The personal question of a good life finds itself in part 'solved' by interpretative self-knowledge about what we already are and have become (a young adult, for example, cannot totally reinvent himself; he must take into account an identity that already exists).

Second, the question of the meaning of life constitutes itself a personal variable. Some will only deal with this question in an unconscious manner. Others will explicitly probe the point and purpose of their life. Some will only relate to this question when most things have already passed by, namely in the final phase of life. Others will be smart enough to deal with this question in the earlier and middle segments of existence (obviously, the most effective role of an evaluative reception of oneself is played out in the context of an ongoing life, when it is still possible to redirect and revise things; when the direction of value, perfection, and meaning matters in a most vital way).

Third, it is not automatically so that an individual, after considering the question of a worthy or good life, will decide to follow the way of perfection. One may, for example, opt for hedonism or capitalism. Many of us will never come to read a treatise in perfectionism, will even resist perfective philosophy altogether. Of course, perfectionism hopes that a plain self — whether he or she has read perfectionist literature or not — will, more often than not, come to lead a life that is significantly defined by implicit perfective concern (according to the later MacIntyre plain selves are spontaneous proto-Aristotelians). However, such a development is never guaranteed. In our social environment we cannot fail to meet a myriad of perfective and non-perfective selves, of maximising and non-maximising perfective selves, and so on.

Unity and flexibility

For a complex perfectionism the central aim is to weave a life story that is healthy and liveable (Kenyon & Randall 1997). The idea of a maximally unified life story — with its almost deadening sense of coherence — does not fit in with normal existential complexity. One author notes:

> When I try to imagine maximal integration I find myself imagining something either desperately simple or intolerably suffocating. I picture new strands of stories with unforeseeable implications being smothered to avoid potential conflict or threat; I picture tired stories being dutifully tended and maintained because they are integral to the existing plot (Walker 1998: 121).

To be sure, important segments of unity and coherent fields of concern and stability are necessary in any successful perfective life (there is also the basic fact of organic unity). Radical fragmentation simply does not provide sufficient opportunity for worthy projects of perfection to develop (such projects take time, often stretch over many years, and may need explicit planning). Unity is, thus, a very relevant standard. But it is certainly not the only one.

The relevant level of unity is strongly dependent on the particular perfective situation of a person. Bob Dylan's life, for example, lacks overall unity. But the best possible perfective option for him, given his talents, seems not to have been a life organised as a firm unity (Hurka 1993: 140). Dylan has created meaning and original perfection according to other perfective standards, such as richness and creativity.

140

Different relevant applications of perfective standards can be expected to arise for each individual.

Existential and moral being

An existential perfectionism is inclined to strongly focus on self-perfection, on what we can personally accomplish. However, perfective theory knows well enough that both the dimensions of personal and moral being must have a say. An individual life of personal perfection can only emerge through the moral and contributive labour of numerous others — moral being is a fundamental source of personal perfective being. Consequently, radical self-realisationism is not a rational option. We all must activate a level of moral concern and activity. This is an elementary perfective obligation, without which human community would deteriorate

Between the poles of radical egoism and total self-sacrifice a life of personal perfection is to be carved out. Certain of those lives will carry deeper and more regular moral opportunities than others. For some, moral being will indeed be a deep part of one's personal career (a nurse's role, for example, involves a much higher degree of moral experience than the perfective life of a gardener). Serving the needs of others can, in fact, be a source of personal satisfaction — this is a point highlighted in the ethic of care movement. For others, self-actualisation will not have a direct moral tone (it can be assumed that a concert pianist is intensely concerned with his or her own quality of performance and musical perfection). However, it is also true that perfective self-development may provide perfective benefits beyond oneself; it can have a positive effect on the community at large. Self-perfection is not automatically non-moral or anti-moral. In fact, stubborn failure to develop one's basic and higher perfections is bound to oblige others to come to our aid — this failure is immoral.

We can conclude that perfective persons will be characterised by moral concern in different degrees and according to different qualities. There is a minimal level of moral duty to which everyone ought to adhere (law and basic moral being), but beyond that level we also discover a fertile, differentiated field in which moral perfection can be an original form of personal perfection (Gandhi) and in which strong personal perfection may possess an extended communal value (Mozart).

Perfective democracy

Finally, the question of personal perfection automatically leads to the question of perfective democracy.

If a plurality of personal perfections is what we need to accept, respect, protect, and stimulate, then democracy presents itself as the best communal option. To be sure, democracy will always constitute an imperfect instrument for dealing with problems of perfection and imperfection, but in its imperfection it is likely to be still the most productive political constellation available to deal fairly and constructively with pluralities and problems of individual and communal need, personal striving and moral demand. Democracy beyond perfective minimalism should be concerned with the creation of perfective opportunity (without falling into the hands of elitism and dogmatism). A perfectionism characterised by democracy may give guidance to a democracy characterised by perfection (and vice versa).

Perfective democracy is likely to accept Bertrand Russell's plea that in society there must be ample scope for 'constructive activity' (1960: 250). Russell's sense of constructiveness thematically anticipates a later proposal, namely that of MacIntyre's sense of perfective practice.

In the next chapter we will direct our attention to the issue of constructiveness in perfective practices.

CHAPTER TEN —
HUMAN PERFECTIVE EXISTENCE — iii:
PERFECTION IN PRACTICE

We are more real when all our energies are focused,
our attention riveted, when we are alert,
functioning completely, utilizing our (valuable) powers.

— Robert Nozick

Having obtained a perfective language of perfection, and a perfective natural-
istic and personalistic framework, it is now proper to focus on perfective being
in the distinct context of practices as defined in MacIntyre (1981).

There is an intimate connection between perfective and practical being.
Practices are the central ingredients in any culture of perfection. A closer study
of the life of practice will take us to the place where many of our most subtle
perfective appraisive judgements are produced, where the general framework
of perfective naturalism for humans is translated into the personal ways of significant perfective existence, and where human satisfaction and happiness are
likely to emerge to the fullest.

Existence within practices constitutes the most adequate and continuous
source for human perfective development and accomplishment. A good human
life, personally as well as morally, is in large part defined by active involvement in perfective practice. Keeping this in mind, I will in this chapter analyse
and extend MacIntyre's concept of a practice. My aim is to walk in the direction of a fundamental perfective praxiology, which manages to highlight the
cultural and perfective importance of practices.

In a preliminary step, before undertaking our analysis, it is good to underline the difference between MacIntyre and Polish praxiology as worked out in
the thought of Kotarbinski (1963) and his followers. Kotarbinski's praxiological theory is concerned only with techniques of efficient work and action, with
maximum effectiveness and economy. One does not find any constructive reference to the aretaic and moral dimensions of practical being. Effectiveness and efficiency may even come to oppose moral and aretaic capacities. As Kotarbinski
states:

> The tasks of praxiology are by no means identical with those of ethics, since emo-
> tional evaluations in general and moral evaluations in particular are not involved.
> What is more, praxiological truths are a source of ethical uneasiness, since the
> mode of action most likely to succeed is frequently at odds with the immediate
> reaction of noble feelings (1983: 29).

We should, of course, not resist effectiveness and efficiency. These standards are legitimate ingredients in any perfective accomplishment. The point is, however, that isolated attention to effectiveness and efficiency disrupts the full and varied perfective content of practical experience. We need efficient, effective practices, to be sure, but an authentic practice also includes other standards — moral, aretaic, and creative standards. Effectiveness means nothing without further teleological orientation, without deeper perfective experience.

Kotarbinski offers testimony to an influential modern view on the idea of practical being — a view we also find exemplified in Taylorism (and Fordism). Kotarbinski, not surprisingly, mentions Taylor's views on scientific management as a primordial version of praxiology.

The cardinal difference between Kotarbinski and a rich perfective sense of practice immediately shows itself in MacIntyre's definition of a practice as

> any coherent and complex form of socially established cooperative human activity through which goods internal to that form of activity are realised in the course of trying to achieve those standards of excellence which are appropriate to, and partially definitive of, that form of activity, with the result that human powers to achieve excellence and human conceptions of ends and goods involved, are systematically extended (1981: 175).

In the following I will constructively and critically consider different implicit and explicit points in MacIntyre's definition. Note: in line with the perfective framework of chapter 5, I will automatically drop MacIntyre's reference to (standards of) excellence and substitute (standards of) perfection for it.

Being active

A first general point to underline is MacIntyre's overall sympathy for the active self as a perfective figure. While the meaning of contemplation is certainly not foreign to his thought, he explicitly breaks open classical perfectionism and its focus on the philosophical way of contemplative being. There are many ways to reach a valid form of perfective existence. The self of perfection can be involved in different projects relating to a wealth of activities — intellectual, physical, familial, sportive, occupational, or otherwise. Personal fulfilment consists in doing things of value.

We may expand MacIntyre's sense of active being with different suggestions.

We are naturally built to act, to transform things, and to spend our energies in different ways. Our life of action is basically connected with our organic way of being. We have to actively respond to things. Enduring stillness is not an option for us (significant moments of spiritual contemplation, valid in their own setting, cannot cancel the organic duty as well as the psychological necessity to act).

It is simply good to be enterprising with regard to activity. In fact, as long as we do not act, we do not know ourselves. To remain sincere, intention has to throw itself into execution (Blondel 1973: 187). Only through action does value become more than an idea. The perfective good is largely active: to achieve it one must do things (Hurka 1993: 57). Activity constitutes the road from promise to perfected selfhood; things need to be undertaken. We do not find people becoming qualified in medicine only by thinking about it; one becomes a physician only through a continuous process of activity characterised by failure, development, setbacks, and achievement. Human accomplishment requires the workings of acquired perfection, and acquired perfection implies effort. Moreover, to have acted does not dispense one from acting again. There is no radical perfective retirement from being active in one way or another. A deterioration of perfective selfhood is often caused by lack of effort and initiative. Sustained lack of action is ultimately bound to take away levels of acquired perfection and to result in a deterioration of spontaneous organic perfection, mental as well as physical.

While on the one hand significant moments of rest (and tranquility) are needed, certainly in our nervous world, one can on the other hand appreciate MacIntyre's praxiology as a critique of contemporary forms of passive selfhood. More and more, we run the risk of turning into the passive observers of electronic recordings of distant events. Often we do not find it anymore in us to respond to events in the world by way of active engagement. To some degree the contemporary Western self has lost its sense of initiative. In my opinion one may propose the idea of practice as a perfective means to become more active again.

In another way, however, MacIntyre exactly criticises a current manner of 'feeling active' — not unlike Erich Fromm, who notes:

> Our whole culture is geared to activity — activity in the sense of being busy. The trouble is that most people who think that they are very active are not aware of the fact that they are intensely passive in spite of their 'busyness'. They constantly need the stimulus from the outside, be it other people's chatter, or the sight of movies, or travel and other forms of more thrilling consumption excitements (1971: 13).

This critique, of course, does not contradict the perfective stress on being active. The point is to be active in an *authentic* sense.

Practical existence plays a strong role in the formation of concrete human identity. Only in particularised and meaningful settings, such as practices, may we begin to build up a significant life course. Flourishing human lives are in large part defined by involvement in activities of a certain kind, namely activities in which one discovers and seeks to fulfil original perfective opportunity. An important way through which people find meaning in their lives is by becoming deeply involved in activities that afford them scope and depth. Practices offer such engagement in a nontrivial manner. Allowing us opportunities for the realisation of perfective depth and wholeness, practices can be regarded as islands of perfective fulfilment. Finding meaning and direction in life is not only a matter of receiving and producing perfective qualities in complex actions and in special domains, but also of choosing one way rather than another. Practices permit us to specialise. Without them we run the risk of will becoming formless and of not achieving distinction in action. This is important. One has to choose between trying

> to partake of all that is good, but at the price of not being able to master anything, or to be in full possession of a limited number of excellences while benefiting from the presence of what other men produce. If we are not to be dilettantes or poetasters we cannot do better than to take the second of these alternatives (Weiss 1967c: 142).

Obviously, not everything in human life is, or should be, a matter of practice and complex action. A large part of human existence is spent in simple routine activities — sleeping, washing up, going to work, cleaning the house, and paying the bills. Some of those simple activities may be part of a practice, but many others stand on their own and do not really seem to belong to practices. Returning home from work we sit and rest in a chair without wanting to do anything. Waking up, we may lie in bed, not yet getting up. We are then not sitting or lying in order to achieve something in terms of practice (Tatarkiewicz 1976: 99). The point in human existence is to have sufficient presence of authentic practical involvement; it is not possible, nor desirable, to be completely embedded in practice each and every minute of the day.

Practical plurality

A second point to bring up as an essential factor is the plurality of practices. We need to install a praxiological perfectionism based on a diversity of fertile perfective practices.

Contemporary perfectionism forcefully reacts against classical contemplative perfectionism. There are numerous human achievements beyond contemplation. The perfective good permits many kinds of content (Hurka 1993: 167). Contemporary perfective praxiology, in the style of MacIntyre, breaks through the classical distinction between *poeisis* on the one hand, and *praxis/theoria* on the other. Forms of making, too, can constitute activities with worthy intrinsic perfective ends. MacIntyre confirms a sense of praxiological plurality. He underlines that contemplation is one (interpretative) practice or craft among others (MacIntyre 1990: 61-62). Philosophy is a craft among crafts, a cognitive master-craft perhaps, but a craft nonetheless; it is social practice embedded in and reflective upon other forms of social practice. And as practice or craft, philosophy shares properties with other practices such as fishing and furniture making. Practices are intrinsically worthy of admiration. They are worth doing in themselves because they confirm

146

and extend human powers in an original way. Think of being active in the practical settings of farming, fishing, architecture, music, chess, and so forth.

An important point is, on the one hand, to let all practices be and not to focus on playing them out against each other. Principally, it is important to recognize that the practice of a Zulu dance is no less fully human than the practice of Russian ballet (Plamenatz 1975: 353). Each fulfils a different combination of perfective standards, On the other hand, however, we must insist on the differences between practices. Each practice is characterised by deeply unique experiences, qualities and goods. The competence and inclination of individual selves will determine which practices come closest in meeting one's best powers and deepest ambitions. Practical destinies are created in the course of our experiences and activities.

In our praxiological scheme the following quote of Martha Nussbaum — which stretches things a bit too far — should be qualified:

> I really do not understand very well the language of higher and lower functionings that the perfectionist tradition glibly endorses; 1 understand that certain types of scientific ability are worthy of public support because society needs them; but that they are higher and more intrinsically valuable than the activity of a farmer, or a mother, or a sweeper of the streets, smacks to me of casteism and elitism, and I don't buy it. I think that there is a way of doing all these functions that include capabilities for sociability and practical reason (2000: 129).

This is a generous view, in part confirming MacIntyre's plurality of practice, but I think it is difficult to deny that even while a sweeper of streets may find some psychological (and moral) satisfaction in his or her activity, it remains very unclear how the work of cleaning up the streets can be organised according to standards of complex perfective practice. No complex achievements are available it seems to me, even when there may be some room for sociability and practical reason. With Nussbaum I think we should indeed walk beyond perfectionist contemplative elitism, but it is not fruitful to throw ourselves in the hands of a radical equality of activities without any sense of distinction and evaluative differentiation. Cleaning up the streets is for most people not an intrinsically rewarding job (which is not to say that streets ought not to be cleaned up — there are numerous intrinsically uninteresting activities that need to be done; perhaps they should be justly divided among citizens). Not every activity can be or become a practice.

Practical togetherness

Practices constitute structural versions of human togetherness. The dimensions of cooperation and sociality are essential.

In most practices we work and interact with others. Or we have, at least, in the past interacted with others in the development of our practical expertise — this is true even for the loneliest artist. And one is likely to continue to find renewed inspiration exactly in interaction with other artists and the public. The practical self is a social figure and practice, typically, is a social union (Rawls 1999: 460). Standards of practice are socially developed. Individual innovations and deviations are in communal context accepted, popularised, revised or rejected.

Beyond intra-practical sociality, each kind of practice needs help from, is influenced by, or contributes itself to other practices (inter-practical sociality). Literary paradigms, for example, have crossed over from novels to plastic art and vice versa. The practices of fishing and farming make it possible for others to give a more prolonged attention to their own complex projects. Some practices are specifically subordinated to the ends of other practices. Think, for example, of the relation between the pharmaceutical and medical practices.

Another socializing dimension of practice lies in its effect on the moral and social qualities of human persons. Practices are forms of social life destined to produce practical selves with abilities of moral and social perfection. One acquires practical reason through involvement in practices, which impose norms and hereby break through the circle of self-desire. Practices are, thus, a source for 'reworked desires' (MacIntyre 1998b: 121). For example, a good hockey-player playing in a team will not hesitate to pass to another member better placed to score instead of only seeing his own, more limited opportunity. The practical self learns in such context to go beyond its own perspective (MacIntyre 1988a: 140-141). Lack of immersion in practice will have severe consequences for perfective selfhood:

> To cut oneself off from shared activity in which one has initially to learn obediently as an apprentice learns, to isolate oneself from the communities which find their point and purpose in such activities, will be to debar oneself from finding any good outside oneself (MacIntyre 1981: 240).

One other important form of perfective togetherness concerns the principle of complementary perfection (Norton 1976: 10). The true artist will see other artists not as hostile competitors, but as contributors to his or her own development (Kamenka 1963: 111). The best in a person, notably within practices, is supposed to bring out the best in others (Hurka 1993: 176). Moreover, persons with different complementary qualities, focused on different role demands, can reach special degrees of perfective cooperation. Think, for example, of the accomplishment of cooperative activity within fishing crews, string quartets and teams of research scientists (MacIntyre 1998d: 240).

Historicity, rationality, progression, authority

A practice implies historical process, rationality, progression, and authority.

First, the practical self participates in a larger narrative, which has been going on before his or her entrance and which will continue afterwards: 'Every craft has a history and characteristically a history not yet completed' (MacIntyre 1990: 127). Practical selves know themselves to be part of projects that extend from the past into the future in such a way that their own activity receives its significance from its contribution to those continued projects. Hence, the individual 'has to recognize him or herself as having a subordinate part, no matter how eminent, in the more than individual projects that constitute the practice' (*ibid.*: 29). Through its historical dimension a practice typically possess perfective depth.

Second, present standards of achievement within a practice are rationally justified exactly in their historical reference: 'To share in the rationality of a craft requires sharing in the contingencies of its history' (*ibid.*: 65). There is a critical, constructive, nontrivial process of reception and transformation of interpretation of ends, rules, standards, conflicts and future possibilities. The perfective rationality of this process lies in the fact that subsequent developments in a practice are considered and defended as improvements beyond earlier ambiguities, failures and defects.

Third, a sense of progression is, thus, essential for the formation of any healthy practice, which is hereby carried by a focus on the best. A deep understanding of any field of human activity involves an increasing revelation of degrees of perfection — to see as less perfect what we previously were prepared to accept as good (Murdoch 1971: 61). As MacIntyre states with regard to practical activities:

> The concept of the best, of the perfected, provides each of these forms of activity with the good toward which those who participate in it move. What directs them toward that goal is both the history of successive attempts to transcend the limitations of the best achievement in that particular area so far and the acknowledgement of certain achievements as permanently defining aspects of the perfection toward which that particular form of activity is directed (1988a: 31).

There are, in fact, two key perfective distinctions which apprentices especially have to learn to apply: between what merely seems good here and now and what is really good relative to us here and now, and between what is good relative to us here and now and what is unqualifiedly good (*ibid.*: 30). The togetherness of these two principles permits one to proceed towards a deeper and better conception of particular practical perfection.

Fourth, past achievement and future possibility constitute the two central poles of praxiological narrative. In such a narrative one is also confronted with the authority of the master who knows what the present standards are and should be, what earlier achievements include, how one can go on beyond what is now the case, and how one can inspire other participants to go further. The individual praxiological story of a participant starts with subordination and training, through development often taking years, arriving at significant moments of accomplishment, perhaps complicated by failures, stagnation and deviations, but also nourished by sudden improvements and creativity. One may end up being received as a master by others. In all cases, however, one remains a participant and, hence, continues to be subordinated in the more than individual project. Praxiological humility should never retreat, although praxiological pride, too, may play a constructive role.

Complexity

MacIntyre turns practice into a perfectively eminent concept. One other essential element contributing to the eminence of practice is its complexity.

Complex projects have more worth and dignity than others. A perfectionist will predominantly be interested in complex, difficult and significant actions, specifically in the context of projects characterized by substantial and original perfective opportunity. Paul Weiss states: 'The best activities are those which are internally variable and have an extended field of operation, for these allow a man's potentialities to be realized again and again' (1967c: 137). Difficult activities have a more elaborated teleology, more steps and sub-strategies (Hurka 1993: 123-125). There is complex subordination of ends and a greater extent (in chess, for example, one considers the whole board and an extended matrix of forces and possibilities). Activities that are complex, intricate and challenging stretch our capacities and satisfy our perfective needs. As Rawls puts it:

> Presumably complex activities are more enjoyable because they satisfy the desire for variety and novelty of experience, and leave room for feats of ingenuity and invention. They also evoke the pleasures of anticipation and surprise and often the overall form of the activity, its structural development, is fascinating and beautiful (1999: 374-375).

Throwing a ball with some skill is, thus, not a practice, while a game of soccer is. Planting turnips and bricklaying also fall outside the realm of practice, while farming and architecture can constitute authentic practices. Other examples of practice are painting, chess, the work of historians, the enquiries of physics, biology and chemistry, fishing, and the creation of family and community (MacIntyre 1981: 175). The range of practices, according to MacIntyre, is quite wide. Each of these practical enterprises implies a complex set of means, ends, goods, skills, virtues, challenges, demands, and opportunities for perfective development and social interaction. One may speak here of integrative practices characterised by teleo-affective structures comprising hierarchies of ends, tasks, projects, beliefs, emotions, moods, and the like (Schatzki 1996: 99).

A question concerning judgement about authentic complexity immediately arises. Some may argue that an activity such as bricklaying is a practice. Persons involved in bricklaying will themselves perhaps be inclined to sense a degree of complexity in their job. They will insist that 'outside opinion' concerning the simplicity of bricklaying is simply irrelevant; only bricklayers can really understand the complex subtleties of laying bricks. It is clear that one has to be careful here. The point is neither to underestimate nor to overestimate complexity. But the problem is, of course, that things are not always clear and stable. First, a certain project or activity may be on its way towards a complex practical structure (through inclusion of new challenges and possibilities) or it may be involved in a process of de-praxiologisation (through productionist mechanisation, for example). In other words, something may be complex now but not in a later period (and vice versa). Second, there is also the issue of particular context. In some cases, bricklaying appears to gain in complexity — namely in the context of restoring old and complicated buildings involving material, aesthetic and historical challenge. In other instances, however, it is hard to escape the perception of bricklaying as a rather simple activity. What remains here as an issue is whether the activity of bricklaying as such fundamentally gains in practical complexity or whether bricklaying rather stays what it is whereas the larger context of the restoration of old buildings offers a supplementary and distinct experience of complexity which, considered strictly, is not part of the bricklayer's direct content (but which belongs more to the challenges of other persons — think of architects, interior decorators, and art historians.

Let us note, finally, that a significant part of the complexity of a practice has to do with the activation of particularised, specialised and regionalised capacities, many of which resist full articulation in terms of explicit rules and propositional theoretical vision (the articulation of theory and regulation is itself a practical cognitive undertaking resisting a full reduction to theory and rules). Practical intelligence and concrete capacity resist easy and total translation into propositional knowledge:

> Many of us know how to ride a bicycle but lack the propositional knowledge of how that behavior is carried out. In contrast, many of us have propositional knowledge about how to make a soufflé without knowing how to carry this task through to successful completion (Gardner 1993: 68).

Polanyi refers to a sense of connoisseurship (1974: 54-55). The doctor's diagnostic skill, for example, is an art of doing as much as it is an art of knowing. It can only be communicated by example, in the course of experience and under the rule of a master. The aim of skilful performance is achieved by the observance of a set of rules which are not known as such to the person following them (*ibid.*: 49). Think of swimmers regulating their breathing. The way it happens is important, but most swimmers do so without knowing. There is a knowledge that is not formulated in rules. To be able to function we need non-reflective knowledge. A pianist should not be focused on his fingers otherwise he or she won't be able to play. There is a sense of non-articulative equilibrium within different practices (Gadamer 1993: 58). Think of tree-sawing, which in its older form is based on an internally unified configuration in which the movements of the two tree-cutters have fused to become, as it were, one single rhythmic flux of movement. Each practiced skill possesses something of the experience of equilibrium. We can also refer to the practitioner's reflection-in-action, which is a reflective conversation with a unique and uncertain situation (Schön 1983: 130). A practitioner tries to adapt the situation to a certain context through a web of moves. These moves produce unintended consequences and allow the situation to 'talk back'. Possessing a repertoire of examples, images, understandings, and so on, one can interpret a unique situation as similar to and different from other situations. This constitutes reflection-in-action, something that again resists summary in terms of well-defined rules.

The question of flow

It is relevant to compare MacIntyre's sense of complexity with Mihalyi Csikzsentmihalyi's influential theory of flow in activity (Csikszentmihalyi 1988). MacIntyre does not mention this element, but one may assume that it highlights an important psychological dimension found in the practices. However, the critical point is that flow seems to contradict the eminent position of complexity. We need to clarify the relation of flow and complexity.

A state of flow has to do with a match between capacity and activity and leads to vital engagement with the world. The universal condition of flow is that a person perceives a balance between challenge and skills. There is something to be done and one is capable of fluently doing it. This ultimately produces a sense of autotelic motivation, that is, the doing of something for its own sake. The goal is then the experience itself rather than future rewards or ends that lie further. The mountaineer, for example, does not climb in order to reach the top, but develops the project of trying to reach the summit in order to climb. Any form of action to which a skill responds can produce flow and autotelic experience.

This point appears to contradict MacIntyre's demand for complex action, since one can assume many simple activities to become autotelic (and therefore intrinsically valuable) by offering opportunities for flow. However, Csikszentmihalyi offers at least three supplementary points that bring the issue of flow again in the neighbourhood of complexity.

First, as a matter of fact, many of his examples do concern the experience in flow in the context of practices (he often refers to scientists and artists).

Second, flow cannot sustain itself for a longer while in all too simple activities. For Csikszentmihalyi every action might engender it, but at the same time no activity can sustain it for long unless both the challenges and the skills become more complex. An increase of complexity is a necessary condition of prolonged possibility of flow. More even, the experience of flow itself will constitute a new incentive for producing complexity, since to keep enjoying flow a person needs to find new challenges: 'The desire to keep enjoyment alive forces us to become more complex — to differentiate new challenges in the environment, to integrate new abilities into our repertoire of skills' (Csikzsentmihalyi et al. 1993: 15).

Third, Csikszentmihalyi's theory of flow and autotelic activity is situated in a larger eudaimonic framework of community, creativity and talent. Flow alone does not guarantee a happy life (Csikszentmihalyi 1999). It is perfectively important to find flow 'in activities that provide a potential for growth over an entire life span' (*ibid.*: 826). One may, for example, also find flow in activities that in the long run distract one from existential enjoyment and happiness — think of vandalism and gang fights.

We can conclude that the theory of flow on the one hand sheds light on autotelic experiences in simple activities that have not been covered in MacIntyre's theory — driving one's car, washing dishes, and so forth. This provides a valuable supplement. On the other hand, the theory of flow does confirm the role of complex activities in the development of human perfection, meaning, and happiness.

Levels of practical being

For the sake of thematic precision we need to distinguish between levels of practical being (MacIntyre does not address this issue).

There is first of all the concept of a practice (MacIntyre's definition). Second, there are the different kinds of practice, that is, the numerous projects and enterprises that are supposed to fall under the concept of practice (think, for example, of medicine, architecture, chess, portrait painting, and so forth). Third, although MacIntyre regards the criteria for the identity of practices as in important respects transcultural (1992: 19) — one can, for example, refer to European and Japanese painting as recognisable instances of the practice of painting — it is in my opinion relevant to, at least, include a level of the different cultural organisations of activities belonging to one and the same sense of practice. It is obvious that some of the internal goods of Japanese painting may be quite different from those of European painting (MacIntyre's point is that painters from different cultures can appropriate those other internal goods). A fourth level of practical being has to do with the organisation of a practice in the context of different movements and specialisations. This level is very visible in the artistic practices — think of the difference between the movements of impressionism and futurism; think also of the difference between portrait and landscape painting — but each practice is to a variable degree characterised by the presence of movements and specialisations. In a fifth step one may refer to the level of concrete, particular instances of a practice. This level is important, because some concrete instances will come closer to the authentic sense of practice (as established on the first conceptual level). For example, one medical office may exemplify the practice of medicine accurately while another instance in important aspects does not. It is possible that a particular medical office fails even to meet the minimal standards of practical being. One is then simply confronted with a simulacrum of practice, not with the real thing. The individual members of a concrete practice constitute a sixth level of practical being. Each individual is bound to play a smaller or larger role within a practice, and to perform in better or worse ways (role perfection). Different possibilities introduce themselves. One may be part of a real practical setting without being psychologically and morally in tune with the demands and goods of this setting. Or one may possess an authentic practical integrity, however in a (very) poor setting that hardly deserves to be called a practice.

Distinguishing between these levels of practical being is necessary to be able to discern certain possible perfective and imperfective tensions and to properly define what is exactly going on in a particular circumstance.

Internal goods

The soul of a perfective practice lies in its unique internal axiological structure. We need especially to refer to the presence of internal goods

An authentic form of a practice is defined by the presence of what MacIntyre calls internal goods. Every practice is complex, but not every complex activity constitutes a practice. Internal goods embody the most essential qualitative ingredient of practices. They are internal for different reasons (MacIntyre 1981: 176).

First, an internal good is only to be *fully* identified and recognised by the participating members of a practice. Those who lack such immersion are deemed to be less competent as judges of internal goods (however, I assume — although MacIntyre does not bring it up himself — that a good literary critic, while not himself a novelist, will manage to capture the concrete perfections and imperfections of a certain novel; he must somehow stand in close contact with important aspects of the practice of writing novels).

Second, an internal good can only be articulated and defined in terms of a specified practice and by means of examples from such a practice (or a very similar practice).

Third, an internal good can only be experienced and achieved within a particular practice. For example, one cannot concert the creative energy and quality of being typical for a painter (something that belongs to the internal axiology of the practice of painting) into the composition of an opera. The main point is that an internal good cannot be received outside a particular practice (with the exception of practices that are very similar and share some internal goods) (*ibid.*: 176). This implies, for example, that a new practice is destined to create new goods. Many original values are created and maintained in the social practices (Raz 1999: 204).

MacIntyre's analysis permits the articulation of at least four kinds of internal goodness (1981: 177).

There are first of all the achievements of perfection that exhibit human aesthetic, imaginative, intellectual, and physical powers at their highest. In line with MacIntyre it can be argued that these achievements of perfection refer to the presence of three kinds of internal goods — a) the perfective state of a product or a final result, b) the perfective state of certain means used in establishing the product or final result (a new technique or a refined method), and c) the perfective state of one's personal capacities that has been achieved while reaching for perfection of product/ result and of means (for example, strategic imagination, the achievement of a certain highly particular kind of analytic skill) (*ibid.*: 175).

Besides these three internal goods MacIntyre also refers to a certain particularised way of life within a practice. This constitutes a fourth type of internal good. A fisherman's life can only be experienced in depth in the context of a fisherman' s practice. The life of a painter implies a distinct and inimitable combination set of ends, challenges, strivings, interactions, experiences, possibilities, capacities, and emotional states (including flow). In chess or in a similar game we find the experience of a specific kind of competitive intensity (*ibid.*: 176). Each practice to a substantial degree introduces inimitable existential goodness.

One can connect the inimitable internal existential goodness of a practice with the dimension of axiological richness, that is, with the presence of 'mixed-value goods' (Raz 1999: 212). A good practice is constituted not by one value or standard, but by a complex and subtle togetherness of standards and values. For example, in the practice of dancing one may experience the togetherness of humour, particular environment, ingenuity, companionship, creativity, cultural particularity, and so on. Exactly the intermingling of these factors produces an existential internal good not to be found anywhere else.

For MacIntyre the internal goods are intrinsic values. As experiences of perfection they can and ought to be enjoyed for their own sake. They provide deep satisfaction and strongly contribute to experiencing one's life as being a happy one. Perfective praxiology include the enjoyment of hedonic experiences, but is essentially focused on delight in noble activities, that is, delight in activities that are undertaken for the sake of their intrinsic worth.

In such a context the human self is able to have invaluable experiences of 'personal expressiveness' (Waterman 1993). Stephen Darwall offers a fine illustration of this:

> I think of a photograph I clipped for the *New York Times* [...] It shows a pianist, David Golub, accompanying two vocalists [...] All three artists are in fine form excercizing themselves at the height of their powers. The reason I saved the photo, however, is Mr. Golub's face [...] When I look at the photograph of David Golub, I don't question that he appreciates the fineness of his playing, but I doubt that this is the main object of his delight. Rather, I imagine that what his smile primarily reveals is an appreciation of values that make music-making a noble pursuit — values like the beauty and power of the music he and his colleagues are creating, values that give music significance or worth (1999: 177-178).

One could argue, with reason, that there are practices that will include deeper opportunities for the experience of noble activity (science, art, sport), but any practice should include a degree of noble activity; otherwise we are confronted with a very serious lack of internal goodness, which could even bring us to cancel the application of the concept of a perfective practice to a particular enterprise.

Internal goodness also provides practices with the crucial element of objective impersonality. In practices it not a matter of individual decision to define something as a standard of internal goodness. It may take years even to be able to see and rationally discern what the authentic particularized perfective standards are within a practice and how they could be approached or adequately transformed. These standards will have to be personally appropriated. They will then become an intimate part of one's subjective way of being. Standards of perfection are, in this case, not enforced from without but come to constitute the innermost core of one's civilised life (Desmond 1990: 91).

Finally, internal goods are forms of common good (MacIntyre 1998d: 239). Different forms of internal good — for example, a new achievement or a new method — can be shared with everyone else, whereas an increase in external goods (power, for example) always means that someone else will have less of it. It is also the case that my practical performance does not prevent someone else from also performing in a practice. About this, Russell notes:

> A man who eats a piece of food prevents anyone else from eating it, but a man who writes or enjoys a poem does not prevent another from writing or enjoying one just as good or better (1977: 80).

Internal goods, consequently, are 'neither mine-rather-than-yours nor others'-rather-than-mine, but instead are goods that can only be mine insofar as they are also the goods of others' (MacIntyre 1999: 119).

External goods

MacIntyre also refers to another type of goods in practices, namely the external goods (MacIntyre 1981: 178). They are contingently related rewards that may derive from successful participation in any practice. Think especially of status, power, and richness. Those goods, typically, can also be received in different ways outside a practice; one can always find alternative means for achieving such goods. In other words, they can be objects of desire prior to and independently of desire for practical perfection.

External goods often are explicitly produced and experienced at the expense of internal goods. My dominant inclination towards profit will limit or even destroy my own sense of internal goodness and/or that of a person working for or with me. MacIntyre refers to a highly intelligent child who is tricked into learning chess and in attempting to win by being offered money for sweets as a reward. The external reward is a reason for the child to try to cheat (profit). However, after a while the child may discover and identify with internal goods specific to chess. The reasons for playing and winning will then change; attempts to cheat would only result in defeating oneself. It is clear, of course, that in many situations people — children as well as adults — simply continue to (predominantly) focus on external goods.

MacIntyre goes so far as to say that an immensely skilled chess player ranking with the grandmasters, but caring only about winning and about the external goods attached to winning, will not (anymore) be able to reach the internal goods of chess. The good of winning, and of the external goods attached to winning, can after all be received in many other games. Far less skilled players may even achieve the internal goods of chess much better than the immensely skilled player (MacIntyre 1984: 274).

Perhaps its is necessary here to qualify Macintyre's argument in some respects. It is unlikely that a highly skilled player can win without recognition of some degree of internal goods (certain achievements). It may also be the case that such a player will produce certain accomplishments that really belong to the realm of internal goodness, even while the player may not appreciate his own actual accomplishment in terms of internal goodness. Nonetheless, it can certainly be argued that he still plays a constructive role with regard to the perfective progression of a practice. It is also likely that such a grandmaster will still be able to recognize some aspects of internal goods, even if only in a context of axiological ambiguity and dissonance. The satisfaction attached to accomplishment in terms of internal goods will have faded, but not completely. It is a satisfaction to which, one day perhaps, he will able to return.

MacIntyre is not arguing that authentic practices should leave the realm of external goods behind. All is a matter of degree and hierarchy. External goods undeniably are a means for the protection and prolongation of practices. Structural concern with, and distribution of, external goods is to be organised in the contributive context of institutions (MacIntyre 1981: 181). Chess, medicine and physics are practices. Chess clubs, hospitals and universities are institutions. MacIntyre speaks about a single causal order between a practice and its structural institution. No practice can survive for long when not supported by an institutional context. In fact, an institution in very good working order is itself an instance of a practice (namely a form of practice involved in the making and sustaining of a practical community). If a practice needs an institution that properly deal with the handling of external goods (money, division of power, prestige and reward), an institution can in turn only remain perfectively healthy when connected in the right manner to the practice for which it has been created and organised in the first place.

All in all, MacIntyre continues to deeply distrust external goods and institutional being. Institutions are always a source of potential distortion of perfective practical being. Due to the institutional focus on external goods, a practice always runs the risk of being threatened in its authentic core. Ideals of practice are vulnerable to the acquisitiveness and corruptive power of institutions (*ibid.*: 182).

MacIntyre's distrust of external goods shows itself in his rejection of any perfective appreciation of financial management as an authentic practice. For MacIntyre financial management cannot withstand the magnetism of the external good of money — money is never a neutral object. There will always be a strong inclination in financial management to treat money as an end and not as a means. Money does in this respect not at all function like chess pieces that are simply used to achieve perfection in the game of chess. In my opinion MacIntyre exaggerates the situation. He should, at least, allow for the possibility of financial managers being involved in finance as a perfective practice. Think of financial managers working in an institution focused on a practice of helping the poor — the invention of a new technique of collecting money can then be appreciated as a fine internal good.

Kinds of practice

The question of financial practice introduces another issue, namely that of different kinds of practice. The main point to note, really, is that MacIntyre has not sufficiently responded to several questions.

It is clear that financial practice will provide another structural set of 'internal' perfective possibilities (and possibilities of deviation) than a purposive productive practice such as fishing or baking or medicine. It is not altogether clear whether finance belongs itself to the field of *productive* practices, which are defined in terms of material production — whether it be an object (fish, bread, etc.) or a state of affairs (health). Can money be regarded a material product or a state of affairs?

Subsequently, it is also not clear whether fishing, baking and medicine are purposive productive practices in exactly the same sense as the artistic practices (painting, architecture, poetry, literature, etc.) or the theoretical practices (sciences, philosophy, etc.). Surely, the production of bread or fish offers far less possibilities in terms of distinct internal goodness than a work of art or a new theoretical vision (bread is bread, now and forever — the opportunity for perfective experimentation seems limited). And the reaching of a state of health is strictly defined in terms of an established organic structure of a body, whereas an artist has much more space in which to manoeuvre.

There are also the self-contained practices. The value of these practices immediately lies in their doing as such, not in the accomplishment of a further end, product, or state of affairs. One can refer to playing music or sport.

Again, we are confronted with ambiguities. Most adult forms of sport and playing music constitute performative practices. Sport could then perhaps be regarded as being defined by an end beyond the activity of sporting, namely to entertain a public. And what is the point of music if not also to play for a public? Clearly, the aim to let others enjoy one's 'self-contained' practical performance is, to say the least, an important sub-ingredient of teleological consciousness. Moreover, do purposive practices like fishing, medicine, art, and philosophy not also essentially include activities that are done for their own sake (flow, the experience of complexity, the internal good of experiencing a certain life of activity, etc.)?

Finally, many practical involvements in society are undertaken in the context of occupational being. Is there a structural difference between occupational and non-occupational practices? One may assume that many of the productive practices will be part of the world of work. The artistic practices, perhaps, may be found more regularly outside the societally organised field of occupational being (the 'lonely' artist, van Gogh). However, if an artist is paid for his production can we not regard his activity as a form of work? What about the occupational status of the performative practices?

The relation between work and practice continues to bother MacIntyre in different ways. On the one hand, he confirms that we all need productive work and that unemployment is not a good thing (1979). On the other hand, he realises that most forms of contemporary work are organised as non- or anti-practices, due to the 'self-aggrandizing and self-protective attitudes and activities characteristic of developing capitalism' (MacIntyre 1998c: 233). Occupational structure may endanger the quality of practice altogether (institutional pressures, focus on external goods, productionism without sense of quality). But it can also be argued that occupational institutional structure offers the necessary stability and continuity to certain practices, which otherwise would fail to live up to their promise (advanced medicine).

MacIntyre's phenomenology of practice, so much has become clear, has not yet reached its limit of articulation. In times to come, it will be quite important to further an exploration of the different kinds of practice in relation to their perfective qualities and possibilities, and to study more closely the relation and tension between the world of practice and the world of work. As MacIntyre himself has noted:

> The question which is perhaps the most important that you could put to me is that of how the concept of a practice must be further developed, if it is to be as philosophically fruitful as I hope that it may be (1998f: 273)

Practice and virtue

The necessary inclusion of aretaic being turns practice into something other than a collection of skills. Practice is more than skill performance.

No virtues without practice. According to MacIntyre practices provide the arena in which the virtues are exhibited and receive their primary definition (see chapter 10). In turn, there is also no practice without the presence of the virtues. The virtues are a necessary ingredient of practical being. Without aretaic being, practices will all too quickly fall into the hands of institutional and external distortion. MacIntyre observes that

> The integrity of a practice causally requires the exercise of the virtues by at least some of the individuals who embody it in their activities; and conversely the corruption of the institutions is always in part at least an effect of the vices (1981: 182).

Virtuous members are needed to protect (a proper interpretation of) the authentic ends and internal goods of a practice. Non-virtuous members will, in fact, silently count on the virtues of others for the practices to flourish (*ibid.*: 180).

There is also a functional and essential role of the virtues with regard to the educational, social, and historical dimensions of a practice. Training in a practice implies a role for the virtues of perseverance and humility and patience. Working together with others implies a role for moral and social virtues such as justice and friendliness and responsibility. Historical development of practices implies that its ends will evolve (there is no fixed scheme once and for all). The virtues are again of vital importance in guiding the historical process.

If virtues are to be present and to be active in certain ways in the fields of practice, can it not be argued that they become themselves achievements that deserve the title of internal good? On the one hand, this seems not to be the case. Virtues are supposed to be at work in every practice and also beyond practices altogether. Hence, they fail to match the definition of an internal good. On the other hand, virtues will receive particularised content in a practice. Hence, a special way of applying virtues in an individual, practical context could perhaps be proposed as constituting an achievement in terms of an internal good. This is a question that needs to be further explored.

Evil in practice / Evil practice

Besides the fact that a practice may contain non-virtuous members, there is still the larger problem that certain practices are as such perhaps capable of producing evil and that certain practices may in fact be forms of evil practice.

According to certain critics of MacIntyre, torture undeniably may count as a practice (Frazer & Lacey 1994: 274). It can be organised as a coherent, complex, socially established project. One could even argue that there are internal goods to be realized. Presumably there can be torturers who practice with artistry (Weinstein 1985: 94). The executioner is then a craftsman.

MacIntyre himself allows the possibility of an evil practice (1981: 186). However, he is also quick to qualify this possibility. He is not convinced, for example, that torture and sado-masochistic sexuality could really match the structural description of a practice with internal goods. Nonetheless, it is clear for him that, as a matter of fact, many types of practice may be *on certain occasions* be productive of evil. The desire to excel can always corrupt. Honourable resort to war (military practice) may turn into savage cruelty. In practices one may sometimes find a lack of justice (discrimination of women and minorities, for example), and certain practical enterprises may have negative consequences for the life of virtue beyond the confines of a practice. The authentic exploration of wilderness, in which the ability to be ruthless in driving oneself and others may be a condition for achievement and even survival, could very well require cultivation of a certain insensitivity to the feelings of others. This disposition is likely to turn into a vice in other settings (MacIntyre 1984: 275). Here, an actual practice would then be the source of vice and immoral being.

The possibilities of evil within practice indeed highlights the fact that a particular practice, or a particular instance of a kind of practice, or a particular member of a practice, may always stand in need of moral criticism (MacIntyre 1981: 187). The solution is to offer serious space for a critical reception of the different practices. It is obvious that practices that systematically produce vice and evil should be reformed and, if necessary, eliminated (bull-fighting comes to mind). This is something to be decided within the contours of legal, moral, and political practice. The political constellation of a society is itself, of course, a practice that may stand in need of criticism. In fact, MacIntyre's critique is that the modern state does not at all function anymore as a proper practice.

The deterioration of practice

The facts that practices may produce evil, that its members may not be sufficiently virtuous, that institutions and external goods may come to dominate the scene, that we nowadays live in societies without a real practice of political being, confront us with a final problem.

According to MacIntyre practices are culturally universal. Perfective naturalism is likely to confirm this point. We are as organisms capable of organising practices, and the cultural nature of our being is itself to be prolonged by involvement in practices. However, since modernity we observe a radical marginalisation of the practices. On this, MacIntyre writes:

> Practices, as I understand them, are a universal feature of human cultures, although in some they may be radically marginalized and their significance deeply obscured. What this may prevent and does prevent in the cultures distinctive of modernity is the development of an Aristotelian understanding of the significance of practices in terms of the whole life of an individual and the lives of communities (1994: 287).

In modern times we seem to have predominantly entered a society ruled by the concept of 'getting on', without a sense of perfective internal goods and without a strong sense of activities that can be done for their own sake.

Although confronted with so many signs of deteriorated practice, MacIntyre continues to have faith in the ultimate vitality of practice. Human nature and culture is such that a sense of practice will continue to subsist in different places. Local 'Aristotelian' revivals of practice are in fact recurrent. It is exactly to these places, which constitute little perfective communities, that we have to turn for a renewed moral, aretaic and perfective consciousness.

MacIntyre is on the one hand dark in his analysis of contemporary society, perhaps too dark, but on the other hand he does live with a sense of hope. He is, in any case, not ready to give up on the ideal of practical perfection, of perfection in practice. The hope for perfection, in MacIntyre's view, is directly linked with the possibility of a revitalised practice, notably with the possibility of constructing 'practice-based forms of local community that will be able to survive the insidious and destructive pressures of contemporary capitalism and of the modern state' (MacIntyre 1998a: xxxi.).

In his own way, so we may conclude, MacIntyre delivers a utopian message — a message fed by the fundamental insight that to give up on the future of practice would be to abandon significant human perfective existence altogether. This insight immediately provides a link with the next chapter, which will be concerned with the question of future perfection and perfective possibilism.

CHAPTER ELEVEN —
HUMAN PERFECTIVE EXISTENCE — iv:
FUTURE PERFECTION

> *L'impossibilité d'éliminer toutes contraintes*
> *nous dit qu'il n'y a pas de meilleur des mondes.*
> *Mais elle n'interdit pas la possibilité d'un*
> *monde meilleur.*
>
> — Edgar Morin

The density, ambiguity and complexity of the current world —with its relative perfections, grades, degradation, imperfections and anti-perfections — is destined to lead to moments of nervousness, anxiety, despair, sadness and disappointment, but also permits a positive reception of what could or should become the case at a later time. Relative perfection implies future perfection or perfective possibility. The question at hand is to receive future perfection in an appropriate manner, beyond the radical options of optimism and pessimism. In this chapter I will propose different segments of a perfective possibilism or a theory of future perfection. I will clarify the relevance of ideals, propose hope as aretaic perfection in the context of a melioristic perspective, and suggest a contemporary sense of utopian being.

The conception of how things could be perfectively better — in myself, in others, or in the world at large — first leads to the question of ideals.

Living with ideals

Perfectionism is concerned with the extent to which future perfection is welcome. To conceive perfective possibility in whatever context means to set up an ideal. An ideal is something valuable and desirable, worth our sustained attention. We are eager to work for the constructive realisation of ideals, because such a realisation makes our lives better. However, a positive reception of ideals and idealisation is not universally shared. It is especially informative to listen and respond to John Dewey's resistance to perfective idealisation.

In numerous passages Dewey warns us that we become victims of ideals more often than we care to realise. The pathology of idealised perfection runs deep and presents itself in common activities and practices. As soon as an idea of quality is appraised it has the tendency to evolve into something beyond concrete realisation:

> The quality of the ideal is exalted till it is something beyond all possibility of definite plan and execution. Its sublimity renders it inaccessibly remote. An ideal becomes a synonym for whatever is inspiring and impossible [...] the ideal is hardened by thought into some high, far-away object. It is so elevated and so distant that it does not belong to this world or to experience (Dewey 1983: 178).

The search for an ideal of perfection will cause us to neglect the only place where the good can be experienced, this is, in the here and now. A physician, for example, is on a wrong existential track as soon as he begins to guide his activities of healing by an articulated picture of perfected health. Such a picture quickly becomes an abstract and lifeless interpretation. Idealised goals are likely to lead to a psychological state of pessimism and frustration. Karen Horney offers one confirmation for Dewey's negative reception of idealisation in her characterising the perfectionist as

> a person who believes he has a warranted claim to an inheritance; instead of making constructive efforts in living, he puts all his energies into a more effective assertion of his claims. In the meantime his actual life loses interest for him; he becomes impoverished; he neglects all that could make life worth living. And so the hope for future possibilities becomes more and more the only thing he lives for (1950: 62).

While resisting distant idealisation Dewey does on the other hand propose his own alternative sense of the ideal. Hence, he is not against the notion of the ideal as such, only against revelations of supreme and static perfection.

Ideals in a proper, non-pathological form are needed for their directive force and sense of further development. We do need direction and progression. Living ideals offer to us a constant warning not to be content with an accomplishment as it stands (Dewey 1978: 379). We should always be on the look out for what is better. Dewey is in his own way a perfective thinker, a perfectionist for whom the movement of progression as such replaces the idea of a shining perfection, a perfection that never can be reached. A perfective ideal is for him not a remote goal. Ends as they emerge must only be received as tentative and swift sketches, without a sharply idealising ambition. Only in the form of flexible constructions can ends or ideals functionally direct our activities. These flexible constructions are to be situated in a process of 'present reconstructing' (Dewey 1983: 195). The critical issue in this process is to stay very close to present troubles, experiences and possibilities, while seriously recognising possibilities of development resident in each concrete situation. The point is never to direct ourselves away from the concrete situations, which need the 'perfecting care of attention and affection' (Dewey 1978: 378) A physician, for example, in examining a patient, should use only what he has in the moment of practice discovered about actual cases of good and ill health — discoveries which contribute to an evolving sense of the ideal.

Flexible ideals will not distract us from the real meaning and experience of being active. A *summum bonum* automatically turns our efforts into means without inner significance. This is important for Dewey. What matters most is the present activity and its intrinsic satisfaction. Enjoyment in the act of building — the appreciation of using and experiencing our abilities in the present — constitutes our most authentic goal, not the fact that a certain end (the built house) is approached or attained. Another important element in Dewey's sense of activity is the fact that it is defined as an ongoing process in which one flexible end leads to another. Ends pull us in a certain direction, but when things are done there is not a phase of enduring satisfaction, only the appearance of new direction and fresh ends. Dewey states, for example:

> A mariner does not sail towards the stars, but by noting the stars he is aided in conducting his present activity of sailing. A port or harbor is his objective, but only in the sense of reaching it, not taking possession of it. The harbor stands in his thought as a significant point at which his activity will need redirection. Activity will not cease when the port is attained, but merely the present direction of activity. The port is as truly the beginning of another mode of activity as it is the termination of the present one (1983: 156).

Dewey's critique of exalted ideals and his flexible sense of ideal clearly are not without rational point. However, I do not find his proposal convincing. Pathological investment in future states does exist, to be sure, and we must try to avoid it, but it is not clear to me why each more sustained conception of a future perfective state would automatically have to exemplify an abnormal investment. Is it not the case, rather, that we need different varieties of ideal — some like Dewey's flexible ends, others more in the form of a perfected vision with an enduring ambition. Such ideals, too, are quite necessary in many different practices and disciplines. Think of medicine. This practice would drastically simplify without reasonably sustained and calm focus on perfective purposes and standards. Ongoing reflection on goods beyond pointillist attention is something we are capable of and which plays an important role. A sketchy concern often is not sufficient. Perfective ideals of a more enduring kind do not automatically distort our daily realities of relative accomplishment and concrete experience. They may fruitfully guide our activities while activities continue to improve the formation of ideals. Deeper perfective ends are not at all foreign to the basic experiential structure of human life (Bollnow 1968: 83). Moreover, the experience of teleologically approaching a worthy end is itself ineradicably an ingredient of the actual satisfaction we enjoy while being active.

Furthermore, Dewey neglects the positive role of deeper ideals as inspirational perfective models. Ideals of a more enduring kind are not destined to succeed — they are meant to be excessive (Sartori 1987: 68). It is not at all a defect of an ideal if its ideal situation and actual implementation diverge greatly (Nozick 1990: 284). This is not what ultimately matters in the formulation of ideals of perfection. Its point is to be a practical tool for maximum movement or progression — a higher ideal inimitably influences what will concretely happen. Aldous Huxley concludes that 'the most valuable ideals are possible, but unrealizable' (1957: 263).

Note that this sense of ideal is only intended to be impossible in one sense (the impossibility of absolute perfection). The ideal that humans should have ten legs, for example, can never be actualised because it directly and unambiguously contradicts the possibilities inherent in our human nature. But the ideal that humans should have an equal level of educational opportunity is not against human possibility in this manner, even if we know that it is in actual life impossible to reach the level of full equality. Nonetheless, it is rational to strive towards it as much as possible. One may argue that even excessive ideals, not destined to succeed in one way, are in another way, paradoxically perhaps, still focused on 'ideal perfection only in so far as there is some possibility and therefore some hope of actualizing it' (Feibleman 1979: 383).

Dewey's sense of the ideal, so we may conclude, is to be included in a larger, plurivocal theory of perfective ideals. There is a role for flexible as well as enduring ends and ideals. Both know their pathological versions; it is likely that exactly a one-sided focus on one type of ideal will lead to pathology.

Optimism and pessimism

Perfective possibilism resists the options of optimism and pessimism. There are, of course, many definitions of optimism and pessimism. I will take these terms to refer strictly to attitudes of certainty with respect to the better and best on the one hand, and to the worse and worst on the other hand. Both options, in the definitions given, distort the authentic position of perfective ideals, of perfective possibilities.

A moderate optimist will say that a better state of being is already there to a significant extent, or that we are without a doubt moving towards a better state. A radical optimist will say that the ideal situation is already fully there, or that we are without a doubt moving towards the best.

A moderate pessimist will say that things are bad, or are moving towards the worse. A radical pessimist will say that things are at their worst, or are moving towards the worst. Perfective ideals, then, have no meaning since they will never be actualised, certainly not to a substantial degree.

Beyond optimism ad pessimism, perfective possibilism proposes the balanced virtue of hope as an alternative option.

Hope as aretaic perfection

Let us situate and define hope as a perfective virtue.

Perfective hope is aretaically relevant exactly because all is not well. It would not constitute a virtue in a world of complete fulfilment and perfective satisfaction. There can be no hope without a hunger to be full, a hunger that could not arise if we do not have a current poverty in one way or another. Hope as virtue would also fall away in a world of total evil and degradation — in such a world there is nothing to hope for. Our hunger to be full would never meet significant opportunities for perfective progression. Fortunately, in reality as we know it there is a functional role for hope. Persons cannot really carry on without hope. We do not function well when we feel that life has grown into 'a tissue of impossibilities' (James 1982: 131). Considered existentially, it is clear that the loss of hope will end in the loss of striving, next comes passivity and then death. Activities like study and thought require an ongoing enthusiasm and, thus, a form of hope (Royce 1920: 109). Progression as imagined possibility is vitally important. For this reason it can be said that hope holds a cardinal perfective position in human existence. Perhaps, it is even one's duty to have a sense of hope, since only from this point of view can one be active and do what one can. Hope is a necessary condition in our many perfective practices.

How does hope arise?

In childhood we live with numerous expectations based on certain regularities of fulfilment (Bühler 1969). These early expectations come close to optimism, but whereas optimism is a conscious expectation that goodness will arrive, expectation in a child is a spontaneous, almost unconscious ingredient of the child's uncompromised way of being. As we grow older fulfilments of expectation become less probable. The simple circle of expectation and satisfaction begins to lose its relevance in many aspects of life. A sense of expectation is, of course, bound to continue to psychologically hold in basic events of different kinds. Often, future development is predesigned into present structure — we live in a world of expectation (Rescher 1998: 70). It would be quite foolish not to spontaneously expect the bus to arrive the next morning, to expect to wake up in the morning, and so forth. However, expectation beyond childhood will always be coloured by some (minimal) sense of the uncertain. Particles of insecurity are bound to infiltrate the remaining bastion of expectation. In other more eventful and dramatic situations, which contain broader teleological possibilities and developments, the simplicity of expectation is bound to give way, or ought to give way, to the complexity of hope.

Hope is fundamentally different from simple expectation and optimism. The earlier expectational self has not sufficiently experienced disappointment, and the optimistic self artificially attempts to continue the pleasure of anticipating secure outcome. Hope only intends to claim that a certain imagined state of affairs is desirable, possible and perhaps even likely, but never that it will necessarily, totally and definitively arrive.

What is the specific content of hope as complex aretaic disposition?

It is first of all fruitful to define hope as a virtue in terms of meliorism. The world permits possible betterment. A melioristic self will 'look towards a world of the future which is always capable of being better than in the past it has ever been' (Feibleman 1952: 316). Things can improve, to some degree, but this is never guaranteed. Meliorism, as a perspective in which hope receives proper content, strongly qualifies eighteenth- and nineteenth-century perfectibilism focused on believing in infinitely extendable improvement — morally, scientifically and technically. Such perfectibilism is more relevant than the classical ideal of perfection according to which 'a man who had once seen the form of the good or achieved union with the one had no greater perfection left to hope for' (Passmore 1975: 158), but, nonetheless, it fails in other aspects. Most of us will nowadays resist the triumphant idea of a *perfectibilité indefinie*, aware as we are of the possibilities and actualities of failure and regression. Quality, once achieved, may fade away in a next phase. Moreover, in life gains often combine with losses; we stand in the field of the mixed. There is no total progress of humanity as such. Negative implications of progressive developments often hide in the back, but they are nonetheless present (Kwant 1986: 61). As Emerson notes:

> The civilised man has built a coach, but has lost the use of his feet. He is supported on crutches, but lacks so much support of muscle. He has a fine Geneva watch, but he fails of skill to tell the hour by the sun (quoted in Perry 1975: 408).

Hope, in a melioristic perspective, also stays away from the idea of total negativity without the possibility of perfective progression. For the pessimist, positive realities and possibilities have gone, or were never there to begin with. It is quite unlikely that a human being can psychologically sustain complete pessimism. This is not how we are structurally built. Even persons with tragic lives may still choose to focus on positive possibilities and achievements in others — this is one method to psychologically cope with one's own sense of impossibility and darkness.

A next point to note is that we develop the aretaic trait of hope only because we are creatures of valuation and teleological direction. The future matters to us in a certain way. We do not hope for the arrival of undesirable states of affairs. Hoping that an enemy will become terribly sick is, in fact, to consider an undesirable state of affairs (for others) in terms of a desirable state of affairs (for oneself). Hope finds its deepest ground in being able to welcome the future, believing that there are things worth attaining, receiving, experiencing. One could hope that different negative things will not come true but this is a derivative form of hope, to be reformulated as hoping that the good that already is will not get disrupted. The existential relevance of hope is especially connected with our own teleological strivings. The human self is a 'system of purposive behaviour emerging from a persistent hope' (Hocking 1928: 46). It is important for us not just to assimilate and to be satisfied with what we have, but also to undertake projects and to fulfil our aspirations. A human being is a colony of possible selves, crowding to become actual projects (Markus & Nurius 1986). One may, of course, direct one's hope towards many things — including trivial and less important things, but the perfective self will be particularly concerned with significant possibility in oneself (and in others). Our ideal self is

> the insistent charge issuing from self-awakened desire, that our original power be answered for and actualised in ways more qualitatively adequate than those provided by the self as given fact (Desmond 1987: 47).

The desire for improvement and progress holds a structural position within our cognitive and conative way of being. Even the most negative self is bound to have experienced the workings of positive teleological inclination in earlier stages. One could perhaps suggest that even the suicidal self still desires a future positive state, a state of rest?

Another relevant point concerns the connection between action, risk and hope. We normally do not begin to act without an intimation of possible success. Action requires a sense of hope; our activities need a sense of hope because of the experience of risk. Confonted with conflicts and uncertainties one must dare, and one can only dare in a spirit of hope. We cannot escape the numerous maybe's on our way. As William James states:

> So far as a man stands for anything, and is productive or original at all, his entire vital function may be said to deal with maybe's. Not a victory is gained, not a deed of faithfulness or courage is done, except upon a maybe; not a service, not a sally of generosity, not a scientific exploration or experiment or text-book, that may not be a mistake. It is only by our persons from one hour to another that we live at all (1979: 53)

Only to act on the basis of secure outcome is not a valuable way of living for us. Josiah Royce notes: 'It is a cowardly soul that needs the certainty of success before it will work. It is a craven who despairs and does nothing because what he can do may turn out a failure' (1920: 131-32). The melioristic self prefers the hard and uncertain way with its eyes open. This preference is an important characteristic of a self properly focused on the possibility of future perfection.

A final point to mention is that hope is focused on possibility according to different shades of likelihood. Considering a desirable state of affairs to be extremely unlikely still includes a (very) minimal sense of the possible. We are confronted with an almost inactive form of hope — perhaps it is better not to speak of hope. Considering a desirable state of affairs as extremely likely implies an enthusiastic and full sense of the possible. We, then, have a maximal form of hope, though without falling into the hands of absolute certainty (otherwise we would have left the virtue of hope). In between we find those many gradations, combinations of hope and doubt that occupy us most in everyday existence. Hope is not a naive trait, implying an indiscriminate hopefulness. Our life experience is a cocktail of good and bad. In intensely tragic situations perplexity and desperation, a sense that nothing is possible, may come close to being our most appropriate response. Indeed, we should not be more hopeful than a situation legitimately allows for. Perfective hope in its proper form always includes a blending of patience and initiative:

> Hope is neither passive waiting nor is it unrealistic forcing of circumstances that cannot occur. It is like the crouched tiger, which will jump only when the moment for jumping has come (Fromm 1971: 9).

Without appropriate patience we encounter disappointment all too quickly. The disappointed self may subsequently come to refuse perfective progression as such. It is important that we hope for the right things in the right way. A good choice of goals is important.

Utopian vision

A balanced perfective self will have perfective hope, not only in relation to private issues, but also with respect to concerns bigger than oneself. Otherwise hope becomes an egotistical enterprise. The articulation of a wider possibilist vision is part of an adult experience of perfective hope. It is one thing to hope that I will find parking space this evening, and quite something else to hope that our nation is on the verge of something good. 'Big hope' involves us in larger projects and intentions aimed at comprehensive ends situated in a distant future. This broader time frame may, in one way, even allow us to escape the numerous disappointments that emerge in the different circumstances of personal life (Russell 1984: 181-182).

A broader vision constitutes a utopian perspective. The utopian imagination constitutes a cure for the temporal narrowness of ideology (Ricoeur 1986b: 17). It offers a wider basis for human cognitive focus, inspiration for action, and emotional flourishing. Beyond private hope, utopian explorations refer to ideals in the context of communities, societies, and the earth at large (ecological utopias!). A utopian vision is a mental exercise with a broader reference — it is a 'serious play' (Ruyer 1950: 4). Utopia typically goes beyond parochial concern. It enlarges the breadth and degree of perfective possibilism. Utopias are characterised, not only by the perfective standard of richness, but also by the standard of scope.

Not all utopian visions are focused on significant perfection. One can think of a hedonist utopian proposal, envisaging future humans who will constantly experience bodily and psychological pleasure. But such a proposal is unrealistic. Most people do long for meaningful effort in ways not addressed in hedonism. The will to find meaning is something else than a need for basic gratification. We need difficulties. Beyond entertainment we desire achievement. Basic goods have a sound place in utopian articulation but utopian possibility implies a surplus beyond elementary pleasure. The installation of such a surplus is what turns a particular utopian vision into a significant imaginative and critical enterprise, which can stimulate the attention of many and has the capacity to lift us up beyond our current state.

The necessary connection between utopian vision and perfection comes sharply in focus from the side of perfectionist theory. If perfection is what we (should) cherish most in ourselves and others, and if there indeed is much unfinished perfective business, then it is a matter of logical expectation that we will be seriously focused on general and social (and global) visions concerning what we still could or should accomplish in future times. In a first step we may be critical of the factual situation, but critique does not exist without a sense of a norm, that is, a sense of what ought to be (Kwant & van Houten 1976: 12). It is therefore natural to expect that an elaborated critique will lead, and be based on, an equally elaborated picture of where we should get. This is a form of utopian expression.

However, not every model of utopian articulation is relevant today.

We are not interested in the static character of classical utopias or in the nightmare vision of a totalitarian and technological utopia. Radical utopian consciousness inadequately applies aesthetic order to the realm of politics. It neurotically desires to build a world that is free from all disorder and ugliness (Popper 1974a: 165). Static and absolute utopian models, giving rise to impossible efforts to realize the perfect ideal, may in fact provide liberal minimalists, who desire no strong action, with an intellectual comfort.

We should not wish to concern ourselves with a total and frozen picture of where we should arrive at once and for all. This is the end-state model of perfection (McKenna 2001). The annihilation of change in the context of a perfect utopian community seems unavoidable:

> For if a change is a change for the better, then the previous state of the society, because surpassable, wasn't perfect; and if a change is a change for the worse, the previous state of society, allowing deterioration, wasn't perfect (Nozick 1974: 328).

By now, we should know well enough that there is no perfective state once and for all. If we still long for utopian exploration today it is for (unfinished) stories of complexity, differentiation and development. Contemporary utopian consciousness should consequently transcend the traditional utopian fondness for fixed patterns of perfection (Kateb 1973: 239). A perfect standardisation of life also denies humans one important ingredient of happiness, namely the experience of freedom and variety (Tatarkiewicz 1976: 280).

It is relevant to refer to one version of the 'paradox of perfection'. We are confronted with the idea of the perfection of imperfection (Tatarkiewicz 1992: 18-21). Absolute perfection ends up with the static result of complete fulfilment. Perfection is seen to be reachable, development comes to an end and we need nothing else. We enter a stage of 'catatonic quiet' (Walhout 1978a: 242). Ceaseless improvement is therefore proposed as authentic perfection. To have reached a so-called ultimate and definitive state is only to enter the imperfection of not being able to improve. The paradox of perfection introduces perfection as a psychological issue. Human beings would not mentally survive the fulfilment of their worthy aims, the accomplishment of all their relevant qualities. Such a state would eliminate all sense of adventure and narrative. As John Ruskin has noted, to banish imperfection is to paralyse vitality (quoted in Pye 1968: 61). Incompletion is what makes us tick, even while it also remains true that we do need substantial moments of perfective success; if everything always fails we would live in a world without meaning or direction. Cioran, too, sharply criticises the psychological irrelevance of classical utopian articulations, depicting a kind of human being we would not like to become or which we do not even recognise as a real person (this brings to mind the principle of minimal psychological realism). He writes, for example:

> Les enfants eux-mêmes y deviennent méconnaissables. Dans 'l'état sociétaire' de Fourier, ils sont si purs qu'ils ignorant jusqu'a la tentation de voler, de 'prendre une pomme sur un arbre'. Mais un enfant qui ne vole pas n'est pas un enfant (1960: 109).

One cardinal problem for contemporary utopian consciousness is, thus, to find new content and new modes of expression. On the one hand we do not accept a finalised picture, that is, a 'perfectionist obsession that retrains and restricts the possibilities of change, instead of serving as a liberating tool of change' (Klaic 1991: 5). On the other hand we do still need inspirational signposts of one kind or another, signposts that transcend a pure dystopia. Many are nowadays hesitant about what to seek. Our current situation invites the following interpretation:

> We have arrived at a station when something has come to an end and when reconsideration of our destiny is imperative. Spiritually, we are in a period of what I propose to call reflective dusk. Before us is the impenetrable darkness of night. It may still last long to the dawn when a new orientation in the world can be clearly articulated (von Wright 1997: 13).

Edgar Morin confirms this interpretation. We live in a time of the unknown future, and cannot even provide our present with an accurate face. We only manage to speak about *post*-industrialism or *post*-modernism (Morin 1991c: 18). Signposts on a larger scale, so it seems, must await new possibilities of articulation.

In the meanwhile, of course, it has some practical value to discern more sharply what it is we definitely wish to leave behind in utopian consciousness. At least three critical questions come to mind, questions concerning the connections between utopia and religion, between utopia and science, and between utopia and revolution.

Utopia and religion

The first question deals with utopia and religion.

MacIntyre (1953) connects a fundamental philosophy of possibility (Marxism) with a sense of prophecy. Prophetic discourse originally belongs to religion. Religious prophecy is characterised by the fact that it can come true in unexpected ways and that it is guaranteed by trust in a prophet who exemplifies a purposeful pattern in his life. The positive reception of prophecies and prophets is essentially a matter of faith, not of scientific accuracy or philosophical argument. While MacIntyre properly insists on the distinct relevance of a secular language of human possibility, his reference to prophecy may rather set us on a wrong track. It is not clear which aspects of religious prophetic language could be carried over into secular discourse. I do not think we should put our trust in a philosopher or novelist or artist according to a manner of faith. When dealing with a possibilist or utopian philosopher, we will look for depth and relevance in his writings. We will also critically estimate his personal actions and societal engagements. And this may eventually install a deepened reader's trust — a trust that is not a form of religious faith, but an aretaic and existential response to wisdom and quality of expression.

There is another religious aspect in a fundamental philosophy of possibility. There seems to be a functional similarity between Marxist possibilism and Christian salvation (Wessell 1979). The Marxist, so it turns out, is only the 'minister of a different idol' (Desmond 1990: 43). Christianity has on offer a fundamental interpretation of man and world by way of a dramatic scheme of sin and redemption. Especially in Marxism this scheme seems to have been translated into a philosophical narrative of alienation and liberation, and in a metaphysics of history and destiny. The proletariat, for example, is given the soteriological task of totally reversing duality and initiating a higher unity (Wessell 1979: 208). Marxism is the form under which the concepts of traditional Christianity have entered into the modern world (MacIntyre 1953: 5). It came to occupy this place due to the gap opened up by the marginalisation of the Christian world-view. Marxism is defined by a similar interpretational ambition. According to Yack (1986) Marxism's interpretational ambition was not caused by a direct intention to imitate Christianity's breadth. The Marxist scheme of bondage and liberation is only the ultimate result of an attempt simply to clarify why things in society have gone so fundamentally wrong. Nonetheless, in its own way Marxism has ended up with something structurally similar to Christianity, however indirectly or unintentionally.

Today, the mythopoetic narrative of Marxism has in large part fallen away as a valid cultural scheme. Hermeneutically, it is for many difficult to sustain the defence of a broad mythical scheme of bondage and liberation — a scheme to be held with religious passion.

Now that religion and Marxism have disappeared as general existential options for so many, is it not better to give up the utopian formulation of possibility? I think not. A sense of larger and wider possibility, however vague, is still relevant. People remain entangled in histories and continue to be confronted with experiences of change and transformation. As soon as one has learned to imagine situations differently, one has also learned to conceive future possibility. We cannot escape a focus on the future. Human consciousness — if it wishes to find or to create direction and meaning — is bound to continue to express fundamental possibility, if only in a more cryptic form. We need to continue our capacity for possibilism. Leaving utopian consciousness behind will only benefit those powers that have a strong interest in the future as an extension of the present.

Whatever the direction of future utopian evocation it is likely that it will to some degree imply the idea of a meta-utopia (Nozick 1974). The idea of a utopian society should essentially include the idea of a society of utopianism, that is,

> a place where people are at liberty to join together voluntarily to pursue and attempt to realise their own vision of the good life in the ideal community, but where no one can impose his own utopian vision upon others (*ibid.*: 312).

Rorty conveys something similar when he writes that the idea of a perfected society should not be organised according to a pre-existing standard, but as 'an artistic achievement, produced by the same long and difficult process of trial and error as is required by any other creative effort' (1999: 270). Toffler, finally, refers to the 'thousands of conscious, decentralized experiments that permit us to test new models of political decision-making at local and regional levels' (1981: 452).

This study is grounded in the hope that — through experience, dialogue, wisdom, and pluralist experimentation — contemporary possibilist consciousness would come to rationally confirm the content of a complex perfectionism.

Utopia and science

A second question deals with the relation between scientific prediction and utopian vision.

Scientific prediction is interested in what necessarily shall become. The practice of prediction automatically leads to the formulation of supplementary hypotheses when events do not happen to arrive as predicted. But this is not how utopian vision should proceed.

Prediction in human affairs is in many aspects inadequate. It is of course true that I can predict that I will now move my hand and subsequently do so. In the very short range prediction works well enough. It is in fact excessively rare for somebody to announce a movement he is going to make and to die the next moment. In this little sphere a man is a lord by knowledge and power (Geach 2001: 85). But in the broader ranges — think of historical, moral and perfective development — accurate and certain prediction constitutes something of a lost battle. Human selves live by virtue of numerous regularities — we have legitimate social and personal expectations — but the point remains that one can always come to act differently and in unexpected ways. Our life stories, and human history as such, are shot through by unannounced events and unforeseen actions. Such unpredictability

> is not to be overcome by more human cleverness, but only by a greater humility, by a greater recognition of the limitations of human thought and action. To ask that one's vision of society shall have the certainty of natural science is always to pass beyond the bounds of that humility (MacIntyre 1953: 71).

There are different sources of human unpredictability (MacIntyre 1981). There is, for example, the nature of radical conceptual innovation. A prediction that in ten years' time the wheel would be invented would mean that it had already been invented. Radical newness cannot be announced. This point has an impact on the course of human history (Popper 1961: vi-vii). History is strongly influenced by the growth of knowledge, and the growth of knowledge includes cognitive innovation that resists prediction. This means that we cannot predict the future course of human history.

There is also the unpredictability of one's own future actions (MacIntyre 1981). This sense of unpredictability arises when one has not yet decided which alternative actions to undertake. Other observers may have the feeling that they can predict what I will do, but they will not be able to sufficiently estimate the impact of their actions and interpretations on the decisions made by me. Imagine someone telling me his prediction of my future action. This would offer to me an opportunity to change my decisions and actions contrary to the predicted course. And these changes are not foreseen in the prediction.

Finally, trivial actions often have an unexpected influence on larger events (*ibid.*). These actions and contingencies cannot be adequately taken into account in our predictive plans for the future. We simply do not have complete knowledge about all the possibilities of cause and effect.

Another issue is that, although we are pragmatically interested in future developments, one might on the other hand wonder whether it would be such a fine thing to be able to foresee the future in each dimension. As Nicolas Rescher has pointed out:

> How much would we actually want to know about the future — at any rate about that relatively near-term future that is most relevant for the lives of ourselves and those we know and care about? Would we really want to have foreknowledge of the suffering that the yet unturned pages of time and circumstance hold in store for us and our children and their posterity — the catastrophes and misfortunes and suffering that await us all? (1997b: 117).

Innovation, an unexpected response to earlier predictions, the unforeseen influence of smaller events, and the undesirability of full foreknowledge, all ensure that personal and social anticipations with panoramic ambition can play only a limited and provisional role. If it relies too much on prediction for the construction of its essential message, utopian discourse will get into trouble all too quickly.

It is certainly true that adult utopian explorations should seek support in scientific views. Ecological utopian vision, for example, should develop a dialogue with scientific interpretations of what is actually happening with our ecosystem. But the perfective and moral message that will follow in response to such a dialogue is itself not something that can result in the structure of a prediction. To wish that goodness becomes reality is only to articulate desirable development, not certain development. The vital insight is to articulate relevant possibilities as utopian ideals that are not so much bound to come, but that *ought* to come (Bauman 1976: 17). This is a matter of moral imperative, not of scientific prediction. A person may have the potentiality to produce great things, but that does not imply that he will do so. Perhaps, one perfectively and morally hopes he will, but there is no guaranteed outcome.

It is also important to underline that utopian statements about the future can be active factors in actually shaping the future. As Paul Weiss notes:

> A universal peace is but a figment of deluded spirits, a prelude to a fable; but were all men to feel the heat of the idea within them, we would soon have a glowing testimony to folly (1967b: 290).

In Zygmunt Bauman we read a similar point:

> Far from being just predictions, passively waiting on bookshelves to be compared with the actual course of events they avowedly tried to foresee, our statements about the future become, from the start, active factors in shaping this future (1976: 10).

The 'dreamy' language of future perfection contributes to the realization of actual perfection.

176

A third question deals with the relation between revolution and utopia.

Utopian vision should not accommodate the myth of radical revolutionary practice as conceived in radical communism. Such a myth — suggesting the fantasm of a unique, global and total event — locks us up in a magical conception of political action (Ricoeur 1970: 26). Revolutionary consciousness thinks itself fully assured in its own possibilist message and subsequently aims at a total realisation without accommodation. It responds to the question of pace by opting for an avalanche rush. In his radical attempt, the revolutionary is likely to become a butcher (Desmond 1990: 47). He is also likely to turn a large part of the current generation into an instrument for the creation of a future generation. Utopian revolution can be dangerous; in particular, in response to the violence of revolutionary perfection of the mythic kind one may be inclined to propose a return to a non-utopian society that is less perfect.

Foundational revolutionary certainty is to be resisted. According to a hermeneutical conception of knowledge we are confronted with a plurality of interpretations through which we make our way toward a rational, but never absolute perspective on human possibility and perfection. Hermeneutics also stresses the impossibility of completely leaving one's tradition in favour of something totally new without relation to what came before. Human existence is a play of habit and shock, of continuity and transformation.

The limitations of human knowledge, however, should not push us toward stubborn minimalism. Popper offers the alternative option of the 'piecemeal engineer', who 'knows like Socrates how little he knows' (1961: 67). Such an engineer will work little by little, step by step. Popper only wishes to back up policies that address the neutralisation of basic evils and suffering. The only thing we can do is to make life a little less terrible and a little less unjust in each generation. I believe we can and should be less minimal than this. It is likely that making life only a little less unjust will benefit the powers that be all too much. The eminent historian David Carr, who cannot be accused of being someone with communist sympathies, is firm in his criticism of Popper:

> The status of reason in professor Popper's scheme of things is, in fact, rather like that of a British civil servant, qualified to administer the policies of the government in power and even to suggest practical improvements to make them work better, but not to question their fundamental presuppositions and ultimate purposes. This is useful work: I, too, have been a civil servant in my day. But this subordination of reason to the assumptions of the existing order seems to me in the long run unacceptable [...] Progress in human affairs, whether in science or in history or in society, has come mainly through the bold readiness of human beings not to confine themselves to seeking piecemeal improvements in the way things are done, but to present fundamental challenges in the name of reason to the current way of doing things and to the avowed or hidden assumptions on which it rests (1981: 155).

Moreover, the neutralisation of suffering and injustice is a central issue, but the lack of significant perfection will also result in deep human misery. Human beings suffer intensely from lack of perfective opportunity beyond basic needs. Perfective striving is not a luxury good. The organised production of perfective opportunity does not have to invite totalitarian utopianism. There is quite a difference between producing free perfective opportunities for everyone and forcing a population to strictly accept a hierarchy of previously established perfective goods.

A strategy of only little improvements is especially an inadequate option when confronted with crises (crises that may be, and often are, caused — at least in part — by the stubborn political refusal to consider and implement more drastic measures). A real crisis reveals that something has seriously gone wrong, and is thereby likely to effectively put in motion more drastic forces of transformation (Morin 1984: 139-153).

It should be clear that not all types of revolution are equally invalid. We must distinguish between the option of revolutionary action in democratic and dictatorial settings. In authentic democratic settings revolution never seems a valid option (this is perhaps one reason why dictatorial regimes are inclined to hide behind a democratic smoke-screen). Revolution, however good its original intention, is always a dangerous project: it is a risky, destructive and invariably tragic undertaking. Revolution is bound to disrupt the whole process of community. Fundamental societal breakdown will produce negative effects and the innocent will suffer along with the guilty. Revolution is only a very last resort, and in principle this stage is never reached in democracy. Authentic democracy aims to develop political structures characterised by sufficient constraints on abuse and sufficient possibilities for revision. This is the perfective utopian ideal of democracy. It is clear, however, that we cannot achieve freedom by merely wishing it (MacIntyre 1960: 23). In democratic contexts this suggests a reformist approach — a gradational meliorism situated between the poles of conservatism and revolutionism. But acts of reformism inside and outside the established political institutions can at times take a muscular form.

In dictatorial regimes the situation is completely different. Here, no other legitimate option may be left than to take the road toward revolution. But revolutions of this kind do not have to be mythic and foundationalist. The immediate revolutionary challenge may simply be to destroy the current regime of terror. It would be foolish not to accept the relevance of revolution in this case. But other considerations play a role. Revolutionary attempts have some tendency to fail. Intense suffering, including the suffering of those who did not participate in revolution but in whose name rebellion was undertaken, will be the outcome. Revolution as a response to tyranny better sees it as its highest duty to avoid failure. A failed revolution may be worse than no revolution at all. Moreover, successful revolutionary practice is subsequently confronted with the duty to install a new politics, but the qualities and virtues of the revolutionary self are one thing, while setting up a stable and continuous institutional framework is quite another. The relevant perfective capacities of the revolutionary self need to give way to those of the institutional and moderated self. Revolution often begins to fail exactly after the moment of its initial success.

The future of possibilist thought

We can conclude that our reception of future perfection is itself carried out in better and worse ways, and can thus be improved upon. We must come to dream in a proper sense, and this most definitely means leaving behind fanaticised or frozen versions of purpose, ideal, progress, and utopianism.

But we should make sure not to leave behind the language of future perfection as such. The language of future perfection or perfective possibility itself constitutes one of our most worthy possibilities. The future should interest us in a variety of ways. In general, we should never fail to be involved in strategies of 'futureness' (Toffler 1980: 378). In particular, it is important not to desert the perfective struggle in refusing to dream. We must always will more than only to try 'to make an uninspired peace with our shabby selves' (Desmond 1990: 20). This implies, among other things, the capability of creating longer projects, focused on ends that lie much further in time. Without this capacity it simply is impossible to accomplish great things (Nuttin 1980). Indeed, the disappearance of ideals, hope and utopia would lead to a life 'without purposes of a sort in which one can appropriately take reflective satisfaction' (Rescher 1987: 44).

What to hope for still? In a sense, for hope itself. Three suggestions might direct a contemporary form of hope. The first suggestion is that most of the great changes and improvements have been 'victories of the improbable' (Morin 1984: 460). The second is that, as humans, 'we are still beginners, and for that reason may hope to improve' (Medawar 1974: 127). This means that we have not exhausted all our human possibilities. The third suggestion is that making a better world will always be a highly relevant project, exactly because a best world is out of reach. The work of perfection is never finished.

CHAPTER TWELVE —
ENVIRONMENTAL PERFECTIONISM:
NATURE AND NARRATIVE

*Storied residence does not begin
with humans.*

— Holmes Rolston

It is appropriate to end this study with an exploration of non-human perfection. The world of perfection is not confined to human existence. It is important to take this point more explicitly into account.

The question of non-human perfection introduces the idea of an environmental perfectionism. Such a project stands in a complex relation to perfectionism as philosophical anthropology. On the one hand, we are the only creatures who speak about perfection. Our interpretation of nature, perfective or otherwise, unavoidably is a *human* effort. In this sense the project of an environmental perfectionism deserves a place within a broader existential perfectionism. On the other hand, the application of perfective concepts to realities beyond the human necessarily implies issues *beyond* anthropology. The claim that non-human perfection is out there — even while based on human interpretation — leads to a fresh perfective environmental dynamics, which runs against any radical humanistic attempt to confine perfection to our way of being (Scheers 2003).

The establishment of a non-human perfective realm offers certain impulses for a redirection of perfective anthropology as such. If we are not perfectively alone in the world it is likely that we shall have to broaden our human moral obligations, and work toward a respect for and a restoration of natural perfection. Our perfective capacity to interpret nature as involved in perfection leads to a radically transformed human responsibility for otherness. In this sense, one may define environmental ethics as 'the most altruistic form of ethics' (Rolston 1988: 341).

The idea of non-human perfection has already been suggested in the contexts of perfective hermeneutics (chapter 2) and perfective naturalism (chapter 8). Here, I will focus on one specific issue, namely the application of the perfective concept of story to the lives of plants and animals. My analysis aims to develop natural content for a concept *most commonly* associated with human perfective existence. We consider ourselves to be the heroes of narrative being.

The implications for environmental perfectionism are significant.

If we, in one way or another, can break through the idea that only humans are connected with the dignified realm of story, we will have obtained one more argument in favour of the fundamental insight that there is original meaning and perfection out there, beyond our cultures and cities.

A natural extension of narrative being is important for another reason too. The influential movements of narrative ethics and ethic of care focus on the fact that moral concern for others is strongly determined by the degree and manner in which we manage to appreciate these others in terms of a significant story. If it can be established that narrative being also applies to parts of nature we will in fact provide a thematic ground for an enlarged human moral concern for the non-human.

My aim in this chapter is to reach an adequate perfective sense of bio-narration (also see Scheers 2000). I will cover the issues of human narrative existence, non-human otherness, anthropomorphism, bio-narration, and the duty not to remain silent.

Heroes of narrative being

Numerous studies underline the deep connection between narrative and humanity in the context of different academic disciplines such as psychology, history, literature, religion, law, and so forth. Narrative being and construction seems to be everywhere in human existence. Roland Barthes writes that

> le récit est présent dans tous les temps, dans tous les lieux, dans toutes les sociétés; le récit commence avec l'histoire même de l'humanité; il n'y a jamais eu nulle part aucun peuple sans récit; toutes les classes, tous les groupes humains ont leur récits [...] international, transhistorique, transculturel, le récit est là, comme la vie.

We, indeed, are the products of a long and distinguished history of narrative mind. Our narrative development is perhaps a cultural adventure of which we do not know the final outcome. Through early enculturation, human selves receive a semantics of action and a hermeneutics of narrative selfhood. We are introduced to narrative concepts such as project, event, intention, coherence, obstacle, agent, habit, action, opponent, helper, together with basic plots of failure and success, of adventure and tragedy. We are narratively educated to speak about, and live in, time in certain ways. We learn to connect episodes and basic actions in larger schemes. By way of plots, the past, present and future are interconnected in a meaningful whole. The narrative paradigm permits us to understand human purposiveness. In a sense humans are doomed to be teleologically minded: we cannot choose not to be acquainted with purpose and direction. Our sense of narrative destiny resists such neutralisation. Narrative as interpretative, semiotic and practical perfective capacity strongly determines our place in this world, permitting us to make sense of ourselves and of historical processes in the world.

Where are we now in narrative history?

Narrative man has become a city-dweller, and it is as city-dweller that we experience the world itself as defined by particular stories. For a long time now many of us, certainly in the Western world, have left the cosmological stories behind. Urban narratives are mostly concerned with human actions, conflicts, and victories. We tell stories about ourselves to others, others tell their stories to us. Most things in cities serve human life stories.

The shining world of human perfection and narration is characterised by an imperial urge. In this regard we are the 'universal dominant creature' (Shepard 1998: 242). By way of our ambitions, capacities, practices and occupations we have transformed, and continue to transform, the world into a symptom and symbol of humanity. We are drastically rewriting the book of nature according to our technological and economic plots. There is a real danger that we will end up with an almost total inclusion of nature into human history. Industrial anthropocentric humanism seems to live by the following rule:

> Anything other than the human is not to be acknowledged as finally other. Indeed if anything intimates its otherness, nature for instance, this is not taken as refutation. Any such intimation of resistant otherness becomes rather a spur pricking the strong self to place *itself* in that space of otherness. Here we have a *program* for the historicization, humanizing of such otherness, such that once again man can be said to recognize nothing but himself' (Desmond 1987: 33)

Non-human others

A critical problem arises thus: what, indeed, is the place of the non-human other in the narrative world of humanity?

One's most common other is someone quite similar: other human selves. We have no real difficulty in interpreting other humans in terms of narrative being. They tell stories like we do; their communication and existence are structured in terms of narratives like ours; they act and suffer in similar fashion and they, too, interpret us as instances of storied being. Between humans there is a spontaneous narrative reciprocity. We do not only receive each other in narrative fashion, in fact we insist upon it. We demand from each other action and expression according to competences that in their togetherness constitute storied existence. We are expected, for example, to be able to tell life stories — this is a primary criterion for being accepted as a normal human being.

Plants and animals constitute more distant others. Our interpretation of them runs quite a different course. We exhibit at least two different attitudes.

On the one hand, we are strongly inclined to deny living non-human nature a life of meaning. This is the most influential form of human interpretation of plants and animals (in line with industrial humanism). Mostly convinced that plants and animals in their difference from us do not embody story, we refuse them significance altogether. Why take account of organisms that cannot tell stories? We give ourselves the right to use 'nature without meaning'. For example, we reduce animals to tools, toys and products. They become instrumental values, contributing to the fulfilment of our needs and desires. Animals, as well as plants, are interpreted according to a radical scenario of contributive perfection, without serious regard for original teleology — natural perfection is then simply conceived in terms of nature made useful to man's purpose (Passmore 1974: 28). Pigs are piled up in trucks as if we are dealing with a collection of boxes. In supermarkets and restaurants we find living lobsters bound and positioned in rows, one upon the other. The reduction and instrumentalisation of nature and natural entities constitutes a vast chapter within human productionist history.

On the other hand, notably in our connection to certain animals, we are at times prepared to draw a narrative picture. We are agreeably surprised by the complex way of being of a chimpanzee, and we treat our domesticated animals in ways resembling our relation to other human beings. We speak to cats, dogs and birds, and sometimes even — albeit far more cryptically — to our cherished plants. In the case of animals that are close to us, we may even expect fragments of humanised behaviour and consciousness in return. This return is never fully there, but we continue the projective habit. Some will perhaps applaud the narrative humanised approach to the animal and vegetal world, and consider it a form of hermeneutic generosity (especially when compared to the aggressive reductionism of industrial humanism). The underlying idea is that the project of humanisation enhances a positive treatment. However, while in comparison with industrial interpretation of plants and animals every other kind of interpretation indeed seems more kind, one must wonder whether in this case we do not simply introduce another form of interpretative violence. An anthropo-narrative treatment of animals (and plants) is in the end not a good thing. We mean well perhaps, but might do more wrong than good. There is a great risk that the authentic needs and projects of non-human creatures will remain unrecognised. We project human meaning into what in many aspects is different from us, and these differences do not get a serious voice in uncritical narrative projection.

If anti-narrative reductionism and anthropo-narrative projectionism constitute forms of misunderstanding plants and animals, can we attempt to proceed toward a more adequate understanding of vegetal and animal existence? A response to this question must first pass through the question of anthropomorphism.

The question of anthropomorphism

The claim that reductionism and projectionism are forms of misunderstanding natural otherness automatically implies the option that we can somehow arrive at a better interpretation of plants and animals. However, even while we are of good will and will the good, we may be so much captured by human categories, moods and perceptions that the human interpretation of nature will always constitute a distortion of one kind or another. A radical constructionist will stress that everything we see and articulate must be an invalid human projection. This means that we can never receive nature in at least some of its original aspects. In that case each understanding is as good as any other. There are no better and worse interpretations of nature, only human constructions without rational underpinning.

However, as we have seen earlier (perfective hermeneutics), human interpretation is characterised by perfective capacity, opening up different possibilities beyond radical distortion — also in relation to non-human otherness. It is clear that we cannot escape the human sense of reality — we cannot observe the world without human categories, and we cannot articulate aspects of animal and vegetal otherness without the use of human words — but the productive play of similarity (shared earthliness) and resistance (difference) can continue to aid us in the development of a better interpretation of plants and animals.

Constructionist projectionism is based on the assumption that there is a radical gap between plants/animals and humans. Once an absolute gap is accepted, the human interpretation of the non-human obviously is destined to go wrong, since our interpretation is *ours* and can therefore only confirm the gap. But it is not clear whether the gap is so great. There seem to be interpretative bridges too.

Plants, animals and humans do belong to one and the same planet; we are all creatures of the earth. Hence, it is not trivial to consider the earth as a basic source of similarity. The fact that we are fellow-voyagers with other creatures suggests that categories of human mind may sometimes be deeply appropriate to the order of non-human being. Notably between animals and humans one discovers vital similarities — drinking, sleeping, eating, fighting, running, and so forth. It is highly unlikely that we are completely cut off from all aspects of ways of being of animals and even of plants. Plants, too, have a life of nutrition, which we can understand to be as it is. We know ourselves what nutrition functionally means. This is also the case for other functions. The function and form of the nose of a dog, for example, is similar to that of a human being (Popper 1990: 30). To some degree, therefore, our own experience of organic and earthly being is likely to serve as a productive hermeneutical key, enabling us to reach out to points and purposes of non-human existence. The application of human words, combined with a sense of terminological adaptation, is not automatically to be taken as misdirection. It is invalid, for example, to regard the application of terms such as 'surprised' and 'bored' to animal being as totally unacceptable (Serpell 1996: 167). There appears to be a benign role for some kind of anthropomorphism, based on a reasonable and subtle application of human terminology to natural entities. We reach a plurivocal appreciation of anthropomorphism. There are better and worse versions of it.

The principle of resistance (difference), too, plays a benign role in the human interpretation of plants and animals. We cannot directly enter the way of being of bats, but we may manage to become aware of how a bat moves and flies and eats. Through its actions it provides us with an expressive testimony of its power to be. We use human words and look with human eyes, but what we see is not human. Vegetal processes and animal movements are capable of resisting many of our interpretations. The experience of resistance introduces the recognition of difference, sometimes the recognition of particular difference in dimensions that in a more general sense are similar.

It is good to psychologically appreciate the similarity between human and non-human creatures. The experience of similarity allows us to situate and anticipate events and structures in the world beyond ourselves. It is also good to experience and appreciate resistance and difference as this makes the world a wonderful place. Terrestrial richness is an important perfective value.

The hermeneutics of vegetal and animal being opens up opportunities beyond anthropomorphism as distortion. While applying certain human experiences, and terminologies, to the world of plants and animals we have the capacity to sift out better and worse interpretations of non-human otherness, a capacity specifically based on the interaction between experiences of similarity and difference. The practice of interpretative ethology is based exactly on our ability to understand the abilities of others (Wilder 1996).

Being capable of interpreting nature beyond radical constructionism, we are subsequently confronted with the moral task of interpreting nature as best as possible. Interpretative benevolence embodies a stubborn project, namely the attempt to discover original meaning and perfection wherever it may be found. An authentic benevolent interpreter will want to see as much significance as possible. This moral inclination involves 'a founding trust in the inherent worth and significance of the other' (Desmond 2001: 355). One will be positively inclined to read plants and animals in the light of meaning and perfective value. About this positive inclination, Maurice Maeterlinck writes:

> A trouver hors de nous une marque réelle d'intelligence, nous éprouvons un peu de l'émotion de Robinson découvrant l'émpreinte d'un pied humain sur la grève de son île. Il semble que nous soyons moins seuls que nous ne croyions l'être. (1943: 113)

And William Desmond writes in similar vein:

> So monkeys and parrots, rats and killer whales live being's intelligibility? Instead of alarming our conceit or inciting it, the human self, even in its distinctiveness,

need not be in estrangement from the rest of creation. A profound kinship with things is engraved on us. This might be cause for joy and for ethical respect (1990: 163).

The principle of interpretative benevolence, as in one aspect exemplified in Desmond and Maeterlinck, offers an alternative to the minimalist principle implied in Lloyd Morgan's canon, which says that in no case may we interpret an action as the outcome of the exercise of a higher faculty, if it can be interpreted as the outcome of the exercise of a lower one (quoted in Walker 1985: 56). However, uncritical adherence may come to blind us to the occurrence of genuine cleverness and ability (Wilder 1996: 34). To be sure, one must remain cautious and critical while ascribing perfections to plants and animals, but one should be equally concerned with a positive recognition of perfective richness and originality whenever this presents itself as the most relevant option. The most likely ascription is the one that takes into account the most evidence, and this ascription may very well lie beyond the law of parsimony (Walker 1985: 58).

Each time again it remains to be seen which human terms are possibly applicable to which forms of vegetal and animal being. We need to show prudence in our ways of application. To express processes of perfection and meaning in plants and animals we will have to look for words embedded in human dictionaries. And while using human words to describe and characterise nature different reasons for and against should be taken into account. There may be good reason not to apply a certain term, or to apply it only in a very transformed sense. A process of critical and constructive consideration forms the basis of a benevolent interpretation of nature.

This brings us to the central question: can we rationally defend an application of narrative being to the natural world? To answer this question it is relevant to consider narrative being in relation to three principal layers of nature: inanimate nature, plants, and animals (note: I will ignore the being of cells and fungi; this is, of course, something that we need to include in a more complete version of the theory of bio-narration). My analysis will make use of the narrative phenomenology of nature in Wilhelm Schapp's seminal study *In Geschichten verstrickt* (1976).

Narrative being and inanimate nature

A first basic group of objects are inanimate things. They constitute the non-vital outside world.

Can we say these objects imply a radical form of otherness, which cannot be bridged by narrative interpretation? We have to make a distinction between objects that are not in any way transformed by human hands and man-made objects intended for use.

The first kind, things not (substantially) transformed by human hands, has a pervasive presence in our human (life) stories. Alpinists, for example, need mountains to experience their adventures. The life stories of sailors are intimately connected with water. But mountains or seas or other inanimate realities (a stone, the ground we walk on) are not involved in their own stories and histories. Mountains, as physical structures, are not alive. We appear in the stories and histories of other persons and they appear in ours. Our way of narrative being implies reciprocal co-entanglement. Non-living objects, too, appear in our stories but there is no real meeting of stories. These objects have no separate narrative standing (*ibid.*: 3). In fairy tales mountains speak, and we refer to mother earth or complain that nature strikes back, but these metaphors do not literally define earth or nature in terms of personality.

It is important to set aside the idea of panpsychism. Hegel speaks of a natural crystal as possessing an inner vocation and a free force of its own. Peirce considers matter as effete mind. Husserl refers to material nature as the totality of sleeping monads, in which instinctualities are somehow present in a dormant manner. These thinkers do not exactly intend to characterise inanimate entities as proto-humans; nonetheless their expressions are somehow inclined to sneak in 'smart elements'. I do not think this is a good idea. It is much better to straightforwardly celebrate material nature in terms of systemic being. Physical being is organised being. This sense of organisation might in a way tempt us to apply terms such as information and finality and habit (Morin 1977: 262). However, we are not really confronted with germs of mentality, only with something that may have the appearance of being teleologically and informationally processed. But stars and crystals have no ends and vocations. The only thing we can say is that there are physical conditions of systemic formation. Certain interactions take the form of interrelations and subsequently turn into systemic organisation. In organised physical being new qualities rise up, making the system more than a sheer collection of parts. Think, for example, of the integrity of ecosystems (Westra 1994). An ecosystem is itself a non-living system (although it does contain living elements) with emergent togetherness.

The non-narrativeness of inanimate being should certainly not prevent us from admiring its organisation and systemic perfection. Matter does matter. The project of a land ethics rightly includes a respect for the workings of soil, water, mountains, and so on. (Leopold 1967). A river is something that emerges and has value as a concrete form of physical and eco-systemic being. A physical system implies material versions of the perfections of composition, completeness, purity, continuity, richness, scope, and so forth.

The second kind of non-living objects are material things created or transformed by humans (Schapp 1976: 11) — a hammer, a chair, a street, a house, or a factory. Objects like these, which are intended for use, also have no narrative existence in their own right. However, unlike untouched natural objects they directly refer to human narratives in a determinate manner. They serve a purpose in the development and maintenance of human life stories. They are conceived by our minds and fabricated by our hands, according to a scheme of contributive perfection. The otherness of use-objects constitutes a collaborative otherness, serving our needs and stories.

Plants and animals, too, often become a part of the realm of objects to be used. When we cut down a tree or kill an animal, we mostly do this in an effort to introduce these entities in the realm of instrumental being. However, the reality of living entities brings us ontologically and morally beyond material things and inanimate objects.

How to define the place of organic being within the narratio-sphere? A fundamental distinction has to be made between plants and animals. I will first concentrate on the being of plants.

Narrative being and plants

Non-human organic life in the form of plants confronts us with another level of existence. Living organisms as such require a new level of description. In the same way that we cannot understand a human organism without seeing it as being entangled in histories, so too is it impossible to say something essential about plants, or to come in contact with them in a fundamental sense, without somehow entering the realm of history and story (*ibid.*: 125). This is a fundamental claim in the narrative phenomenology of Schapp: each plant is a history, and a history invites (and can in fact only be adequately articulated in) a narrative. Aldo Leopold, too, refers to 'the hundred little dramas of the woods and meadows' (1967: 32). Human beings may certainly speak about trees in non-narrative ways, but then they are bound to ignore much of what is going on with plants in its vital aspects.

The life of a plant, for example, has a beginning, middle and end. Many things happen with and to plants. Confronted with an oak we sense a texture of histories (*ibid.*: 131): a storm may threaten the oak's existence, rain provides renewed opportunities, insects may make its life difficult. A tree is a history of progress and decay, a history to be captured in a narrative (to be told by humans). Vegetal history places plants within the narratio-sphere — not as entities that narrate and interpret narratives, but as entities having existences that deserve and, in fact, need to be narrated by humans. Each plant is a 'central history', entangled in the histories of others (including humans), and in which others (including humans) are entangled (*ibid.*: 136). Plants are historical beings objectively, but do not know this subjectively (Rolston 1994: 179).

A narrative view on plants cannot simply be taken for granted. We have accepted that inanimate things cannot be (directly) included in the realm of narrative being. A flame or a cloud may sometimes move as if animate, but clearly we have no difficulty in realising that flames and clouds are not alive. The idea of a flame or cloud narrative is at most an amusing thought. The question is now whether we should not receive plant narration in the same way. Plants move even less than flames and clouds. They remain where they are, passive and immobile. Is the lack of mobility in plants not a sign of non-narrative being, of a being without a dramatic history?

This question leads to a basic issue: what are the minimal conditions for the presence of narrative being? When is it possible, and indeed necessary, to formulate the reality of something in terms of a story?

One important issue to be pointed out in favour of a narrative interpretation of plants is the fact that plants, unlike flames, are involved in sustained efforts-to-be. In Ricoeur's hermeneutic phenomenology (1969) we find this term applied to human existence, but it can be extended — or rather, it can be brought back — to the realm of organic being. The notion of effort-to-be lies behind the human perception of the difference between stones and plants, between flames and plants. It functions as an ultimate concept. But how do we know whether this ultimate concept is not a fiction? It is fruitful to turn to Ricoeur's discussion.

For Ricoeur the interpretation and estimation of a particular human narrative life unavoidably takes the structure of a hermeneutic circle. How do we sense that certain events and movements are versions of meaningful action and narrative history? This is only possible when we presuppose and believe that these events and movements are expressions of a sustained effort to-be. How to sense an authentic effort-to-be? Only through a fair or benign reading of a sequence of events and movements that suggests an effort-to-be (we hereby make use of our own experience as effort to be). Sensing others as human efforts-to-be is never a matter of rigid truth. Already our own feelings about our powers are not a matter of objective certainty. We feel assured about ourselves and this assurance rests on an affective form of trust without complete epistemological confirmation. This sense of trust can also be applied, I think, to the life of plants. Plants do not speak. They do not move or act like humans. But there are visible aspects in plants, which human beings are able to read and which testify that something significant is going on.

To be able to receive these signs it may be helpful to break through human versions of development. We live with a rapid rhythm, but the time in which plants develop is often situated on another scale. In nature documentaries we are sometimes confronted with an accelerated film about trees or flowers. We observe then in a few minutes how a tree develops, what happens to it, how it recovers or fades away. This artificial acceleration makes visible to us the historical texture of a tree; it confronts us in a very direct way with 'die ganze Dramatik des Lebens' (Max Scheler, quoted in Corbey 1988: 27). Observing growth, blossoming, development, recovery, or decay, it is not impossible for human beings to sense vegetal expressions of an effort-to-be. Plants may not have organs of perception, hands and legs, a nervous system, and independent mobility, but there are a sufficient number of signs giving expression to a functional way of being. A plant uses relevant ingredients in its surrounding, something that we do not see in stones. And the form of leaves is not mechanically caused through erosion. The combination of gravity and the physical being of raindrops leads plants, as evolutionary entities, to create forms of leaves that make the water fall in a way most convenient for the plant's roots. These and many other things suggest that one may regard plants as 'original concretions of the original power of being' (Desmond 1995b: 506).

There are, thus, many things that matter to a plant, even if a plant itself cannot mentally conceive its own values. As an effort-to-be a plant is nothing less than an axiological entity. With life values enter the world (Popper 1990: 50). Some things in the world are contributively valuable for the identity of a plant (water, minerals, earth, sun), while other elements are contrary or neutral to its existence (certain insects for example). The point is that a plant preserves its life as a good (Rolston 1994: 194). Vegetal beings are values for themselves because, once given to be, they maintain their integrity and strive to perpetuate themselves (Desmond 1995b: 513).

It is, once again, obvious that a plant cannot itself apprehend its good or its ends, but in our human interpretation of plants we can arrive at the idea of a vegetal axiology and teleology on the basis of the hermeneutics of similarity.

The dimension of values and ends deepens the connection between the vegetal realm and narrative being. The dimension of narrative — as we know it best in the context of human reality — is itself defined by essential reference to values and ends. Narratological studies bring to light that human narratives are axiologically and teleologically structured. Heroes are defined as entities striving for certain things or situations and trying to avoid others (Bremond 1966). Without values and ends, situated in time and space, there would be no dramatic history to be told since what happens would not matter to anyone. Since only living organisms are axiologically and teleologically structured, and since narrative is concerned with values and ends, one may arrive at the idea of a *vital* narrative: the medium of story is taken to offer an adequate instrument for the interpretation and articulation of the already existing histories of living creatures such as plants. As Rolston notes, the logic of life is biography emplaced in geography (1994: 178). *Bios* is history that deserves a narrative interpretation. We arrive, thus, at a narrative ontology of vegetal being.

One important aspect of vegetal history is the presence, even if only a minimal sense (when compared to animals and humans), of 'narrativeness' (Morson 2003). Narrativeness refers to elements such as eventness, unpredictability, possible futures, and suspense. Narrativeness is the plurivocal dimension in actual existence that makes narrative articulation necessary. For example, the present moment matters to plants. A sudden event can turn things around, for better or worse. These events cannot be predicted with absolute certainty, even if plants have much more predictable lives than animals and humans. Plants, too, have possible futures. Vegetal histories are processes that may evolve in different ways, due to obstacles, sudden events and contingency. Each vegetal species is organised in response to regularities *and* contingencies of earthly being. This unavoidably introduces the element of suspense. There are ends and goods to be sustained and protected. Plants are organically directed towards survival, but things can go wrong. There is the presence of danger and risk. Ultimately, danger is deadly danger. Life stories, in this sense, are death stories. What is alive will cease to exist, and what can die is embedded in a history characterised by drama.

The narrative interpretation of plants holds a fragile but real position. In different aspects, one must admit, there may be a very fine line between benevolent interpretation and distorting projection. I am aware that the practice of bio-narration with regard to plants could in certain respects imply an invitation to unconsciously sneak in certain human elements. Nonetheless, on a deeper onto-logical level, I think it is legitimate to hold on to an application of story and life story to the world of plants. Plants do not tell stories, do not have capacities of planning and self-reflection, do not know themselves as narrative beings, do not possess individuality like humans do, but they, too, are involved in histories characterised by effort, events, opportunities, obstacles, capacity, quality, success and failure, better and worse, value and disvalue, mutualism and antagonism. We need narrative because there are significant things to narrate.

I am not insisting that we should discover an adventure or tragedy in every leaf that falls on the ground — a hyper-narrative interpretation of vegetal existence is not what we should seek. We need a sober conception of bio-narration. The main issue is perhaps simply to accept that narrative being in one way or another applies to the ontology of plants, without necessarily getting involved in, or being able to articulate, very concrete narrative interpretations of particular plants. Wilhelm Schapp seems to suggest this hermeneutic option when he writes the following about the histories and stories of plants:

> Wir müssen uns damit zufrieden geben, daß diese Geschichten zu uns herüberwe-hen wie die klange einer fernen Musik, die wir nicht mehr in Noten wiedergeben können, von der wir nur sagen können, daß sie Musik sind, Musik die uns anspricht (1976: 134).

Narrative being and animals

After plants we enter the realm of animal being. Earlier narrative findings remain valid. Animals are also efforts-to-be. There are animal goods. There are elements of narrativeness in the animal world. The hermeneutics of testimony is equally relevant. Clearly, the histories and life stories of animals are far more complex than those of plants. They can be expected to provide us with more intense opportunities for narrative interpretation.

We quickly sense the difference between the animal and non-animal world. Ethological studies of animal behaviour constitute a scientific discipline in its own right. One says of a man or of an animal that he behaves in a certain way. One does not really say this of a plant. It is not difficult to guess why. Animals do not only develop through time but, much more visibly than plants, are involved in differentiated forms of action, effort, and skill. Animals move, fight, run away, look for partners, and protect their offspring. There are involved in an alert and self-moving life. Animals have to react to a world of foreseen and unforeseen events. This is one reason, for example, why there could never emerge any animal that moves by 'wheels':

> Wheels work on highways where the terrain is predictable. In a forest, or anywhere where the terrain is irregular, one may encounter an obstacle that wheels cannot negotiate, but which legs, which are more flexible than wheels, can. If the world were predictable, we would see a wheeled cheetah rolling after a wheeled antelope down the highway of the Serengeti. But animals have evolved to react to a world of radical contingency (Morson 2003: 65).

The complexities of action which we observe in the animal world provide us with a deeper opportunity — in combination with issues such as development, teleology, axiology, and suspense — to grant narrative being to animals. The narrative demands of behavioural existence are, as it were, inscribed in the animal bodies.

According to narratological theory, the relational dimension is central to narrative being on the human level. We live with friends and enemies, with helpers and antagonists. The relations and conflicts with others are extensively dealt with in our stories. In animals this dimension is also available in a varied manner, much more so than in the world of plants. One can think of togetherness, battle, flight, mutualism, antagonism, and other forms of interaction. The play of interaction, mutualism, and antagonism strongly adds to the drama of animal histories, and brings them closer to what we experience on the level of human histories and stories.

Animal action, interaction, mutualism, and antagonism is especially made possible by, and complexified in, two other animal competences, namely semiosis and interpretation.

It could be argued that plants, too, are involved in semiosis and interpretation. However, most bio-semioticians (see Deely 1990) are inclined to argue that *non-virtual* semiosis and interpretation may have a presence on the level of inter- and intracellular being, but not on the level of plants as organic totalities.

It is in any case clear that the interpretative and semiotic competence of animals is played out in a distinct, extended, and varied manner not found in plants.

Animals could not sustain their active and interactive lives without communication, expression, and interpretation. Information is of vital importance. And social relations, such as the formation of alliances, presuppose communicational skills. Creatures of the same species must be able to locate and identify each other. This happens through the production of signs, which may convey information about what niche an animal occupies in a territory as well as its status in a social hierarchy (Sebeok 1972: 130). There are intimidating and decoying signs, signs of submission and authority.

In the 'higher' animals (chimpanzees, dogs, cats, dolphins, whales, etc.) we may find the more complex communications and sign-productions, but semiosis comes in numerous shades and forms. It is also present in spiders, bees, and all other animals. Take, for example, the dance of the honeybee, which is a semiotic means to inform the hive about places where to find food, water, and nesting sites. The dance is primordially an indexical sign, since location and distance of the place determine the direction of tail vibration. But the bee dance is also involved in a form of iconic sign-behaviour, since there is an underlying similarity between distance of the place and the speed of the dance. Finally, the presence of various dialects of bee dancing may also suggest a sense of symbolic semiosis, that is, of sign-production grounded in conventions. Many theorists are inclined to doubt the presence of symbolic conventions in animal semiosis, because this is regarded to open up a possibility of animal culture and innovation. However, ethological research does come up with interesting findings concerning differences in tool behaviour of chimpanzees, arbitrariness of tail work in dogs and cats, and the presence of dialects in bird songs.

Interpretation equally has a pervasive presence in animal action and interaction. Animals live in species-specific *Umwelten* (subjective environments) (von Uexküll 1980). They are the concerned builders of their environment. The world experience of a fly, for example, is structurally different from that of a bat or a scorpion. Each kind of *Umwelt* is defined in a functional circle of perception and operation. Animal environments are constituted by interplay between things noticed and things acted upon. Animal meanings are imprinted upon objects. Some things or aspects do not exist in certain *Umwelten*; and the same object may constitute a different reality in different *Umwelten*: a table for humans is a thing to lie under for dogs. Specific interpretation defines the histories of animal kinds. Interpretation is a concrete testimony of the effort-to-be — interpretation matters to an entity, which through interpretation testifies that aspects of being matter to it. Each animal is an organic centre from which activities of interpretation radiate. We are confronted with organic versions of the hermeneutic circle. Needs, interests and capacities give rise to a certain *Umwelt*, and the *Umwelt* refers to, demands, and makes possible certain capacities and interests.

With his hermeneutics of animal being Uexküll provides us with a fine perspective on the book of nature as 'ein unerhort reiches Gewebe von sich überschneidenden und ineineinder eingepaßter subjektiven Umwelten' (1980: 377). Each *Umwelt* permits, and pushes for, certain selective interactions with and responses to elements of otherness, elements which often are a part of other *Umwelten*. The differentiated interpretative life of animals explains much of the drama each animal will experience (obstacles, opportunities, friends and enemies). To know an animal's way of interpretation is to know much of its storied existence.

The presence of semiosis and interpretation provides us with two essential links to human narrative being. Think of our stories. Communication and miscommunication, lies and deceptions produced by strategies of sign-behaviour, interpretation and misunderstanding, in large part define what happens in our lives. Many of our conflicts and victories are defined by semiotic and interpretative activities. Human narration itself is a semiotic and interpretative enterprise. Semiosis and interpretation in humans is for a large part played out on the level of the natural languages, something that is not available in animals, but the main point is that there is a clear and varied life of semiosis and interpretation beyond the linguistic way of being.

The human interpretation of animals, when directed to our house and farm animals, may be deeply coloured by a hermeneutics of similarity. When, for example, human beings work together with a dog or a horse in farming and in other practices, we sense processes of mutual understanding. Dogs and horses seem to construct the outside world or environment to some degree similar to our own experience of an outside world. But many other kinds of animal species are not near to us at all — in a geographical as well as in a psychological sense. Then, we are bound to experience deeper gaps and discover much less similarity. From a human perspective there are more and less transparent animal histories. The plot used to describe the life of a tick, capable of waiting in a tree for years until a mammal passes by, involves humans much less than plots applied to the lives of dolphins or horses. However, so Schapp insists, the gap with distant animals will never be so radical as to make completely impossible any understanding of animal being in terms of a history that can be narrated to some degree (1976: 137).

With Heidegger (1983) one can more strongly underline the otherness of animal being. He points out, for example, that the connections of animals to the world are radically different from the qualities of human perception and understanding). A lizard looks at a stone, warmed by the sun, as something to lie on, but it is highly doubtful that it sees the sun as sun, or the stone as stone. It only knows 'lizard things'. Animals do not see something as something, but as things to catch or eat. They do not experience and create linguistic meanings and totalities like humans do. Animals are therefore poor in world (*weltarm*), while humans are world-forming (*weltbildend*). Moreover, animal orientation is especially characterised by drive and release of tension. An animal, unlike humans, is captured in a confined *Umring*. It senses objects only in function of momentary inclination. Animals are situated in an enveloping immediacy. William Desmond writes, in a similar vein:

> Animal desire seeks definite objects — food, shelter, sex. It repeats itself — now briefly satisfied, in a moment it will spring up dissatisfied again. It repeats itself in a circular way — the animal moves through the round of nature, alternating endlessly between lack and repetition (1995a: 76).

It is indeed obvious that animal interpretations, actions, signs, and histories are not identical to human ones. It is quite legitimate, with Heidegger, to stress qualitative differences. Think of human reflection, language, creativity, and freedom. We may have an *Umweltfreiheit* not available in animals.

However, something is found in animals, and we should honour this as such. Let us guard ourselves against any quick tendency to simply regard animal properties as 'deviations', as 'lower capacities' considered from the normative standpoint of human experience.

Weltarm seems to imply such an evaluation from a human perspective. Heidegger himself is, in fact, bothered by this evaluative implication and in part does his best to perfectively turn the tide. In different passages he stresses that animals do not themselves suffer from their lack of interpretative openness to the world. As such animals fulfil their capacities with complete adequacy. In this sense, one may consider each species as perfect in its own terms. Heidegger states: 'Jedes Tier und jede Tierart ist als solche gleich vollkommen wie die andere' (1983: 287). This point brings Heidegger again one step closer to Uexküll, who writes: 'Jedes Lebewesen besitzt seine Spezialbühne, die genau so real ist wie die Spezialbühne des Menschen' (1980: 355).

The hermeneutic combination of similarity and difference, while offering a serious space for the uniqueness of human experience, should never bring us to ignore the functionality and perfective status of animal stories and life stories, which ultimately have their own point and purpose (this point, of course, also applies to vegetal being). For example, for us the life of a tick is likely to appear extraordinarily boring, but from the perspective of the tick, leading a life of functional simplicity, the nervous complications of human life might be regarded as needless deviation. It all depends which — and whose — perfective standards we wish to apply. If the perfective aim is only to survive, amoebas would be the thing to be (Midgley 1978: 152).

It is an essential ingredient of adult moral consciousness to let things be according to their own (implied) standards:

> A well-bred salmon will love the life of a salmon, which after all, is the only life it can know. The life cycle for it may seem to be its own point, with no further

purpose, no further achievement external to it, needed to establish its rational credentials. To insist that without permanently preserved achievements and lasting monuments, the life of a salmon is absurd, is a piece of parochial prejudice on the part of human beings (Feinberg 1992: 3 10).

In their own functional context, animal perfections are valuable — not as poor imitations of human performance, but as competence and virtuosity not our own (Rolston 1994: 104). In their particular settings animals are masters, and may even exemplify a *superior* capacity:

> Many other animals outdo us in the range of sensuous attunement of eye or ear or nose. They sense a presence, where we feel nothing but the vacant wind; they see a prowler haunting the darkness which for us is only black night; they scent the coming of the thunder clap, while we balm heedlessly in the sleepy sun. Biologically they are on the alert, while we just picnic (Desmond 1995a: 72).

It is best to perfectively propose a plurality of 'vital norms'. Human narratives about animal histories do well to accept the perfective originality of animal ways of being. We may not be capable of existentially abandoning our own vital norms, but it seems possible for us to sense, at least, that a bat or a snake is characterised by its own set of norms and goods. Animal life stories exemplify specific varieties of perfective teleology, quality, and capacity.

The duty not to be silent

The general point made in this chapter is that we are not islands of perfection and meaning in a desert of nothingness (Midgley 1978: 19).

Putting aside a direct narrative interpretation of material nature, we can endorse the introduction of life stories on the level of vegetal and animal being. Somewhere between the radical denial of narrative beyond humanity and an uncritical, humanised application of narrative to the non-human lies an interpretative middle of narrative natural being.

It will continue to be true that one may always doubt the relevance of human terms, such as narrative, for the interpretation of nature, plants and animals. Ultimately, one may end up without any conceptual means to say something about the non-human. But not speaking about nature will simply lead us to ignore its original qualities. The duty not to be silent is a moral task occupying a central position in any ethical system, so too in environmental perfectionism as a moral perspective. We need benevolent interpreters who continue to bring up the issue of natural perfection and meaning, hereby embracing the conviction that we did not invent natural meaning, but that 'the world has always meant something. It just didn't know it' (Hoffmeyer 1996: 146).

In principle, plants and animal are very capable of taking care of themselves — if only we let them be. The best we can do, one could argue, is to leave nature alone. Perhaps we should even withdraw from certain quarters of the earth or at least shut down our industrial activities in the important ecological areas. And to convince ourselves that we should eventually withdraw, as to some degree I think we certainly should, it is important to realise that plants and animals are original projects of perfection, and authentic members of the narratio-sphere.

It is important never to shut our eyes to the perfective fact that 'to kill a species is to shut down a unique story' (Rolston 1988: 145).

CONCLUSION

With an eye on the development of a complex theory of perfection I have in this study attempted to establish the following.

In the first three chapters I have highlighted the position of interpretation in human and perfective existence, the inescapable perfective aspects of interpretation, and the interpretative nature of perfective theory. I have concluded that, on the basis of an evolutionary hermeneutics, it is possible to develop a contemporary reading of perfective language and human perfective existence.

An explicit connection between interpretation and perfection can be expected to have fruitful effects for the further development of both hermeneutics and perfection. I have been concerned mainly with the theory of perfection, but one may have the hope that in times to come hermeneutics could take a more systematic perfective form. A direct perfective appreciation of interpretative existence would have to include a renewed reading of the hermeneutic tradition — a tradition that already harbours many explicit perfective moments. A hermeneutics informed by perfectionism may, in turn, be expected to stimulate the further, rational development of a perfectionism informed by hermeneutics.

In the next four chapters I have developed a contemporary language of perfection. It has been made clear that one can continue a positive conception of perfection, that perfection is a degree-concept with a specific content, that it is important to install a differentiated perfective language that aims to fit the actual complexity of human appraisive consciousness, and that a varied aretaic perfective terminology — in the framework of a realistic personology adequate to the needs and possibilities of fallible selves — can survive situationist criticism.

In a third set of chapters I have clarified different aspects of human perfective existence. I have first of all offered an argument in perfective naturalism — a general argument that has been complemented with certain suggestions concerning the personal or individual aspects of human perfection. I have also sketched a perfective praxiology in dialogue with Alasdair MacIntyre. My aim has been to highlight the invaluable role of practices for the development of human perfective existence. Finally, I have proposed a melioristic and perfective reading of possibilist consciousness. My aim has been to underline and explore the position of 'future perfection' in human existence.

It is obvious that other elements could have been included in my analysis of perfective language and existence. It is equally obvious that certain elements touched upon deserve a more extensive exploration. The language of perfection could be further explored in its relation to axiology. The aim would be to reach a systematic perfective axiology. It is necessary, also, to develop a perfective theory of moral concepts. One should in particular envisage the possibility of a plurivocal ethics concerning itself with the definition of and relation between principal moral ingredients such as duties, rights, virtues, values, and consequences. Furthermore, questions concerning existential wholeness, life plans, self-interpretation, fulfilment, happiness, and so on, could be systematically explored in the framework of a narrative eudaimonism, that is, a theory focused on the interpretation and formation of perfective life stories. It would be good, too, to apply the model of perfective practice in different fields — not only work, but also, for example, the world of sport. The question of meaningful work, in particular, could become part of an extended review of the project of an occupational perfectionism. We would then have to include issues such as the idea of work, quality of work, professionalism, the idea of craft, Taylorism, deskilling, moral dynamics in occupational roles, economics, unemployment, and so forth. Finally, I have not dealt with the political implications of perfectionism and with the perfective implication of politics. This is something that needs to be addressed in a possible future attempt.

In a last chapter I have introduced the project of an environmental perfectionism by way of a defence of bio-narration with regard to plants and animals. My aim has been to underscore a benign extension and transformation of human concepts (such as 'life story') with an eye on a perfective interpretation of non-human nature. Beyond the tenets of a radical constructionist perspective I have insisted upon the point that there are better and worse ways to interpret nature. A bio-narrative understanding of plants and animals is one way to honour the life of meaning and perfection in nature.

At a later time it would be good to enrich the project of an environmental perfectionism with the development of a perfective theory of the conservationist self, in dialogue with Aldo Leopold and other ecological thinkers. Natural conservation, as a human perfective practice, may offer a conceptual setting for a defence and analysis of eco-systemic consciousness, environmental virtues, a larger sense of earthly community, and a narrative and aesthetic appreciation of nature. It is clear that the development of a systematic environmental perfectionism constitutes a most urgent challenge.

The many suggestions for extension make one thing visible. Perfectionism itself is in a permanent state of relative perfection. We continue to be confronted with numerous demands for improvement. The process of perfecting perfectionism will never know a definite ending.

BIBLIOGRAPHY

Adler, A. (1933), *Der Sinn des Lebens*. Vienna.

Alexander, P. and Gill, R. (eds.) (1984), *Utopias*. London.

Allport, G. W. (1955), *Becoming*. New Haven.

—, (1956), *Personality*. London.

—, (1961), *Pattern and Growth in Personality*. New York.

Anderson, E. (1993), *Value in Ethics and Economics*. Cambridge (Mass.).

Annas, J. (1993), *The Morality of Happiness*. New York.

Applbaum, A. (1999), *Ethics for Adversaries*. Princeton.

Arneson, R. J. (2000), 'Perfectionism and politics'. *Ethics* 111.

Arnold, Matthew (1965), 'Culture and Anarchy'. In *The Complete Prose Works of Matthew Arnold*. Vol. 5. Ann Arbor.

Aschenbrenner K. (1971), *The Concepts of Value*. Dordrecht.

—, (1974), *The Concepts of Criticism*. Dordrecht.

—, (1983), *Analysis of Appraisive Characterization*. Dordrecht.

Ashbee, C. R. (1908), *Craftsmanship in Competitive Industry*. Campden.

Aspinwall, L. and Staudinger, V. (2003), 'A psychology of human strengths'. In Aspinwall & Staudinger (eds.) (2003).

Aspinwall, L. and Staudinger, V. (eds.) (2003), *A Psychology of Human Strenghths*. Washington, DC.

Attfield, R. (1987), *A Theory of Value and Obligation*. London.

Baier, K. (1988), 'Radical virtue ethics'. In French (et al.) (1988).

Baltes, P. and Freund, A. (2003), 'Human strength as the orchestration of wisdom and selective optimization with compensation'. In Aspinwall & Staudinger (eds.) (2003).

Barthes, R. (1977), 'Introduction à l'analyse structurale des récits'. In R. Barthes (et al.). *Poétique du récit*. Paris.

Bauman, Z. (1976), *Socialism: the Active Utopia*. London.

Bekoff, M. and Jamieson, D. (eds.) (1996), *Readings in Animal Cognition*. Cambridge (Mass.).

Blanchette, O. (1992), *The Perfection of the Universe According to Aquinas*, University Park (Penn.).

Blatt, J. (1995), 'The destructiveness of perfectionism'. *American Psychologist* 50.

Blondel, M. (1973), *L'action*. Paris.

Bollnow, O. F. (1958), *Wesen und Wandel der Tugenden*. Frankfurt am Main.

—, (1968), *Einfache Sittlichkeit*. Göttingen.

Bond, E. J. (1996), *Ethics and Human Well-Being*. Cambridge (Mass.).

Bontekoe, R. (1996), *Dimensions of the Hermeneutic Circle*. Atlantic Highlands.

Booth, W. (1988), *The Company We Keep*. Berkeley.

Bovone, L. (1993), 'Ethics as etiquette: the emblematic contribution of Erving Goffman'. *Theory, Culture, and Society* 10.

Brandt, R. (1970), 'Traits of character: a conceptual analysis'. *American Philosophical Quarterly* 7.

Bremond, C. (1966), 'La logique des possibles narratifs'. *Communications* 8.

Buchler, J. (1966), *Metaphysics of Natural Complexes*. New York.

Bühler, C. (1969), *Wenn das Leben gelingen soll*. Munich.

Burgen, A. (et al.) (eds.) (1997), *The Idea of Progress*. Berlin.

Carr, E. (1981), *What is History?* Harmondsworth.

Cavell, S. (1990), *Conditions Handsome and Unhandsome. The Constitution of Emersonian Perfectionism*. Chicago.

Chisholm, R. (1977), *Theory of Knowledge*. Englewood Cliffs.

Cioran, E. (1960), *Histoire et utopie*. Paris.

Conly, S. (1988), 'Flourishing and the failure of the ethics of virtue'. In French (et al.) (eds.) (1988).

Connor, S. (1992), *Theory and Cultural Value*. Oxford.

Corbey, R. (1988), *De mens een dier?* Nijmegen (doctoral diss.).

Cottingham, J. (1996), 'Partiality and the virtues'. In Crisp (ed.) (1996).

Crisp, R. (1992), 'Utilitarianism and the life of virtue'. *Philosophical Quarterly* 42.

Crisp, R. (ed.) (1996), *How Should One Life?* Oxford.

Crisp, R. and Slote, M. (eds.) (1997), *Virtue Ethics*. Oxford.

Csikszentmihalyi, M. (1988), 'The future of flow'. In M. Csikszentmihalyi and T. Csikszentmihalyi (eds.). *Optimal Experience: Psychological Studies of Flow in Consciousness*. Cambridge.

—, (1999), 'If we are so rich, why aren't we happy?' *American Psychologist* 54.

Csikszentmihalyi, M. and Robinson, R. (1986), 'Culture, time and the development of talent'. In Sternberg & Davidson (eds.) (1986).

Csikszentmihalyi, M. and Rathunde, K. (1990), 'The psychology of wisdom: an evolutionary interpretation'. In Sternberg (ed.) (1990).

Csikszentmihalyi, M. (et al.) (1993), *Talented Teenagers*. Cambridge.

Darwall, S. (1999), 'Valuing activity'. *Social Philosophy and Policy* 28.

Day, W. (2000), 'Knowing as instancing. Jazz improvisation and moral perfectionism'. *Journal of Aesthetics and Art Criticism* 58.

Deci, E. L. and Ryan, R. M. (1985), *Intrinsic Motivation and Self-Determination in Human Behaviour*. New York.

Deely, J. (1990), *Basics of Semiotics*. Bloomington.

Desmond, W. (1987), *Desire, Dialectic, and Otherness*. New Haven.

—, (1990), *Philosophy and its Others*. Albany.

—, (1995a), *Being and the Between*. Albany.

—, (1995b), *Perplexity and Ultimacy*. Albany.

—, (2001), *Ethics and the Between*. Albany.

Dewey, J. (1978), *Ethics*. In John Dewey, *The Middle Works*. vol. 5. Carbondale and London.

—, (1980), *Democracy and Education*. In John Dewey, *The Middle Works*. vol. 9. Carbondale and London.

—, (1983), *Human Nature and Conduct*. In John Dewey, *The Middle Works*. vol. 14. Carbondale.

—, (1984), *The Quest for Certainty*. In John Dewey, *The Later Works*. vol 4. Carbondale.

Doris, I. (1998), 'Persons, situations, and virtue ethics'. *Nous* 32.

—, (2002) *Lack of Character*. Cambridge.

Driver, J. (1996), 'The virtues and human nature'. In Crisp (ed.) (1996).

Düll, L. (1984), 'Freiheit und perfektion'. *Conceptus* 18.

Eco, U. (1992), 'Interpretation and history'. In S. Collini (ed.). *Interpretation and Overinterpretation*. Cambridge.

Ewin, R E. (1992), 'Loyalty and virtues'. *The Philosophical Quarterly* 42.

Feibleman, J. K. (1952), *Philosophers Lead Sheltered Lives*. London.

—, (1970), *The New Materialism*. The Hague.

—, (1975), *The Stages of Human Life*. The Hague.
—, (1979), *Christianity, Communism, and the Ideal Society*. New York.
Feinberg, J. (1992), *Freedom and Fulfillment*. Princeton.
Feldman, D. (2000), 'Developmental theory and the expression of gifts and talents'. In van Lieshout & Heymans (eds.) (2000).
Fink, E. (1979), *Grundphänomene des menschlichen Daseins*. Freiburg.
Flanagan, O. (1991), *Varieties of Moral Personality*. Cambridge (Mass.).
Foot, P. (1978), *Virtues and Vices*. Berkeley.
—, (2001), *Natural Goodness*. Berkeley.
Foss, M. (1946), *The Idea of Perfection in the Western World*. Lincoln.
Frankena, W. (1973), *Ethics*. Englewood Cliffs.
Frankfurt, H. (1988), *The Importance of What We Care About*. Cambridge.
Frazer, E. and Lacey, N. (1994), 'MacIntyre, feminism and the concept of practice'. In Horton & Mendus (eds.) (1994).
French, P. (et al.) (eds.) (1988), *Ethical Theory: Character and Virtue*. Notre Dame.
Fromm, E. (1971), *The Revolution of Hope*. New York.
Gadamer, H.-G. (1986), *Wahrheit und Methode*. Tübingen.
—, (1993), *Über die Verborgenheit der Gesundheit*. Frankfurt-am-Main.
—, (1995), *Hans-Georg Gadamer im Gespräch*. Heidelberg.
Galston, J. (1991), 'Toughness as a virtue'. *Social Theory and Practice* 91.
Gardner, H. (1993), *Frames of Mind*. London.
Geach, P. (1979), *The Virtues*. Cambridge.
—, (2001), *Truth and Hope*. Notre Dame,
Geertz, C. (1973), *The Interpretation of Cultures*. Chicago.
Gelven, M. (1997), *The Risk of Being*. University Park (Penn.).
Gewirth, A. (2001), *Self-fulfilment*. Princeton.
Gibson, J. (1982), 'Notes on affordances'. In E. Reed and R. Jones (eds). *Reasons for Realism*. Hillsdale.
Ginsberg, M. (1962), *On the Diversity of Morals*. London.
Goldstein, K. (1934), *Der Aufbau des Organismus*. The Hague.
—, (1966), *Human Nature in the Light of Psychopathology*. New York.
Greenspan, T. (2000), 'Healthy perfectionism is an oxymoron'. *Journal of Secondary Gifted Education* 11.
Greisch, J. (1977), *Herméneutique et grammatologie*. Paris.
Griffin, J. (1986), *Well-Being*. Oxford.
Habermas, J. (2001), *Die Zukunft der menschlichen Natur*. Frankfurt am Main.
Hafter, M. (1966), *Gracian and Perfection*. Cambridge (Mass.).
Harman, G. (1999), 'Moral philosophy meets social psychology: virtue ethics and the fundamental attribution error'. *Proceedings of the Aristotelian Society* 99.
Hamilton, R. (1990), 'The aesthetics of imperfection'. *Philosophy* 90.
Harré, R. and Krausz, M. (1996), *Varieties of Relativism*. Oxford
Hartshorne, C. (1962), *The Logic of Perfection*. La Salle.
Heidegger, M. (1963), *Sein und Zeit*. Tübingen.
—, (1983), *Die Grundbegriffe der Metaphysik*. Frankfurt am Main.
Heil. J. (1985), 'Thoughts on the virtues'. *Journal of Value Inquiry* 19.
Heller, A. (1991), 'The role of interpretation in modern ethical practice'. *Philosophy and Social Criticism* 17.
—, (1998), 'The moral situation in modernity'. In A. Heller and F. Fehér. *The Post-Modern Political Condition*. Cambridge.

Helwig, P. (1957), *Charakterologie*. Stuttgart.

Hill, T, (1983), 'Ideals of human excellence and preserving natural environments'. *Environmental Ethics* 5,

Hirsch, E. (1976), *The Aims of Interpretation*. Chicago.

Hocking, W. E. (1928), *The Self*. New Haven.

Hoffmeyer, J. (1996), *Signs of Meaning in the Universe*. Bloomington.

Hollender, M. (1976), 'Perfectionism'. In A. Arkoff (ed.). *Psychology and Personal Growth*. Boston.

Hooker, B. (ed.) (1996), *Truth in Ethics*. Oxford.

Horney, K. (1942), *Self-Analysis*. New York.

—, (1950), *Neurosis and Human Growth*. New York.

Horton, J. and Mendus, S. (eds) (1994), *After MacIntyre*. Cambridge.

Howe, M. (1999), *The Psychology of High Abilities*. Basingstoke.

Hunt. L. (1997), *Character and Culture*. Lanham.

Hurka, T. (1993), *Perfectionism*. New York.

—, (2001), *Virtue, Vice, and Value*. New York.

Hursthouse, R. (1999), *On Virtue Ethics*. Oxford.

Huxley, A. (1957), *Proper Studies*. New York.

Iser, W. (1996), 'Coda to the discussion'. In S. Budick and W. Iser (eds.). *The Translatability of Cultures*. Stanford.

Jankélévich, V. (1977), *La mort*. Paris.

James, W, (1975), *Pragmatism*. Cambridge (Mass.).

—, (1979), *The Will to Believe and other Essays in Popular. Philosophy*. Cambridge (Mass.).

—, (1982), *Essays in Religion and Morality*. Cambridge (Mass.).

Jaspers, K. and Bultmann R. (1954), *Die Frage der Entmythologisierung*. Munich.

Johnson, M. (1987), *The Body in the Mind*. Chicago.

—, (1993), *Moral Imagination*. Chicago.

Juarrero, A. (1999), *Dynamics in Action*. Cambridge (Mass).

Jünger, F. (1949), *Die Perfektion der Technik*. Frankfurt am Main.

Kamenka, E. (1963), *The Ethical Foundations of Marxism*. London.

Kampis, G. (1999), 'The hermeneutics of life. In M. Feher (et al.) (eds). *Hermeneutics and Science*. Dordrecht,

Kaplan, B. (1986), 'Value presuppositions in theories of human development'. In S. Wapner (et al.) (eds.). *Value Presuppositions in Theories of Human Development*. Hillsdale.

Kateb, G. (1973), 'Utopia and the good life'. In Manuel (ed.) (1973).

Keenan, J. (1999), 'Whose perfection is it anyway?'. *Christian Bioethics* 5.

Keith, W. and Cherwitz, R. (1989), 'Objectivity, disagreement, and the rhetoric of inquiry'. In H. Simons (ed.), *Rhetoric in the Human Sciences*. London

Kekes, J. (1988), *The Examined Life*. Lewisburg.

—, (1990), *Facing Evil*. Princeton.

—, (1995), *Moral Wisdom and Good Lives*. Ithaca.

Kenny, A. (1992), *Aristotle on the Perfect Life*. Oxford.

Kenyon, G. and Randall, W. (1997), *Restorying Our Lives*. Westport.

Keyes, C. and Haidt, J. (2003), 'Human flourishing: the study of that which makes life worthwhile'. In Keyes & Haidt (eds.) (2003).

Keyes, C. and Haidt, J. (eds) (2003), *Flourishing: Positive Psychology and the Life Well-Lived*. Washington.

Kilcullen, J. (1983), 'Utilitarianism and virtue'. *Ethics* 93.

Kitcher, P. (1999), 'Essence and perfection'. *Ethics* 110.

Klaic, D. (1991), *The Plot of the Future*. Ann Arbor.

Klinger, E. (1977), *Meaning and Void*. Minneapolis.

Knight, K. (ed.), *The MacIntyre Reader*. Cambridge.

Koestler, A. (1975), *The Act of Creating*. New York.

Kotarbinski, T. (1963), *Praxiology*. Oxford and Warsaw.

—, (1983), 'On the essence and goals of general methodology'. In W. Gasparski and T. Pszczolowski (eds.). *Praxiological Studies*. Dordrecht and Warsaw.

Krampen, M. (1981), 'Phytosemiotics'. *Semiotica* 36.

Kruschwitz, R and Roberts, R. (eds.) (1987), *The Virtues*. Belmont.

Kupperman, J. (1991), *Character*. New York.

Kwant, R. (1986), *Mensbeeld als referentiekader*. Amersfoort.

Kwant, R. and van Houten, D. (1976), *Maatschappijkritiek*. Alphen aan de Rijn.

Lachs, J. (2000), 'Grand dreams of perfect people'. *Cambridge Quarterly of Healthcare Ethics* 9.

Laszlo, E. (1972), *The Systems View of the World*. New York

Lebacqz, K. (1985), *Professional Ethics*. Abingdon.

Lenk, H. (1993), *Interpretationskonstrukte*. Frankfurt am Main.

Leopold, A. (1967), *A Sand County Almanac and Sketches Here and There*. London.

MacIntyre, A. (1953), *Marxism: An Interpretation*. London.

—, (1960), 'Purpose and intelligent action'. *Aristotelian Society* (supplementary volume) 34.

—, (1962), 'A mistake about causality in social science'. In P. Laslett and W. Runcimann (eds.). *Philosophy, Politics, and Society*. Oxford.

—, (1972), 'Hegel on faces and skulls'. In A. MacIntyre (ed.). Hegel. London.

—, (1975), 'How virtues become vices'. In H. Engelhardt and S. Spicker (eds.). *Evaluation and Explanation in the Biomedical Sciences*. Dordrecht.

—, (1979), 'Seven traits for the future'. *Hastings Center Report* 9.

—, (1981), *After Virtue*. London.

—, (1984), *After Virtue* (2nd ed.). Notre Dame.

—, (1988a), *Whose Justice? Which Rationality?* Notre Dame.

—, (1988b), 'Sophrosune: how a virtue can become socially disruptive'. *Midwest Studies in Philosophy* 13.

—, (1990), *Three Rival Versions of Moral Enquiry*. Notre Dame.

—, (1991), *How to Seem Virtuous without Actually Being So*. Lancaster.

—, (1992), 'Colors, culture and practices'. *Midwest Studies in Philosophy* 17.

—, (1994), 'A partial response to my critics. In Horton & Mendus (eds.) (1994).

—, (1998a), *Marxism and Christianity*. London.

—, (1998b), 'Practical rationalities as forms of social structure'. In Knight (ed.) (1998).

—, (1998c), 'The Theses on Feuerbach: a road not taken'. In Knight (ed.) (1998).

—, (1998d), 'Politics, philosophy and the common good'. In Knight (ed.) (1998).

—, (1998e), 'Social science methodology as the ideology of bureaucratic authority'. In Knight (ed.) (1998).

—, (1998f), 'An interview for *Cogito*'. In Knight (ed.) (1998).

—, (1999), 'Social structures and their threats to moral agency'. *Philosophy* 74.

—, (2002), 'On not having the last word'. In J. Malpas (ed.). *Gadamer's Century*. Cambridge (Mass.).

MacKinnon, D. (1978), *In Search of Human Effectiveness*. Buffalo.

Maeterlinck, M. (1943), *La vie des abeilles*. Brussels.

Manuel, F. (1973), 'Toward a psychological history of utopias'. In Manuel (ed.) (1973).

Manuel, F. (ed.) (1973), *Utopias and Utopian Thought*. London.

Margolis, J. (1989), *Texts without Reference*. Oxford.

—, (1996), *Life without Principles*. Cambridge (Mass.).

Margolis, J. (ed.) (2001), *The Philosophy of Interpretation*. Philadelphia.

Magritte, R. (1994), *Les mots et les images*. Brussels.

Markus, H. and Nurius, P. (1986), 'Possible selves'. *American Psychologist* 41.

Maslow, A. (1965), *Eupsychian Management*. Homewood.

—, (1971), *The Farthest Reaches of Human Nature*. New York.

—, (1973), *Dominance, Self-esteem, Self-Actualization*. Monterey.

Matthews, G. and Deary, T. (1998), *Personality Traits*. Cambridge.

McKenna, E. (2001), *The Task of Utopia*. Lanham.

Medawar, P. (1994), *The Hope of Progress*. London.

Meier, G. F. (1996) *Versuch einer allgemeinen Auslegungskunst*. Hamburg.

Merritt, M. (2000), 'Virtue ethics and situationist personality psychology'. *Ethical Theory and Moral Practice* 3.

Midgley, M. (1978), *Beast and Man*. Ithaca.

Mieth. D. (1984), *Die neuen Tugenden*. Düsseldorf.

Morin, E. (1975), *Autocritique*. Paris.

—, (1977), *La nature de la nature*. Paris.

—, (1984), *Sociologie*. Paris.

—, (1986), *La connaissance de la connaissance*. Paris.

—, (1990a), *Introduction à la pensée complexe*. Paris.

—, (1990b), *Science avec conscience*. Paris.

—, (1991a), *Les idées*. Paris

—, (1991b), 'L'astre errant'. In Morin (et al.) (1991).

—, (1991c), 'L'âge de fer planétaire'. In Morin (et al.) (1991).

—, (1991d), 'La revolution totalitaire'. In Morin (et al.) (1991).

—, (1991e), 'Le grand dessein'. In Morin (et al.) (1991).

Morin, E. (et al.) (1991), *Un nouveau commencement*. Paris.

Morrison, A. (1984), 'Uses of utopia'. In Alexander & Gill (eds.) (1984).

Morson, G. (2003), 'Narrativeness'. *New Literary History* 34.

Muller, D. (1994), 'Virtues, practices, and justice'. In Horton & Mendus (eds.) (1988).

Muller, V. (1985), *The Idea of Perfectibility*. Lanham.

Murdoch, I. (1971), *The Sovereignty of Good*. London.

—, (1997), ' The sovereignty of good over other concepts'. In Crisp & Slote (eds.) (1997).

Murphy, J. (1993), *The Moral Economy of Labor*. New Haven.

Musschenga, A. W. (2004), *Empirisch geïnformeerde ethiek*. Amsterdam.

Nagel, T. (1986), *The View from Nowhere*. New York.

Nakamaru, J. and Csikszentmihalyi, M. (2003), 'The construction of meaning through vital engagement'. In Keyes & Haidt (eds.) (2003).

Ng, A. (et al.) (2003), 'In search of the good life'. *Genetic, Social, and General Psychology Monographs* 129.

Nicholson, G. (1984), *Seeing and Reading*. Atlantic Highlands.

Nisbet, R. A. (1994), *History of the Idea of Progress*, New Brunswick.

Nöth, W. (1990), *Handbook of Semiotics*. Bloomington.

Norton, D. (1976), *Personal Destinies*. Princeton.

Novitz, D. (2001), 'Interpretation and justification'. In Margolis (ed.) (2001).

Nozick, R. (1974), *Anarchy, State, and Utopia*. New York.
—, (1990), *The Examined Life*. New York.
Nussbaum, M. (1988), 'Non-relative virtues: an Aristotelian approach'. In French (et al.) (eds.) (1988).
—, (1990), 'Aristotelian social democracy'. In B. Douglas (et al.) (eds.). *Liberalism and the Good*. London.
—, (2000), 'Aristotle, politics, and human capabilities'. *Ethics* 111.
Nuttin, J. (1967), 'Problèmes de motivation humaine. Psychologie des besoins fondamentaux et des projets d'avenir'. *Scientia* 102.
—, (1980), *Motivation et perspectives d'avenir*. Leuven.
Oakley, J. (1996), 'Varieties of virtue ethics'. *Ratio* 9.
O'Dea, J. (2000), *Virtue or Virtuosity?* Westport.
Olthof, T. (2000), 'The morality paradox: choosing not to be moral as a component of moral excellence'. In van Lieshout & Heymans (eds.) (2000).
Pacht, A. (1984), 'Reflections on perfection'. *American Psychologist* 39.
Palmer, R. (1969), *Hermeneutics*. Evanston.
Passmore, J. (1970), *The Perfectibility of Man*. London.
—, (1974), *Man's Responsability for Nature*. London.
Paul E. F. (et al.) (eds.) (1992), *The Good Life and the Human Good*. Cambridge.
Pellegrino, E. and Thomasma, D. (1981), *The Virtues in Medical Practice*. New York.
Perrett, R and Patterson, J. (1991), 'Virtue ethics and Maori ethics'. *Philosophy East and West* 41.
Perry, R. B. (1975), *Realms of Value*. New York.
Peterson, C. (2000), 'The future of optimism'. *American Psychologist* 55.
Pincoffs, E. (1986), *Quandaries and Virtues*. Lawrence.
Pirot, M. (1986), 'The pathological thought and dynamics of the perfectionist'. *Individual Psychology* 42.
Plamenatz, J. (1975), *Karl Marx's Philosophy of Man*. Oxford.
Polanyi, R. (1974), *Personal Knowledge*. Chicago.
Popper, K. (1961), *The Poverty of Historicism*. London.
—, (1974a), *The Open Society and its Enemies*. vol. 1. London.
—, (1974b), *The Open Society and its Enemies*. vol. 2. London.
—, (1990), *A World of Propensities*. Bristol.
—, (1994), *In Search of a Better World*. London.
Puka, B. (1990), *Toward Moral Perfectionism*. New York.
Pye, D. (1968), *The Nature and Art of Workmanship*. Cambridge.
Ramsay, H. (1998), 'Natural virtue'. *Dialogue* 37.
Rawls, J. (1999), *A Theory of Justice*. New York.
Raz, J. (1986), *The Morality of Freedom*. Oxford.
—, (1999), *Engaging Reason*. Oxford.
Renzulli, J. (1986), 'The three-ring conception of giftedness'. In Sternberg & Davidson (eds.) (1986).
Rescher, N. (1987), *Ethical Idealism*. Berkeley.
—, (1990), *A Useful Inheritance*. Savage.
—, (1991), *Baffling Phenomena*. Savage.
—, (1997a), *Objectivity*. Notre Dame.
—, (1997b), 'Progress and the future'. In Burgen (et al.) (eds.) 1997.
—, (1998), *Predicting the Future*. Albany.
—, (2000), 'Optimalism and axiological metaphysics'. *Review of Metaphysics* 53.

Ricoeur, P. (1936), 'Le risque'. *Etre* 2.

—, (1969), *Le conflit des interprétations*. Paris.

—, (1970), 'Il faut espérer pour entreprendre'. *Jeunes Femmes* 119.

—, (1976), *Interpretation Theory*. Fort Worth.

—, (1986a), *Du texte à l'action*. Paris.

—, (1986b), *Lectures on Ideology and Utopia*. New York.

—, (1990), *Soi-même comme un autre*. Paris.

Rolston, H. (1988), *Environmental Ethics*. Philadelphia.

—, (1994), *Conserving Natural Value*. New York.

Rorty, A. (1988), 'Virtues and their visciscitudes'. In French (et al.) (eds.) (1988).

—, (1992), 'The advantages of moral diversity'. In Paul (et al.) (eds.) (1992).

Rorty, R. (1989), *Contingency, Irony and Solidarity*. Cambridge.

—, (1999), *Philosophy and Social Hope*. Harmondsworth.

Royce, J. (1920), 'The nature of voluntary progress'. In J. Royce. *Fugitive Essays*. Freeport.

Russell, B. (1954), *Education and the Good Life*. New York.

—, (1960), *Sceptical Essays*. London.

—, (1976), *In Praise of Idleness*. London.

—, (1977), *Authority and the Individual*. London.

—, (1984), *The Conquest of Happiness*. London.

Ruyer, R. (1950), *L'utopie et les utopies*. Paris.

Sabini, J. and Silber, M. (1982), *Moralities of Everyday Life*. Oxford.

Sandøe, P. (1999), 'Quality of life, three competing views'. *Ethical Theory and Moral Practice* 2.

Sartori, G. (1987), *The Theory of Democracy Revisited*. Chatham.

Schapp, W. (1976), *In Geschichten verstrickt*. Wiesbaden.

Schatzki, T. (1996), *Social Practices*. Cambridge.

Scheers, P. (2000), 'Over levensverhalen'. *Filosofie en Praktijk* 1.

—, (2003), 'Human interpretation and animal excellence'. In W. Drees (ed.). *Is Nature Ever Evil?* London.

Scheffler, T. (1985), *Of Human Potential*. Boston.

Schmuck, P. and Sheldon, K. (eds.) (2001), *Life Goals and Well-Being*. Seattle.

Schneewindt, J. (1998), *The Invention of Autonomy*. Cambridge.

Schön, D. (1983), *The Reflective Practitioner*. New York.

Schweiger, A. (1991), 'Reflections on perception and action'. In R. Hanlon (ed.). *Cognitive Microgenesis*. New York.

Sebeok, T. (1972), *Perspectives in Zoosemiotics*. The Hague.

—, (1994), *An Introduction to Semiotics*. London.

Seiffert, H. (1992), *Einführung in die Hermeneutik*. Tübingen.

Seligman, M. and Csikszentmihalyi, M. (2000), 'Positive Psychology'. *American Psychologist* 55.

Sennet. R. (1998), *The Corrosion of Character*. New York.

Serpell, J. (1996), *In the Company of Animals*. Cambridge.

Shanahan, T. (2004), *The Evolution of Darwinism*. Cambridge.

Shaw, B. (1997), 'A virtue ethics approach to Aldo Leopold's land ethics'. *Environmental Ethics* 19.

Shepard, P. (1998), *Thinking Animals*. Athens (Georgia).

Shickle, D. (2000), 'Are genetic enhancements really enhancements?' *Cambridge Quarterly of Healthcare Ethics* 9.

208

Shuman, J. (1999), 'Desperately seeking perfection'. *Christian Bioethics* 5.

Siegel, H. (1997), *Rationality Redeemed?* New York.

—, (2001), 'Incommensurability, rationality and relativism'. In P. Hoyningen-Huene and H. Sankey (eds.), *Incommensurability and Related Matters*. Dordrecht.

Silverman, L. (1983), 'Personality development: the pursuit of excellence'. *Journal for The Education of the Gifted* 6.

Simon, Y. R. (1986), *The Definition of Moral Virtue*. New York.

—, (1991), *Practical Knowledge*. New York.

Skolimowski, H. (1965), 'Praxiology, the science of accomplished acting'. *The Personalist* 46.

Slote, M. (1983), *Goods and Virtues*. Oxford.

Smitsman, A. (2000), 'Slumbering talents: where do they reside?'. In van Lieshout & Heymans (eds.) (2000).

Solomon, D. (1996), *A Handbook for Ethics*. Fort Worth.

Soper, K. (1993), *What is Nature?* Oxford.

Starobinski, J. (2001), 'La perfection, le chemin, l'origine'. In M. Gagnebin and C. Savinel (dir.). *Starobinski en mouvement*. Seyssel.

Statman, D. (ed.) (1997), *Virtue Ethics*. Edinburgh.

Steiner, G. (1975), *After Babel*. London.

Sternberg, R. J. (ed.) (1990), *Wisdom: Its Nature, Origins and Development*. Cambridge.

Sternberg, R. J. and Davidson, J. (eds.) (1986), *Conceptions of Giftedness*. Cambridge.

Swanton, C. (1997), 'Virtue ethics and satisficing rationality'. In Statman (ed.) (1997).

—, (2003), *Virtue Ethics: A Pluralistic View*. Oxford.

Tatarkiewicz, S. (1976), *Analysis of Happiness*. The Hague.

—, (1992), *On Perfection*. Warsaw.

Taylor, C. (1989), *Sources of the Self*. Cambridge (Mass.).

Taylor, F. W. (1972), *The Principles of Scientific Management*. Westport.

Thom, P. (2001), 'On changing the subject'. In Margolis (ed.) (2001).

Toffler, A. (1980), *Future Shock*. London.

—, (1981), *The Third Wave*. London.

Trianosky, G. (1987), 'Virtue, action, and the good life: toward a theory of the virtues'. *Pacific Philosophical Quarterly* 68.

—, (1990), 'What is virtue ethics all about?'. *American Philosophical Quarterly* 27.

van Lieshout and Heymans, P. (eds.) (2000), *Developing Talent across the Life Span*. Hove.

van Wensveen, L. (2000), *Dirty Virtues*. Amherst.

—, (2001), 'Ecosystem sustainability as a criterion for genuine virtue'. *Environmental Ethics* 23

Veenhoven, R. (1984), *Conditions of Happiness*. Dordrecht.

Vernon, M. (1969), *Human Motivation*. Cambridge.

von Uexküll, J. (1980), *Kompositionslehre der Natur*. Frankfurt-am-Main.

von Uexküll, T. (1984), 'Semiotics and the problem of the observer'. *Semiotica* 48.

von Wright, H. (1963), *Varieties of Goodness*. London.

—, (1997), 'Progress: fact and fiction'. In Burgen (et al.) (eds.) (1997).

Walhout, D. (1978a), *The Good and the Realm of Values*. Notre Dame.

—, (1978b), 'Properties, perfection, and human good'. *The Personalist* 59.

—, (1980), 'Human nature and value theory'. *The Thomist* 44.

Walker, M. U. (1998), *Moral Understandings*. New York.

Walker, S. F. (1985), *Animal Thought*. London.

Wall, S. (1999), *Liberalism, Perfectionism and Restraint*. Cambridge.

Wallace, J. D. (1978), *Virtues and Vices*. Ithaca.

Waterman, A. (1993), 'Two conceptions of happiness'. *Journal of Personality and Social Psychology* 64.

Watson, G. (1984), 'Virtues in excess'. *Philosophical Studies* 46.

Watzlawick, P. (1984), 'The imperfect perfection'. In P. Watzlawick (ed.). *The Invented Reality*. New York.

Weinstein, M. (1985), *Finite Perfection*. Amherst.

Weiss P. (1961), *The World of Art*. Carbondale.

—, (1967a), *Man's Freedom*. Carbondale and London.

—, (1967b), *Reality*. Carbondale and London.

—, (1967c), *The Making of Men*. Carbondale and London.

Weissrnan, D. (2000), *A Social Ontology*. New Haven.

Welchman, J. (1999), 'The virtues of stewardship'. *Environmental Ethics* 21.

Wenger, E. (1998), *Communities of Practice*. Cambridge.

Werkmeister, H. (1967), *Man and his Values*. Lincoln.

Wessell, L. (1979), *Karl Marx, Romantic Irony and the Proletariat*. Baton Rouge.

Westra, L. (1994), *An Environmental Proposal for Ethics*. Lanham.

White, R. W. (1965), 'Motivation reconsidered: the concept of competence'. In I. J. Gordon (ed.). *Human Development: Readings in Research*. Glenview.

Wilder, H. (1996), 'Interpretative cognitive ethology'. In Bekoff & Jamieson (eds.) (1996).

Williams, B. (1993), *Ethics and the Limits of Philosophy*. London.

—, (1996), 'Truth in ethics'. In Hooker (ed.) (1996),

Williamson, D. (1986), *The Perfectionist*. Sidney.

Wolf, S. (1982), 'Moral saints'. *Journal of Philosophy* 79.

Wolters, G. (1997), 'The idea of progress in evolutionary biology'. In Burgen (et al.) (eds.) (1997).

Yack, B. (1986), *The Longing for Total Revolution*, Princeton.

Zagzebski. L. T. (1996), *Virtues of the Mind*. Cambridge.

Zebrowitz, L. (1998), *Reading Faces*. Boulder.